RURAL EXODUS

*A study of the forces influencing the
large-scale migration of Irish rural youth*

DAMIAN HANNAN

GEOFFREY CHAPMAN
LONDON DUBLIN MELBOURNE 1970

Geoffrey Chapman Ltd
18 High Street, Wimbledon, London SW 19

Geoffrey Chapman (Ireland) Ltd
5–7 Main Street, Blackrock, County Dublin

ISBN 0 225 48928 7

First published 1970

This book is set in 10 on 12pt Monotype Baskerville 169

Made and Printed in Great Britain by A. Wheaton & Co., Exeter

RURAL EXODUS

Contents

Foreword

Migration in a country like Ireland has two faces. It is a national problem to be analysed at macro-level, a question of national growth and survival. If things had gone better in the nineteenth and early twentieth century, Ireland today could easily have had twenty or thirty million inhabitants, and ranked well up among the medium-sized nations of the world. Instead, it has four-and-a-half million, of whom three million are in the Republic. The people have drained away, and for this purpose it is the net drain that counts; forty thousand a year in the 1950's, probably around sixteen thousand a year since 1961.

But there is also the very different problem of the individual migrant; who he (or she) is, where he comes from and goes to, what qualifications he has, where he gets the information and contacts which help him to migrate, and how he fares. For this purpose it is the vastly greater total of gross migration that matters. Internal as well as external migration has to be taken into account, since for many migrants this imposes strains as great as, if not greater, than migration abroad. In another Economic and Social Research Institute study, Dr Geary and Mr J. G. Hughes show that at the Census of 1961 from one quarter to one half—according to age group—of all adults resident in Dublin were born elsewhere, mainly elsewhere in Ireland. As Dr Hannan shows in this study, in many parts of Ireland almost everyone at least considers either internal or external migration at some time. The gross movement of migrants will, of course, continue even if nett emigration from the country comes to an end. People will still move from less- to more-rapidly developing parts of Ireland or to areas where their particular qualifications are in demand, and there will still be an exchange of people between Ireland and the rest of the world.

If the gross flow of migration is to be steered to the best advantage, whether by the action of individuals themselves or by Government and voluntary agencies concerned with personal welfare, with an

efficient labour market, etc., it is essential that there should be a
disentanglement of the conditions in which people with different
backgrounds migrate. Men do not migrate for the same reasons or at
the same time of life as women. Farmers, craftsmen, operatives,
clerks, and professional workers all follow different patterns. So do
people with primary, technical or commercial ("vocational"), or
secondary education. So, again, do people living in central localities,
those remote from them, and those in intermediate zones.

The problem is to set up a conceptual framework—a set of
categories, a list of questions, a working theory of how and why
migration happens as it does—which will point out the significant
differences as sharply as possible and show how and where the
factors influencing migration operate. This is what Dr Hannan does
in this book, on the basis of a before-and-after study of young people
in Cavan. What originally were their intentions about migration,
and what actually came of these intentions?

The facts which he brings out about Cavan are interesting and
important in themselves, both for Cavan and for policy on migration
in Ireland as a whole. Vocational education appears, in the time and
place at which he writes, to have been the best bet for securing a job
near home, and secondary education the best for a job elsewhere in
Ireland. For many, primary education proved to be a passport to
the boat for Britain. We can watch in his pages the hesitancy and
second thoughts of many young people about their career and
migration choices, underlining the importance of an education broad
enough to let them choose between many alternatives. This point, as
Dr Hannan notes, could be expected to stand out still more sharply
if his informants had been followed not merely from school into their
first years of working life, but on into marriage and final settlement
into a career.

Few migrants, it seems, move without information and contacts.
Only the secondary educated make much use of official job-finding
procedures. But an informal network of brothers and sisters, uncles
and aunts, is available to find jobs and provide a first contact in a new
place. Where this network has not been established, migration is
blocked; and so it comes about that opportunities in Irish towns
close at hand—such as, in this case, Drogheda—may be neglected in
favour of much more distant centres or migration overseas.

A problem which assumes special prominence is that of young men
from farms who find that the prospects of a job in farming are

diminishing, and who are in any case themselves inclined to reject farming and seek other opportunities, and yet too often have not received the preparation needed to adjust successfully in other places and in careers of other kinds. Too often their education stops at the primary level. They are not encouraged by their families to move out of farming—or out of their district—when young enough to make a good start elsewhere. And too often, also, these problems cannot easily be discussed at home because communication with parents is poor.

On or off the farm, shades of the prison house begin to close about the growing boy and girl. Increasingly, as the time of choice comes nearer, the hard realities of job and income opportunity and family obligations take precedence over considerations of the human quality of the community, considerations which play a significant part in earlier preferences. Girls, not surprisingly, turn out to be concerned less with income opportunities and more with human relations and community facilities than do boys. But for them, as for boys, job opportunities are of key importance, and their range of job opportunities is limited in a way which often pushes them towards migration. They have not traditionally had the same opportunity as boys to qualify in the high prestige skills of the craftsman. Accordingly, they consider manual work in factories (though not in shops) as being low-skilled and of low prestige; they may reject even such openings for skilled manual training as come their way; and they flock into white-collar jobs which often have, necessarily, to be sought away from home.

But the point to underline about Dr Hannan's book is that its importance lies not so much—except for those directly concerned with planning the area of which he writes—in the facts which he brings out, as in the frame of thought which he has developed. The thing of most general and permanent value about his book is his method of analysis: his way of looking at migration motives, taking them to pieces, and laying out information about them and about the problems arising from them in an orderly fashion. It is this which makes his book a significant contribution, not merely to the steering of migration in and from Ireland, but to the theory and practice of migration policy everywhere.

MICHAEL P. FOGARTY
18 March 1970

Preface

> But now the sounds of population fail,
> No cheerful murmurs fluctuate in the gale,
> No busy steps the grass-grown footway tread,
> For all the bloomy flush of life is fled.
>
> Goldsmith, (1727–1774), *The Deserted Village*

Goldsmith's eloquent and nostalgic comment on village decline and the dissolution of the peasant way of life not only foreshadowed a moral concern with this problem which persists up to the present time, but also demonstrates that the phenomenon has existed for well over two centuries in Ireland.

Within Ireland the topic has been the subject of many studies and government investigations, the most recent being the *Commission on Emigration Report*, 1954. The results of these investigations, however, have had little apparent impact on population change. It declined almost continuously from the 1840s right up to the 1960s. The population of what is now the Republic of Ireland numbered 6.53 million in 1841, and only 2.82 million in 1961—a decline of approximately 57 per cent. In 1966 the population stood at 2.88 million, an increase that is apparently continuing right into the seventies.

Curiously, there have been very few anthropological or sociological field-studies of migration in Ireland, despite the stimulus provided by Arensberg and Kimball's work (*Family and Community in Ireland*, 1940, and *The Irish Countryman*, 1937) in the 1930s. Since these disciplines have only recently been introduced to Irish universities this oversight becomes understandable. When the author went to Michigan State University for his graduate work in 1962, a Professor of Sociology had not yet been appointed in any of the universities, and a full scale undergraduate programme had only recently been set up. The position has changed for the better in more recent years and this monograph is one of a series by Irish sociologists published since 1967.

This study attempts to answer some questions about the motives and social structural constraints that lie behind the decisions of young adolescents to migrate from a particular rural community in Ireland. The approach used is, broadly speaking, what could be described as "variable analysis", the use of a small number of theoretically relevant and operationally defined variables which are used singly and in combination to explain variations in migration intentions in a theoretical and statistically meaningful way. These independent variables were selected, on the basis of prior evidence and on the results of initial pilot investigations, as being the most important factors influencing migration. Evidence was subsequently gathered, coded and statistically analysed to see to what extent these variables predicted differences in migration plans. This is, therefore, a very different kind of investigation than that which would be undertaken by an anthropologist, for instance. Although the text may not, therefore, fulfill the promise of simplicity and eloquence suggested by Goldsmith's lines, what it loses in that respect is, I hope, regained in the added rigour of the discussion.

I am indebted to many people in the development and completion of this project, but I can only thank a few of them publicly here. I am particularly indebted to Professor J. Allen Beegle, my academic advisor at Michigan State University, who encouraged and advised me throughout the period of the research and preparation of this manuscript. The research on which this study is based could not have been carried out without the financial support of the Central Statistics Office, Dublin. Dr M. D. McCarthy, then Director of the C.S.O., acted as Chairman of the Irish committee which supervised the utilisation of that grant. His advice and guidance was invaluable at all stages of the research. The help of the other members of the research committee is also gratefully acknowledged: Mr Mac Gearalt, Assistant Secretary of the Department of Education; Professor P. Lynch of the Economics Department, and Dr Conor Ward of the Social Science Department, University College, Dublin.

Further financial assistance was given by the Agricultural Expt. Station at Michigan State University, and this enabled me to complete the initial analysis and writing there. Most of this was presented for a Doctoral dissertation in Sociology. The follow-up study was supported completely by the Economic and Social Research Institute, Dublin. A special debt of gratitude is due to the Director and Board of the Institute for allowing me a few months leave from other duties to complete the writing-up of the first study and who completely financed the follow-up study.

I am particularly grateful to all the administrators and teachers in the primary, vocational and secondary schools in Co. Cavan who are too numerous to mention. They allowed me to interrupt their classes and interview their students, and gave freely of their time in providing records and answering my questions. The study would not have been possible without their cooperation. I am, of course, completely indebted to the respondents and their parents, who, without advantage to themselves, took considerable pains in answering all our queries. I was received in a most friendly and hospitable way that is so characteristic of Cavan people. I only hope that my exposition of the underlying reasons for the problems faced by them in education, job finding and migration will help repay some of the debt I owe them. Finally, I owe special thanks to my wife for her help, encouragement and support at all stages of the research.

DAMIAN F. HANNAN

The Economic and Social Research Institute, Dublin.

Part One—The Main Study

1. Statement of the Problem

Introduction

This is a study of the causes and characteristics of migration from a cohort of young boys and girls who grew up in a typical rural community in County Cavan, Ireland. The County seat, Cavan town, is situated about seventy miles north-west of Dublin. This town forms the centre of the community studied which is located in one of the most economically depressed regions of rural Ireland. Most of the respondents were between 15 and 18 years of age when first interviewed in 1965. The majority had completed their primary education two or three years previously. A small minority started work immediately on leaving primary school, but the majority had gone on for further education. Some of these later dropped out of school, so that, at the time of interviewing, somewhat over one third of the respondents were already working in their first jobs. The remainder were still at school but would take up jobs within six months or so of being interviewed.

The community studied is primarily an agricultural one, roughly sixty per cent of the population being dependent on farming for a living. The farms are small, over half of them under thirty statute acres and many of them at subsistence-level. Although there was a small number of factories in the towns the majority of the non-farm employed were engaged in non-manual work, in service industries, or in farm processing businesses such as creameries or bacon factories. Since the county seat, Cavan town, was the hub of the community the number of non-manual workers is somewhat greater than in many other rural communities.

Almost all the respondents were born and raised in County Cavan. This would also be true for the majority of their parents and grandparents. More than half of their uncles and aunts, however, had

1

migrated from the county, and so had a big proportion of their great-uncles and great-aunts. The respondents comprising the subject of this study, therefore, represent the residue of a once stable community of traditional subsistence farmers and artisans which has been suffering a continuous population decline since the middle of the last century.

Despite this very strong migration tradition, less than five per cent of the age group studied had already migrated by 1965. By 1968, however, almost half of them had migrated permanently from the home community and only one third intended to stay there permanently. The majority of people growing up in this community, therefore, leave it upon reaching adulthood. In this pattern of massive out-migration the area resembles most of the other counties in the north-west and along the west coast of Ireland. Despite this long history of migration from rural Ireland, however, we know far less about it than do other countries with a far shorter history of rural–urban migration and less extreme migration patterns.[1] This lack of knowledge is especially obvious in respect to the feelings and aspirations of the migrants themselves.

The major purpose of this study was to throw some light on the motives involved in the migration of these young people, and on the economic and social constraints forcing them out of their home community. The strategy adopted was to interview a representative sample of a young cohort from a community having a high migration rate, at a time immediately preceding their likely large-scale migration. The main dependent variable to be explained in the study is the migration planning of respondents. By proposing a series of motivational and social structural variables, I hope to make clear why there is variation in these migration plans, why some people plan to migrate and others to stay at home. There are two general research questions explored in the study:

1. What are the main motives involved in the migration decisions of the rural adolescents interviewed?

[1] The Reports of the Commission on Emigration and Other Population Problems, Dublin, 1948–54, is a very extensive economic and demographic analysis of the problem. Connell, K. H., *The Population of Ireland, 1750–1845*, Oxford, 1950; Jackson, J. A., *The Irish in Britain*, London, 1963; Newman, J. (Revd.), Ed., *The Limerick Rural Survey*, Tipperary, 1964; Arensberg, C. A. and Kimball, S. T., *Family and Community in Ireland*, Harvard, 1940; Arensberg, C. A., *The Irish Countryman*, Macmillan, 1937, are some other authors who deal with Irish migration. However, very little systematic fieldwork bearing directly on the problems of migration is found in these works.

2. Do migration decisions, and the motives involved in these decisions, vary systematically with the position of respondents in the social structure of the home community? And, if they do, how can these variations be predicted and explained?

The first question is concerned with what Kingsley Davis called "the motives that migrants carry in their heads".[2] Their personal beliefs, attitudes, aspirations, likes and dislikes are the only variables of importance for this question. Social structural factors, such as social class, educational level, family size or sex, etc., are not of importance in this question, except insofar as their effects are mediated through the more proximate personal motives. They are, however, directly considered in the second question.

An additional research question explored in the last chapter is really based on a follow-up study done three years after the original one. It is concerned with the extent that migration plans predicted subsequent migration behaviour. It is also concerned with the extent to which previous conclusions regarding migration motives and migration differentials, hold also for actual migration.

In the remainder of this chapter each of the first two research questions is explored in turn. From previous research findings, social theoretical considerations, and previous unsystematic personal observations—since I was born into a rather similar community in the west of Ireland—a series of hypotheses are proposed in relation to migration motives and differentials. In the second chapter a more extensive description of the methodology employed and of the community studied is given. The following four chapters report the results of the fieldwork in an attempt to answer the research questions posed above. The seventh chapter summarises and draws the final conclusions from the original study. In the last three chapters are reported the results from the follow-up study and some final concluding observations on the relationship between intended and actual migration behaviour.

THE MOTIVES INVOLVED IN MIGRATION

"Nobody who contemplates the multiplicity of economic, political, social and psychological factors that must enter into the personal

[2] Davis, Kingsley, *Human Society*, Macmillan, 1949, 589–92.

contemplation of any prospective migrant would expect any simple model using only two or three variables to account for everything."[3] This disclaimer by Stouffer, referring to one of his best known writings on migration, applies very strongly to this study. So many considerations enter the decision-making processes of young rural migrants when they first consider moving from their home community that any single investigation could not possibly deal with them all. Besides this obvious difficulty, there is the added problem of effectively investigating the interrelationships between such a large number of variables. For these and other reasons I propose five major motivational variables of importance in the migration choice. I do not claim they are exhaustive, only that they appear to be the main considerations involved. Since the study is equally concerned with exploring differences in migration rates between boys and girls and amongst different social classes and educational levels, etc., only those motivational variables will be considered that show predictable variations with these structural factors. Personality variables that are not directly related to such social structural factors—such as IQ, achievement motivation, etc.—are therefore excluded from this analysis since they are not explanatory in this sense.

Given these restrictions on the type and number of variables allowed into the model, it seems that the most useful framework within which migration decisions could be considered is that proposed by Eisenstadt and elaborated by the US North Central Regional Committee on Migration.[4] Eisenstadt proposed the existence of three stages in the migration process:

"First the motivation to migrate—the needs and dispositions which urge people to move from one place to another; second, the social structure of the actual migratory process, of the physical transition from the original society to a new one; third, the absorption of the immigrants within the social and cultural framework of the new society".[5]

[3] Stouffer, S. S., *Social Research to Test Ideas*, Free Press, Glencoe, 1962, 109–10.
[4] Eisenstadt, S. N., *The Absorption of Immigrants*, Routledge and Kegan Paul, London, 1954, 1–4; Beegle, J. A. (Chairman), North Central Regional Committee Concerning Field Studies of Migration, *Report of Procedures Committee of N. C. 18*, Michigan State University, Department of Sociology, Mimeo, 1957, 2–5.
[5] Eisenstadt, *op. cit.*, 1.

The first stage, the motivation to migrate, is the one focussed upon in this study. It is assumed that migration is motivated, as Eisenstadt put it, by the migrant's "feeling of some kind of insecurity and inadequacy in his original social setting".[6] The migrant is not able to "attain some level of aspiration in his original society, where he is unable to gratify all his expectations or to fulfill the role of his desires".[7] This approach then states that migration results from the thwarting or frustration of certain aspirations in the community of origin, allied with beliefs that it is possible to fulfill these aspirations in some particular alternative community. The migrant does not necessarily feel frustrated in every sphere of his social life, for he may remain attached to his original society and culture in various ways.[8] Thus only certain parts of the total social "field of contact" between the individual and society may be of importance in migration planning. Indeed the continuing attachment of migrants to aspects of their original culture has been observed to be one of the major barriers to successful assimilation into their new society.[9]

The sources of dissatisfaction with one's community of origin, or of attraction to another one, vary very widely. The very different kinds of motive involved in the migration of Polish, American or Iranian Jews into Israel would be a good example of this variety.[10] Other examples are the nineteenth century migration of the central European Anabaptist sects to the United States and Canada; the migration of the more highly educated out of Great Britain and of the poorly educated into it; and the voluntary movement of 'loyalists' back to their mother countries when previous colonies gain independence.

When dealing with rural–urban migration, however, within modernised or modernising European or American countries certain universals appear to be present. Almost all studies dealing with the motives of rural–urban migrants, both in the United States and in Europe, have emphasised the overriding importance of economic

[6] *Ibid.*, 2–3.
[7] *Ibid.*, 2.
[8] *Ibid.*, 2; Shuval, T. J., *Immigrants on the Threshold*, Atherton Press, NY, 1963; Gordon, M. M., *Assimilation in American Life*, Oxford University Press, NY, 1964.
[9] Eisenstadt, *op. cit.*, Shuval, *op. cit.*, Gordon, *op. cit.*
[10] *Ibid.*
[11] *Ibid.*

and social mobility motives in migration.[12] This would hold especially in the case of adolescents about to take up adult occupational roles for the first time. For these, finding a satisfactory job, and achieving an adequate income and a desired style of life are considered to be the predominant variables involved in migration decision-making.

The Irish studies in this area demonstrate an even greater preponderance of economic type motives in migration planning.[13] To quote the Commission on Emigration Report, "emigration has been due to two fundamental causes—the absence of opportunities to making an adequate livelihood, and a growing desire for higher standards of living."[14] The fact that opportunities to fulfill these aspirations are seen to be available elsewhere is also important here. This latter condition could be safely assumed to exist in traditional out-migration areas where most families have relatives, friends and neighbours working and living in Great Britain and the United States.

The demographic evidence on rural–urban migration leads to the same conclusion. Birth rates are generally higher in rural areas, while at the same time technological changes are continuously reducing the labour demand in agriculture. "Replacement rates"— the ratio of new young entrants to the labour force to the actual opportunities available through death and retirement of the older labour force and the creation of new jobs—are usually two to three times greater than available opportunities.[15] This proportion is

[12] *Rural Migration:* Papers and Discussions of the First Congress of the European Society for Rural Sociology, privately published, Bonn, 1959; Krier, H., *Rural Manpower and Industrial Development*, OECD Publication, 1961; *Geographic and Occupational Mobility of Rural Manpower*, OECD Publication, Documentation in Agriculture and Food, Report No. 75, 1964; Beijer, G., *Rural Migrants in Urban Setting*, Martinus Nijhoff, The Hague, 1963; Hofstee, E. W., *Some Remarks on Selective Migration*, Martinus Nijhoff, The Hague, 1952; Lijfering, J. H. W., *Selective Migration*, PhD thesis, Agricultural University, Wageningen, 1967. For the United States see Beegle, *op. cit.*, and for review of studies Hannan, D. F., *Factors Involved in the Migration Decisions of Irish Rural Adolescents*, Unpubl. PhD thesis, Michigan State University, 1967; and for an annotated bibliography, *Migration of Farm People*, Misc. Publication No. 954, Economic Research Service, USDA, Washington DC, 1963.

[13] Commission on Emigration, *Reports, op. cit.;* Newman, *op. cit.;* Arensberg and Kimball, *op. cit.;* Vercruijsse, E. V. W., *The Shannon Hinterland Survey*, Dept. of Sociology, Leyden University, Mimeo, 1961.

[14] Commission on Emigration, *op. cit.*, 138.

[15] Bowles, G. and Taeuber, C., *Rural Farm Males' entering and leaving Working Ages, 1940–50, and 1950–60. Replacement Rations and Rates*, Census Series, Agric. Marketing Service Report No. 22, Washington D.C., 1965.

further increased by the fact that the level of aspiration of rural youth is continually rising so that a considerable proportion of them would not be satisfied with the jobs and incomes of the older 'retirees'. The generally remarked 'declassing' of the small farmer,[16] and a similar much greater fall in status of the farm labourer occupation, both of which have accompanied the economic and market transformation of European agriculture, further reduce the available acceptable supply of occupations in rural areas.[17] These cultural and economic transformations of rural society mean that the majority of farm youth (and practically all non-farm youth in rural areas) are oriented toward non-farm occupations, and toward a level of living and a style of life which increasingly cannot be achieved on the farm; nor, for a considerable proportion, in local off-farm employment.

In this study occupational and income aspirations are considered to be the most important variables involved in the migration decisions of rural youth. Income aspirations are used as an index of general consumption aspirations. Both can vary in the level of aspiration sought; occupations in the status or prestige level aspired to, and income in the amount of wages or salary sought. It is expected that if respondents perceive that occupational and/or income aspirations cannot be fulfilled locally they will plan to migrate. Although both variables are probably highly correlated with each other it is nevertheless expected that they will have major independent effects on migration plans.

Satisfaction with social provisions, another variable popularly regarded as a very important "cause" of migration, is very closely related to these economic motives. It is one of the main causes that some Irish politicians and popular commentators cite for rural depopulation. It refers to the current poverty of social services and social provisions in rural areas (water supply, sewerage, shopping facilities, recreational and entertainment facilities, poor roads, and the inadequacies of local institutions, schools, hospitals etc).[18] Bracey's remarks would suggest that this overemphasis is not restricted to Ireland.[19]

[16] Van den Ban, A. W., "Some characteristics of progressive farmers in the Netherlands", *Rural Sociology* (1957) 22, 210–12.

[17] McNabb, P., *The Limerick Rural Survey 1958–64*, 207–9.

[18] See Newman, *op. cit.*, 251–65, 293, 306; and *Christus Rex* (1961) 15, 20–2, for a review and criticism of this view.

[19] Bracey, H. E., "Some aspects of rural depopulation in the United Kingdom", *Rural Sociology* (1958) 23, 385–91.

It is suggested here, however, that the adequacy of such provisions is very closely related to the characteristics of the local economic system. So, where off-farm jobs are plentiful, these provisions will tend to be adequate, and poor where they are scarce. To improve facilities without improving economic opportunities would be futile. If occupational and income aspirations could be fulfilled locally on a large scale then the resulting improvements in transport and communications would enable people to travel more easily to distant and better shopping and entertainment centres. At the same time many of the other social provisions such as water and sewerage can be purchased privately. If the effects of occupational and income frustration are controlled statistically it is expected that attitudes toward the local social provisions will have little if any additional effect on the migration plans of adolescents.

Vercruijsse's research has shown that where occupational and income aspirations have been satisfied, dissatisfaction with the local social provisions does not usually lead to migration. The counteracting effects of ruralistic values makes for a highly satisfying life in small rural communities, despite some drawbacks.[20]

To summarise the discussion thus far: the evidence for Ireland and for the other Western countries suggests that social mobility and purely economic type motives predominate in the migration decisions of most rural youth. Two major motives of this kind were proposed here—occupational status aspirations, (social mobility), and income aspirations, (consumption aspirations). Although both are probably highly intercorrelated it is thought that they will have major independent and joint effects on migration plans. The combined effects of both variables should explain the greater proportion of variation in migration plans.

Consumption and social mobility motives, however, do not exhaust the list of motives found to be related to rural–urban migration planning. Another independent major dimension of migration is what Roy Francis called "cohesiveness": one's attachment to, or alienation from, the particular personal relationships one has with others in the home community, or the structural characteristics of these relationships.[21] Most of the studies which

[20] Vercruijsse, *op. cit.*
[21] Francis, R., "Relation of theory to data", *Rural Sociology* (1957) 22, 158–66.

were carried out under the aegis of the North Central Regional Committee on Migration in the United States paid major attention to these types of variables.[22] Beegle defined it in terms of "feelings of cohesiveness and security rooted in identification with groups and structures".[23] In most of these studies it was operationalised by a modification of Vernon Davies' "Community Satisfaction" scale,[24] a procedure which was also followed in this study. There are two sources of variation in satisfaction or dissatisfaction with personal relationships locally. The first involves purely personal sources of variation due to feelings of relative deprivation or well-being. These arise from the continuous comparisons people make between their own situation, vis-a-vis family and community relationships generally, to that of others seen as significant reference points for themselves. This is the well-known phenomenon of comparative reference group effects.[25] The second source of disaffection with local structures results from cultural change, and is of a far more fundamental nature. There are major cultural and structural changes occurring within the rural family and kinship group and other rural community groups and institutions.[26] The old traditional patriarchical authoritarian family structure, the local rigid class structure inhibiting social mobility and enforcing clear precedence and deference patterns of behaviour, the strong local neighbourhood groups etc., are all in the process of dissolution. There are, however, great variations between families and small

[22] Schulze, R. H. K., *Community Satisfaction and Migration*, MA thesis, Department of Sociology and Anthropology, Michigan State University, 1960; Cowhig, J., et al., *Orientations Toward Occupations and Residence: A Study of High School Seniors in Four Rural Counties of Michigan*, MSU, AES. Special Bulletin 428, 1960; Goldsmith, H. F., *The Meaning of Migration: A Study of the Migration Expectations of High School Students*, PhD thesis, Department of Sociology and Anthropology, Michigan State University, 1961; Goldsmith, H. F., and Beegle, J. A., *The Initial Phase of Voluntary Migration*, MSU, AES, Rural Sociology Studies No. 1, January 1962; Schulze, R. H. K., Artis, J., Beegle, J. A., "The measurement of community satisfaction and decision to migrate", *Rural Sociology* (1963) 28, 279–83.

[23] Beegle, *op. cit.*, 2.

[24] Davis, V., "Development of a scale to rate attitudes of community satisfaction", *Rural Sociology* (1945) 10, 246–55.

[25] Kelley, H. H., "The two functions of reference groups", reprinted in Swanson, Newcomb and Hartley, et al., (ed.), *Readings in Social Psychology*, Holt, NY, 1952 410–14.

[26] Compare Burchinal, L. G., "The rural family of the future", in Copp, J. H., (Ed.), *Our Changing Rural Society*, Iowa State U.P., 1964, 159–97; and Arensberg, C. M., and Kimball, S. T., *Family and Community in Ireland*, reprinted 1961, Peter Smith, Gloucester, Mass.

communities in this respect. Children who have internalised more democratic urban middle class patterns of relationships within the family or class structure will tend to become highly alienated from these more traditional forms of relationships where they still persist.[27] Variations in these values and in the structure of relationships in their own family and community groups would bring about corresponding changes in attitudes toward the home community, in one case binding them more strongly to the home community, in the other alienating them from it. Both sources of differences— the personal and the cultural—in these attitudes toward personal and institutional relationships in the home community should be reflected in the degree of attachment to or satisfaction with the home community and in migration plans.

The role that this or similar variables played in migration had become apparent even by the 1930s. The unemployed and the economically disadvantaged frequently refused to leave their community of origin for better opportunities, even when aided.[28] A sizeable proportion of those who had participated in the planned migration programmes of the United States Department of Agriculture in the midst of the depression, and who had as a consequence experienced considerable improvements in their economic and social position, nevertheless left these projects for less advantaged positions elsewhere.[29] Unemployed manual workers have also usually shown considerable resistance to migration.[30] More recent research on rural youth who plan to farm has shown considerable cultural differences between them and others who plan to move off the farm. The former have values and attitudes which can only be

[27] Benvenuti, B., *Farming in Cultural Change*, Van Gorcum Press 1961; and Eisenstadt, S. N., *From Generation to Generation*, Free Press, 1961. Both contain descriptions of such cultural changes, and the latter especially describes some of the resulting tensions.
[28] Williams, R. Jr., "Concepts of marginality in rural population studies", *Rural Sociology* (1940) 5, 292–302; and Brunner, E. de S., *The Growth of a Science*, Harper and Brothers, NY, 1951, 51.
[29] Loomis, C. P., "Social relationships and institutions in seven new rural communities in the United States", reprinted in Loomis, C. P., *Studies of Rural Social Organisation*, State College Bookstore, East Lansing, Mich., 1945.
[30] See Lipset, S. M. and Bendix, R., *Social Mobility in Industrial Society*, University of California Press, 1959, 160 for references. In Harris, A. I., and Cleusen, R., *Labour Mobility in Great Britain, 1953–1963*, Government Social Survey, March 1966, 24, nearly half of the unemployed male workers interviewed said they were unwilling to move to other areas to find work.

satisfied in farming and in small gemeinschaftlike communities.[31] On the other hand there is considerable dissatisfaction with traditional family and community roles in rural areas, particularly in the case of women, and this may be a major cause of migration of young farm girls.[32]

The fact that strong attachment to particular people and to the way of life of the home community retards migration has been emphasised in most migration research. The contrary hypothesis, that high levels of alienation from relationships in the home community lead to migration, will be emphasised in this research. The greater the degree of dissatisfaction with community relationships the greater should be the tendency to migrate. It is also expected that such dissatisfied people will plan to migrate, irrespective of their ability to fulfill other aspirations in the community—notably occupational and income aspirations. In a sense it is expected that where such high alienation is present it takes precedence over all other variables involved in migration.

On the other hand it is not expected that people who are strongly attached to the home community will plan to remain, irrespective of the frustration of economic type aspirations. Something close to this idea has been a traditional assumption about the role played by such attachments in migration planning. But with the revolution in modern communication and transport methods, migration, although introducing certain strains into family attachments, does not have such major disruptive effects as originally thought. Attachments can persist and certain types of family interactions

[31] Kaldor, D. R., Eldridge, E., et al, *Occupational Plans of Iowa Farm Boys*, Research Bull. 508, Iowa Agric. Expt. Station, Ames, 1962; Haller, A. O., "Planning to Farm: a social-psychological explanation". *Social Forces* (1959) 37, 263–8; and his later studies published in *Rural Sociology* (1960) 25, 321–33, and (1962) 27, 275–93; Schwarzweller, H. K., "Value orientations in educational and occupational choice", *Rural Sociology*, (1959) 24, 408–25; Addans, N. N. H., "Occupational choice of farm youth on the sandy soils of the provinces of Northern Brabant and Limburg", *World Agricultural Economics and Rural Sociological Abstracts* (1962) 4: 1, 46; Addans, N. N. H., "Which farm boys and girls go into farming", *World Agricultural Economics and Rural Sociological Abstracts* (1961) 3: 2, 218; Boekistijn, C., "Attachments to one's area of residence and migration", *World Agricultural Economics and Rural Sociological Abstracts*, (1962) 4: 1.

[32] Heberle, R., "The causes of rural-urban migration, a survey of German theories", *American Journal of Sociology* (May 1938) 43; Planck, U. ,"The rural youth of Western Germany", *Rural Sociology* (1960) 25; 442–6; Haushofer, H., "The farm woman in the social and economic trends of today", *World Agricultural Economics and Rural Sociological Abstracts*, (1962) 4: 1, 52.

continue even when family members are separated by great distances.[33] The idea of 'migration systems'—of patterns of interaction and population interchanges between a particular community of origin and its daughter "colony" of migrants in a particular community of destination—is based on such interactions.[34] A tentative answer as to why this might be so was suggested by Crawford who showed that where high attachments exist but are accompanied by expectations to migrate on the part of 'significant others' (in this case parents and sibs), then the rate of migration is almost as great as where very low attachments exist.[35] As early as the 1930s Arensberg had proposed a rather similar idea: that the extended Irish family, both in the home community and through its contacts with its migrant members abroad, facilitated and encouraged migration for those children who could not be satisfactorily placed locally.[36] It was expected that the same situation would hold in this case so that high attachments would not necessarily retard migration, because of the counteracting effects of family expectations and support.

The family, however, may play a more direct role in migration. Some individuals have such strong obligations to their families that they are required to stay at home even when they would prefer to migrate. These obligations would include, for instance, binding expectations on some farm boys to stay and work on the home farm where there is a great need for their labour. Alternatively, some girls may be expected to stay and help out in the household or to look after aged parents etc. If this is an important variable in migration planning under American conditions, as Goldsmith found,[37] it is likely to be much more important under Irish conditions where the rural family structure is more patriarchical and the parents exercise much more control over family members. This variable, then, of family obligations, rather similar in its nature to Community Satisfaction, is the fourth variable proposed as influencing migration

[33] Litwak, E., "Geographic mobility and extended family cohesion", *American Sociological Review* (1960) 25, 385–94.

[34] Brown, J. S., Schwarzweller, H. K. and Mangalam, J. J., "Kentucky mountain migration and the stem family: a variation on a theme by Le Play", *Rural Sociology* (1963) 28, 48–69; Hillary, G. A., Brown, J. S. and De Jong, G. E., "Migration systems of the Southern Appalachians" *Rural Sociology* (1965) 30, 1.

[35] Crawford, C. O., "Family attachments and support for migration of young people", *Rural Sociology* (1966) 31, 293–301.

[36] Arensberg and Kimball, *op. cit.*, 145–57.

[37] Goldsmith, *op. cit.*, 221; and Goldsmith and Beegle, *op. cit.*, 85–6.

decisions. It is expected that such obligations will take priority over any personal aspirations. Even if occupational and income aspirations are frustrated, people with such obligations will not migrate.

This variable, therefore, is expected to play a role in migration which is in many ways the converse of Community Satisfaction. The combined effects of both variables on migration planning—low Community Satisfaction causing migration, with high levels of Obligation leading to plans to stay—may explain a considerable amount of the variation in migration plans. Their effects are also likely to be largely independent of one another, since those with strong obligations—usually farm boys—are least likely of all respondents to be alienated.

To summarise the discussion so far, there appear to be two broad categories of motives involved in rural–urban migration: "economic" —occupational status and consumption aspirations; and "solidarity motives"—Community Satisfaction and Family Obligations and expectations. Some of the inter-relationships amongst these variables, as well as their likely direct influence on migration plans, have been spelled out. The evidence for Ireland and for other Western countries suggests that occupational and consumption aspirations predominate in the migration decisions of most rural youth. A minority, however, are likely to be so highly alienated from the community (low Community Satisfaction) that they will probably migrate, irrespective of the local satisfaction or frustration of economic type motives. Much the same situation holds for a corresponding minority of respondents who are expected to have such strong local family obligations that they have to stay in spite of the frustration of any personal aspirations. Table I is an attempt to summarise these hypothesised interrelationships in a simplified tabular form. Variations on the independent variables are given in the marginal positions in the table while their influences on the dependent variable (migration) are given in the cells of the table. As can be seen from this table there are likely to be such clear interactive effects among the variables that a simple linear model of these interrelationships is not feasible.

This completes consideration of the major motives involved in the migration decision. From a sociological point of view, however, these motives themselves equally need explanation: for instance, why some respondents can fulfill occupational and consumption aspirations locally and others cannot; why some people are obliged

TABLE I: A DIAGRAM OF THE RELATIONSHIPS BETWEEN THE DEPEN-
DENT AND INDEPENDENT VARIABLES

	Community Satisfaction			
	High		Low	
ECONOMIC ASPIRATIONS	Family Obligations			
	Present	Absent	Present	Absent
	Migration Decision?			
NOT FRUSTRATED	Stay	Stay	Stay	Migrate
FRUSTRATED	Stay	Migrate	Stay	Migrate

to stay at home and help the family while others are free to migrate if they wish; and why some people are highly attached to the home community while others actively dislike it. The next section, dealing with migration differentials, attempts to explain these problems.

MIGRATION DIFFERENTIALS:
THE STRUCTURAL ANTECEDENTS OF MIGRATION PLANS AND MIGRATION MOTIVES

The question explored in this section concerns the way migration plans, and the motives influencing them, vary with the position of the individual in the social structure of the home community. This study limits consideration to a small number of structural variables, some of them highly correlated with each other. Social class origins and the level of education achieved will, on this basis, be considered together first. Their influences on migration plans and motives will be studied by examining their intervening influences on the level of occupational and income aspiration. Sex differences in migration planning, and the influence of farm or non-farm origin will be explored in the same way, by examining their intervening relationship to the level of aspiration and to local occupational recruitment. In the latter case, however, there are also predictable differences between the sexes and between those from farm and non-farm backgrounds on levels of Community Satisfaction and Family Obligations. The final two structural variables examined deal with the remoteness of respondents' homes from the community's centre and the degree of involvement of individuals in migration systems. In both these cases, also, it was possible to make clear predictions as to their likely relationship to migration motives and plans.

1. Social Class, Education and Level of Aspiration

In any country social class, educational level achieved and level of occupational aspiration are highly intercorrelated variables. The most obvious relationship is between social class and education. If postprimary education is still highly selective by class origin, as in Britain and the United States,[38] it is likely to be much more so in Ireland, where it was not free at the time of the survey (1965). [This position has changed dramatically since 1965. The Irish Government initiated free secondary education from September 1967.] Indeed a report published after this study was completed, showed a very high correlation between educational mobility and social class level in Ireland.[39]

Besides the direct effect of class on education and consequently on aspiration level, specific class cultures are also likely to have independent effects on the type and level of aspiration. The stratification system in Ireland is much more rigid than in the United States. As a result, the cultural and aspirational differences between classes in Ireland should be even more marked.[40] Therefore respondents from different class levels are expected to have achieved correspondingly different educational and aspirational levels.

The relationship between class backgrounds and educational level achieved will be explored in Chapter Three. It is expected that secondary school students should be selected largely from the non-farm middle class and the large farm class.[41] These should tend to undervalue all manual and service occupations, and will aspire

[38] Havighurst, R. J. and Neugarten, B., *Society and Education*, Allyn and Bacon, Boston, 1962; Halsey, A. H. and Gardner, L., "Selection for secondary education and achievement", *British Journal of Sociology*, 4: 1, 60; Stephenson, R. M., "Stratification, education and occupational orientation; a parallel study and review *British Journal of Sociology*, 9: 1, 42; Floud, J., et al., *Social Class and Educational Opportunity*, Heinemann, London, 1956.

[39] *Investment in Education*, Report of the Survey Team appointed by the Minister of Education in October 1966, The Stationery Office, Dublin, 149–53.

[40] Hyman, H., "The value system of different classes, a social psychological contribution to the analysis of stratification", in Bendix and Lipset (Eds.), *Class Status and Power*, Free Press, 1963, 426–44.

[41] *Investment in Education*, *op. cit.*

generally to jobs at the white collar or non-manual level.[42] Vocational schools are generally attended by adolescents from the working class and small farmer class. These should orient male students toward skilled manual and service occupations, and females toward service and lower non-manual occupations. The primary educated should be even more concentrated in the lower levels of the class hierarchy. Excluding those who can remain on the home farm, these have to restrict their aspirations realistically to unskilled and semi-skilled occupations and lower order service occupations.

The next question is how these variations in levels of occupational aspiration affect migration plans? Since the opportunity structure of most rural communities is severely limited at the upper levels, high levels of occupational aspiration should be closely related to beliefs that these aspirations cannot be fulfilled locally. The major channels of vertical occupational mobility become accessible only if aspirants migrate to more urban communities: the quest for social mobility leading to migration.[43]

Of course if rural communities differ in the structure of local off-farm labour markets then there would be proportionate variations in the kind of aspirations that are frustrated. There are also likely to be variations between communities in the structure of the occupational aspirations of adolescents. These are brought about primarily by community differences in educational opportunities. But other social and cultural differences might affect this as well. These are probably some of the reasons why so little progress has been made in research dealing with the selectivity of rural–urban migrants. No attention has been paid to the community differences which influence this selectivity. One must take into consideration both the number *and* structure of occupational opportunities, and the number and structure of local occupational aspirants. If this is not done an equation which takes numbers alone into consideration will give an incorrect estimate, even of the number of potential migrants.

Some direct evidence for this argument exists. It has been shown that it is possible to have a highly developed local educational system which 'trains' students to aspire to occupations beyond the level of those available locally, and at the same time to have

---

[42] Vercruijsse, *op. cit.*; McNabb, *op. cit.*

[43] Kaufman, H. H., *e l.*, "Social stratification in rural Society", *Rural Sociology* (1953) 18, 1.

numerous well-paid, but lower status occupations which have to be filled by immigrants.[44] On the other hand, in poorer rural communities with inferior educational facilities it is equally likely that most of the local white collar and professional occupations will be filled by outsiders.[45] For the community under study, however, occupational opportunities are largely limited to farm, unskilled, semiskilled and skilled manual occupations, service and some lower order non-manual occupations. Less than 19 per cent of adult workers in Co. Cavan, for instance, were employed in non-manual occupations in 1966.[46] Consequently, the higher the level of aspiration, the greater the level of frustration, and the resulting tendency to migrate.

How does this argument relate to education? Because secondary school students have excluded most manual and service occupations from consideration, and vocational and primary educated students have not, occupational frustration and consequent plans to migrate should be much greater in the former case. On the other hand, primary educated respondents should exhibit the lowest level of aspiration and consequently the lowest level of frustration of all respondents. They should also be the most likely to remain on the home farm. Of all educational groups, therefore, they should be the least likely of all to migrate.

Thus the higher the level of occupational aspiration, the greater should be the level of local frustration of these aspirations and consequently the greater the tendency to migrate. The reason why the more highly educated should be more migratory than others would be due to their higher level of aspiration. Controlling for aspiration level, therefore, education, *per se*, should not be related to migration. It is the intervening process of occupational selections that brings about the relationship.

2. Income Aspirations

Aspirations to reach particular occupational status levels have been shown to be related to occupational frustration levels and

[44] Williams, J. L., "Some social consequences of grammar school education in a rural area in Wales", *British Journal of Sociology*, 10:2, 125; Vercruijsse, *op. cit.*

[45] Gerschwind, R. D. and Ruttan, V. W., *Job Mobility and Migration in a Low Income Rural Community*, Research Bulletin 730, Purdue University, Ag. Expt. Sta., 1961. This also appears to have been the case in Co. Cavan up to very recent times.

[46] Census of Population of Ireland, 1966, Vol. IV, *Occupations*, 146-7.

migration plans. This, however, refers only to the relative prestige level of the occupation *per se*. Such aspirations have precedence for the socially mobile or those with high levels of occupational aspirations. Even for these, however, but especially in the case of those with lower levels of occupational aspiration, other related aspirations become very important. The most important of these are likely to be aspirations to reach particular consumption levels relating to income or level of living. This study focusses exclusively on income aspirations, treating them as an index of general consumption aspirations.

Despite the relationship between the level of occupational aspiration and occupational frustration, there is probably in most rural communities a surplus of aspirants over opportunities at almost all levels of aspiration; but proportionally much less so at the lowest (service and manual) levels. It is at this level that consumption aspirations, or motives for economic betterment, become important. The greater part of the decline in rural populations all over the Western world has taken place among the smaller farmers and farm labourers.[47] Much of this off-farm mobility cannot be regarded as being upwardly mobile in a status sense. In fact, much of it results in an apparent decline of occupational status.[48] But many studies also show that it has led to an improvement in economic status.[49] Hence, at this level of occupational recruitment, it is not the absence of occupational opportunities at the status level aspired to that is important (witness the great decline in the self-employed farmer category, and the almost universal complaints about lack of farm labour) but the remuneration of those occupations that are available. Income aspirations, then, should be very important in migration especially at these levels.

Again here it is expected that the higher the level of aspiration, the higher the probability that respondents will feel their income aspirations cannot be satisfied locally; and that such local income frustrations will also lead to plans to migrate.

---

[47] See the OECD Report, *Geographic and Occupational Mobility of Rural Manpower*, *op. cit.*

[48] Folkman, W. S. and Cowhig, J. D., "Intergenerational occupational mobility in a rural area", *Rural Sociology* (1963) 28, 4.

[49] Schwarzweller, H., "Education, migration, and economic life chances of entrants to the labor force from a low income rural area", *Rural Sociology* (1964) 29, 152–67; Landis, P. H., "Educational selectivity of rural urban migration", *Rural Sociology* (1946) 11, 218–32.

In comparison with occupational aspiration, very little research has been done on the factors associated with variations in income aspirations. The hypothesis is that it will vary directly with the same factors that affect occupational aspiration level. But, controlling for these, it is expected that large variations will occur, especially for lower occupational aspirants, where the variable is expected to have its major predictive influence. It is expected that reference group factors would account for most of this variation: for instance, variations in the extent and depth of contact the individual has with significant others working off farms and outside the community; and variations in the cultural orientation of the individual's family, whether of a traditional non-materialistic orientation or a modern urbanised orientation.[50] Here again sex is a factor, with girls having lower levels of aspiration than boys. Since the level of opportunities for girls, however, is much more limited, the influence of this on income frustration will be very limited.

3. Occupational and Income Aspirations and Migration Plans

Occupational frustration (whether the respondent thinks he can get the job he wants in his home community) and income frustration (whether the respondent thinks he can get the income he wants by staying and working in his home community) are proposed here as the major predictors of plans to migrate. Both can be considered in isolation from the level of aspiration. From this point of view, both frustrations can act together, separately, or be altogether absent. When both are frustrated, there should be a greater tendency to migrate than where only one or neither is frustrated. The joint effect of both variables on migration should, in fact, explain most of the variation in migration plans.

It is likely, however, that the effects of Occupational and Income Frustration on migration are not simply additive. Their relative predictive ability is likely to vary with the level of occupational aspiration. In both cases, frustration of aspirations is possible at all levels of aspiration, although much more likely at the upper levels. However, at the upper levels of occupational aspiration, occupational frustration alone is much more likely to give rise to migration plans than at lower levels. At higher levels of aspiration social mobility

[50] Benvenuti, B., *Farming in Cultural Change*, Van Gorcum, Assen, NL, 1961.

R.E.—B

motives are at a maximum, and local opportunities to satisfy these motives at a minimum. At the lower levels of occupational aspiration it is not the absence of some occupational opportunities as such that is important, but the remuneration of the occupation in comparison with similarly unskilled occupations in alternative communities. This latter situation should hold true for a large sector of the population under study—those who have had only a primary education, or a minimum of postprimary education. This group can realistically aspire only to unskilled and semiskilled occupations and to lower level service occupations. At this level of occupational aspiration, income aspirations become very important in predicting out-migration plans. Great differences in remuneration for the same occupation (particularly manual occupations) exist between most rural and urban areas in Ireland; and particularly between rural areas in Ireland and urban areas in Britain. Moreover, the ability to change occupations at the unskilled, semiskilled and service level in order to profit from higher incomes, is much easier than at higher occupational levels.

To summarise the section so far; if we stratify respondents by their level of occupational aspirations, it is expected that: (1) the higher the level of occupational aspiration, the greater the proportion of respondents who believe their occupational and income aspirations cannot be achieved locally; (2) variation in levels of income frustration, however, is likely to be much greater at lower levels of occupational aspiration than is the case for occupational frustration; (3) occupational frustration, however, will be more predictive of plans to migrate at the upper levels of aspiration than the lower, while income frustration *per se* will be more predictive of plans to migrate at the lower occupational aspiration levels; (4) the joint effects of both variables on migration will be greater at lower levels of aspiration since the two independent variables are likely to be least correlated at this level.

4. Community Satisfaction, Class and Educational Level

The higher the educational level (and the social class level) the greater should be the degree of modernisation of values and attitudes. Consequently, given the general traditional structures of the community in question, one would expect that, in general, the more highly educated and those from higher social class backgrounds have lower levels of Community Satisfaction. If so, this would strengthen the already hypothesised relationship between educational level achieved, levels of occupational and income frustration, and migration plans. On the other hand the more highly educated and those from higher class levels occupy a more advantaged position in the community, so that if one views their attitudes from a relative deprivation viewpoint they should be more satisfied. It is difficult to decide *a priori* between these alternatives since it depends on whether cultural change or reference group factors are the major sources of differences in levels of Community Satisfaction. As a result, no clear hypothesis can be proposed. The interrelationships concerned will, however, be explored in the analysis.

5. Family Obligations, Class and Educational Level

Family obligations which require some people to stay at home to work in family enterprises, or in the household, should be restricted largely to those from a farm background. The relationship between family obligations and farm background should be very marked since such obligations are almost by definition limited to people with family enterprises, and farms constitute the majority of these.

Household obligations on the other hand are more evenly distributed but are not expected to be as onerous as the former type. They should also be restricted to girls, while outside work obligations should be equally restricted to boys. Nor is there any reason to believe that those from the more prosperous farms should be less subject to either of these work obligations. In other respects, however, farm size should be related to educational and aspirational level and consequently to migration. Among the non-farm respondents, those from middle class families should be least subject to household obligations while work obligations would be restricted to the small proportion of those with family enterprises.

Regarding the educational level achieved, both these types of family obligations should be generally restricted to those who have received only a primary education. The secondary educated, especially, should be most free from these obligations. The fact that respondents are sent on for such education is itself an indication that they are bound by fewer and less onerous obligations than their peers who are kept at home.

Both in the case of Community Satisfaction and Family Obligations, therefore, the argument proposed strengthens the already clearcut relationship between class, educational level and migration plans. Because of their intervening relationship with aspiration levels and with attitudes and obligations etc., one would expect the more highly educated and those from the upper levels of the local class hierarchy to be more migratory than those from the lower levels. The sex of respondents may intervene here, however, in affecting both obligation and education levels, and the next section considers these possibilities.

SEX AND OCCUPATIONAL BACKGROUND AND MIGRATION PLANS

1. Occupational and Income Aspirations

One of the few consistent findings on rural–urban migration differentials is that rural females are more migratory than males.[51] Why should this be so? Does it hold for all educational levels, and for those from farm and non-farm homes?

For the community under consideration here, the demographic evidence would suggest that this is restricted only to those from a farm background. In the age group 14 to 19 in County Cavan in 1961, there were approximately as many males as females employed in non-farm pursuits, whereas there were nine times as many males as females employed on the farm.[52] In rural farm areas the only usual off-farm occupation available for girls is in domestic service: an occupation of a very low status and employing very few in number.[53] Boys, on the other hand, are disproportionately catered for by farming, from an occupational point of view. At least one boy in each farm family has the opportunity of staying on the farm if he wishes, whereas this is true for very few girls. Since, even for farm girls, the occupational role is almost as relevant for adolescent girls as for boys this means that far more girls than boys are seeking off-farm jobs. On the other hand occupational opportunities in the rural trade centres for males and females are approximately equally

[51] Thomas, D. S., *Migration Differentials*, SSRC Bull. 43, 1938; Hofstee, *op. cit.*
[52] See Tables 6A and 6B, *Census of Population of Ireland*, 1961, Vol. V, *Occupations*, CSO, Dublin, 1964, 154 and 170.
[53] McNabb, *op. cit.*, 173.

balanced, at least as indicated by census figures. Taking the community as a whole, therefore, a relatively greater population of females than males competes for approximately the same number of off-farm opportunities. The frustration of occupational and income aspirations should be much greater, therefore, among females than males and especially among those from farm backgrounds. Can sex selectivity in migration be explained then by a similar selectivity in local occupational opportunities, or is it necessary to go further and locate the reason in the frequently mentioned farm girl's active dislike of rural living?

Herberle's review of German social research on rural migration in the 1930s showed a major sex difference in levels of satisfaction with the farm family way of life.[54] The role of the farm woman became increasingly less satisfactory as the nineteenth and twentieth centuries progressed. Her age-old role as food and clothing processer dwindled in importance as participation in the market increased. However, this original role was replaced by increasing her share of farm-yard work: feeding pigs and calves, milking cows, helping in the vineyards etc. Her jobs appeared to become 'dirtier' and more toilsome as traditional roles declined and as urban values and consumption patterns penetrated the countryside. As a result, the stereotype of the farm woman with the "black apron and wellington boots" has become more powerful. The extra-economic rewards of her roles also declined, as the conviviality of the spinning room, and the festive gatherings of neighbouring women for common tasks were not replaced by compensating patterns of relationships as her economic roles in the farm-yard increased. In fact she became more isolated from her neighbours. Although changes have more recently occurred to reduce the backaches and drudgery associated with the farm housewife's role, the traditional stereotypes persist and militate against farm girls aspiring to a farm role.

Accompanying these changes are others which have greatly increased the participation of farm girls in the labour force, particularly from adolescence to marriage. The old pattern of staying on the farm until marriage has almost completely disappeared with the decline of matchmaking and the dowry system. Therefore, not only have the definitions of desirable occupations changed greatly in favour of off-farm work for women, but the overall importance of occupational aspirations as factors in migration decision-making

[54] Herberle, R., op. cit.

has also increased. It should be remembered, however, that underlying these more apparent occupational changes have been great
structural and cultural changes which transformed rural society
from a self-sufficient peasant economy (where almost all the economic roles of males and females were carried on within the farm
family system itself) to a much more highly differentiated economy
and society. The rural family is approaching the urban industrial
model in a consuming sense and also in terms of the economic role
of its younger female members. In general, therefore, occupational
selectivity is likely to be the main force influencing differences in
migration rates between males and females, although underlying
this selectivity there are major cultural factors involved.

How is this sex selectivity in migration affected by education?
Does it vary with the level of education received, or the status level
of the occupation aspired to? One would expect little difference
between secondary educated males and females in their levels of
occupational and income frustration, or migration plans. The great
majority of these aspire to higher non-manual occupations and these
are notoriously scarce for both sexes in rural areas. However the
situation may be somewhat different for those educated in vocational
schools. Males in these schools aspire to, and get a technical training
appropriate to skilled and semiskilled jobs, while females tend to be
oriented toward lower non-manual ones. It seems likely, therefore,
that males will be better able to fulfill their occupational aspirations
locally than will females. The same situation is likely to hold for
those who have received only a primary education, in this case
because of the sex selectivity of the farm occupation.

To sum up, therefore, sex selectivity in occupational and income
frustration and in migration plans is expected to be concentrated
in the farm sector, and only among those who receive primary or
vocational education. Somewhat similar sex differences are likely to
arise in the case of Community Satisfaction as we will see in the
following section.

2. Community Satisfaction and Sex

Casual observations and corroborating evidence from American
and Dutch studies suggest that farm boys have higher levels of
Community Satisfaction than farm girls. There should be little

difference between non-farm boys and girls.[55] This may be so because farm boys usually have more traditional values than farm girls. This is only partly due to their lower educational levels, and partly also because within both the farm family and the rural community they occupy a more advantaged position relative to their aspirations. Occupationally, farm boys fare better than girls, and their recreational and general community relationships are generally more satisfactory. Social and cultural changes in traditional rural communities, in fact, appear to cause much greater problems of adaptation for females than males. How and why this occurs has not been clearly explained. It is probably an unavoidable consequence of change from a patriarchal family structure and a male dominated community structure. It is likely that the diffusion of "new" urban middle class family ideals throughout the countryside meets a readier response among females than the more advantaged males. Faced with this change, males would have to relinquish power and privilege—and females would have to fight against certain cultural and structural restrictions. In this situation, is cultural change as rapid among males as females? And are age-old structures as easily adapted to the newer run "liberating" demands and aspirations of the young females as to the similar but less disrupting aspirations of the young males? The argument here is that cultural change is less radical among males and that they make the corresponding structural adjustment more easily.

Levels of Community Satisfaction then should be much greater among farm males than farm females while one would expect little difference among non-farm males and females in this respect.

This completes consideration of sexual differences in migration. The following and final section examines the relationship of remoteness to migration.

3. Remoteness and Migration Plans and the Factors Affecting Migration Plans

Since the study is of a trade centre community, distance from the centre (Cavan town) is likely to be an important variable in education and migration. There were no school buses serving the centre

---

[55] See Haller, A. O., *op. cit.*; Kaldor, *op. cit.*; Schwarzweller, H. K., *op. cit.*; Heberle, R., *op. cit.*; Planck, U., *op. cit.*; Haushofer, H., *op. cit.*; Barberis, C., "The matrimonial balance of the agricultural population", *World Agricultural Economics and Rural Sociological Abstracts* (1964) 6:1, 42.

in 1965[56] and the times and routes of public transport buses made them generally unsuitable for the great majority of school-going youth. As a result, most of them walked or cycled to school. Consequently the greater the distance from the centre the smaller the proportions likely to be attending postprimary schools, since these schools are concentrated in the centre. If this were so it would mean that adolescents living nearer the centre are more highly educated and have higher levels of occupational and income aspiration than have those from further away. One would expect somewhat similar consequences from the fact that nearness to the centre should also lead to higher levels of modernisation or urbanisation of attitudes and aspirations. If occupational opportunities are evenly distributed throughout the community this would indicate that greater distances from the centre would lead to lower levels of occupational and income frustration and a lesser tendency to migrate. However, off-farm occupational opportunities are not evenly distributed throughout the community but are concentrated near the centre. As one moves out from the centre, the area becomes more farm dependent and off-farm occupational opportunities become fewer. (See Table III, Chapter 2.) This suggests that those living further from the centre find it more difficult to get a suitable job, and therefore might tend to migrate more. It may be, however, that the more remote respondents commute to the centre to work. As Arensberg suggests, it may be that shopkeepers and garage owners in the centre prefer employing farm youth to working class youth from the town.[57] If this is so, and given their lower levels of aspiration, the more remote the respondent the lower should be the tendency to migrate. It is not possible to make clear predictions here and the analysis will explore both possibilities.

Increasing distance from the centre may also influence sex selectivity in migration. Since the proportion of farm families in the population increases with distance, and since farming is highly selective of males, the difference between males and females in their levels of occupational and income frustration should increase greatly with distance from the centre. Consequently, the greater the distance from the centre the greater should be the sex difference in migration plans.

---

[56] This situation has also changed since the time of the survey. School buses were introduced in 1967.

[57] Arensberg, *The Irish Countryman, op. cit.*, 157.

How should attitudes toward, or the degree of satisfaction with, community relationships be affected by distance from the centre? Available evidence from America and the Netherlands suggests that for males, levels of satisfaction increase with distance from the centre. This tends to occur both because of the increasing proportions of the more traditionally oriented farm males in the population, and secondly because increasing remoteness itself tends to operate as a deterrent to the "urbanisation" of attitudes, by restricting the universe of more urbanised reference groups used as points of comparison.[58] The reverse situation should hold for girls for the reasons already discussed. An increasing proportion of girls are likely to become dissatisfied with their family and other roles as the community becomes increasingly dominated by more traditional farm families and community structures.

The proportion of respondents with high levels of family obligation should also increase with distance from the centre. Since it is expected that these obligations are concentrated among farm males, increasing proportions of farm males should lead to increasing proportions of respondents with high levels of obligation.

The fact that the more remote respondents—especially males— are likely to have high levels of Community Satisfaction and Family Obligation indicates that migration tendencies should decline with distance in their case. If, besides this, distance does not act as a barrier to participation in the centre's labour market one could strongly predict decreasing migration rates for males with increasing distance from the centre. Whether this is so or not hinges on the characteristics of participation in the centre's labour market.

CONCLUSION

This completes the discussion of the more immediate factors likely to influence intentions to migrate, as well as their relationship to some major antecedent social structural factors. A sizeable number of hypotheses have been proposed and the rationale for their probable validity developed. The following chapter includes a brief—largely demographic and ecological—description of the research site and a more full description of the methodology employed. Since educational achievement is such an important variable in the analysis of migration trends, Chapter 3 examines the structure

[58] Haller, *op. cit.*; Kaldor, *op. cit.*; Kelley, H. H., *op. cit.*

of postprimary educational movement of an adolescent cohort in the community studied. Chapters 4, 5 and 6 analyse the results of the interview study of a sample of these adolescents, and examines to what extent the actual situation conforms to that predicted in this chapter. The next chapter (Ch. 7) summarises the results of the first study in terms of the rationale proposed and any changes necessary in this framework are discussed. The lastt three chapters report the results of the follow-up study and the final conclusions of the study.

2. The Area Studied and Methods Employed

Introduction

This chapter describes the area and population studied and the methods employed in data gathering. To put the problem in its wider context, however, we first take a general look at migration from Ireland, and attempt a brief description of the history, economy and population of the country and of the community studied. Then we describe the method of delineating this community and give some details of its population. The particular cohort of adolescents studied is also described here, as well as the method of sampling them. The chapter ends with an account of the data gathering procedures used and of the means of operationalising the main variables, along with some discussion of the errors involved in measurement.

The Irish, of almost all nationalities, seem to have been very migratory from early times. Certainly from the arrival of Christianity in the fifth century our folklore and history is full of stories of the deeds and travels of Irish emigrants, saintly and otherwise. This is illustrated by a story found by Dr Geary, one of the most eminent Irish demographers: in the eighth century an Irish poet, Sedulius, turned up at a continental monastery. The abbot, Strabo, speculated as to why Sedulius had left Ireland, "whether it was due to the unsettled state of the country or the Irish habit of going away".[1] This "Irish habit of going away" has been characteristic of successive generations since that time and any overall consideration of migration from Ireland must consider this tradition of migration from very early times. While the point is not equally of importance in

[1] Geary, R. C., "Present day and future emigration from Ireland in historical perspective", paper delivered under Professor K. H. Connell's auspices to a seminar in the Department of Economic and Social History, The Queen's University, Belfast, 3 May 1968.

this more specific study it should be kept in mind when comparing our situation to that of other countries.

Even before the massive exodus after the Famine, Irishmen had migrated in large numbers abroad. Up to that tragic event in 1845–7, however, the total population had continued to increase from the middle of the eighteenth century onwards.[2] Since the Famine, population decline has been massive, and was almost continuous right up to 1961, when the trend was halted.[3] There has been a slight increase in population from then up to the present time. From 1841 to 1961 the total population of the 26 counties now in the Irish Republic dropped from 6.5 million to 2.8 million; a decline of over 57 per cent in 120 years. This decline has been limited, however, to rural areas since the population of towns with more than 1,500 people has, in fact, increased from 1,002,000 to 1,297,000 in the same period.[4] So the movement has been largely out of agriculture into urban industrial employment. But because industrialisation has been very slow to develop in Ireland, people have had to emigrate. Thus the major fact that emerges from an examination of these population changes is that the growth of urban complexes has been very slow. The rate of rural population decline, although much greater and starting at a much earlier date than in other European countries, has, by and large, proceeded at the general European average since the beginning of the century.[5]

Cavan county, the one chosen for this study, has been one of the worst hit areas. Its population in 1841 was 243,200 compared to 56,600 in 1961; a decline of 78 per cent. While the rate of decline has not been as rapid in more recent census periods, it continued at a steady rate even up to 1966, when the population was 54,000, a decline of almost 5 per cent since 1961.[6]

THE TOWN AND COUNTY OF CAVAN

Cavan is one of the three Ulster counties which remained in the Free State, now the Republic of Ireland, in 1922. The Treaty

[2] Connell, K. H., *The Population of Ireland, 1750–1854*, Oxford University Press, 1950.
[3] Commission on Emigration Report, *op. cit.*, and *Census of Population of Ireland, 1961*, Vol. I, 1963; and Vol. I, 1966.
[4] Commission on Emigration, *op. cit.*
[5] Ibid.
[6] *Census of Population of Ireland*, Vol. I, 1961; and Vol. I, 1966.

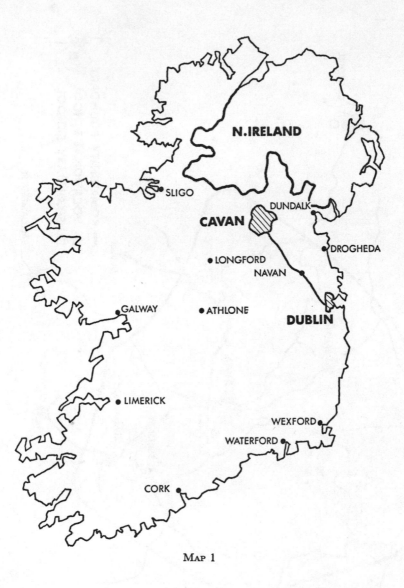

MAP 1

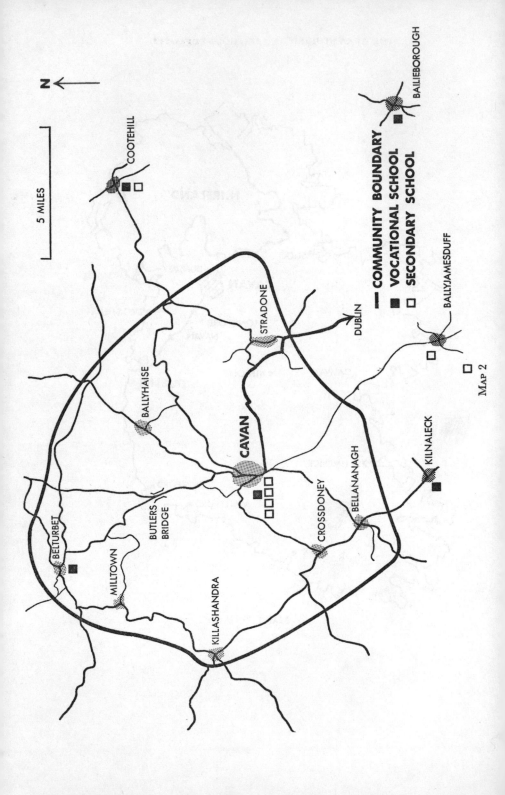

N ←

5 MILES

COOTEHILL

BAILIEBOROUGH

BALLYHAISE

STRADONE

DUBLIN

BALLYJAMESDUFF

CAVAN

BELTURBET

BUTLERS
BRIDGE

MILLTOWN

CROSSDONEY

BELLANANAGH

KILNALECK

KILLASHANDRA

— COMMUNITY BOUNDARY
■ VOCATIONAL SCHOOL
□ SECONDARY SCHOOL

MAP 2

separated it from its six northern neighbours of the province of Ulster by a political border which bore little relation to economic realities. The boundaries of the county touch on this border at many places. Indeed, its establishment at this point has had damaging economic effects on many northern communities in the county. Some trade centres were cut off from their previous hinterlands, and many open country areas were cut off from their market and trade centres.

The town of Cavan is situated about seventy miles north-west of Dublin (see Map 1). Its name derives from an Irish word meaning "a hollow", and is highly descriptive of the topography of the town itself. The origins of the town and county of Cavan go back at least to the tenth century, when the territory known as Breifny was divided into two principalities—East Breifny, the territory of the O'Reilly sept; and West Breifny, the territory of the O'Rourke sept. These two principalities correspond to the modern counties of Cavan and Leitrim respectively, although it was not until six centuries later, in 1584, that East Briefny was formed into the present county of Cavan, and the English administrative county system replaced the original Irish one. The principal castle of the OReillys was situated on Tullymongan hill just outside the present town of Cavan, and it may be assumed that the town originated from the castle.[7]

The community includes the town of Cavan and its surrounding trade-dependent hinterland—the "trade-centre community" as it is termed by rural sociologists.[8] (See Map 2 for its outline.) The main focus of the community is therefore the town of Cavan itself, the administrative centre for the local government of the county. The town had a population of 3,958 in 1961, and 4,205 in 1966. Its primary economic function is as a service and marketing centre for the surrounding farm areas. It has one bacon factory, its major employer; three hospitals which service most of the 'county; the county council offices, many garages and shops which give considerable employment, and a large number of professionals to service the surrounding area. A new engineering factory had just been opened before the survey started but was giving very limited employment and in fact closed down very soon after the survey was completed.

---

[7] Smyth, T. S., "Municipal charters of the town of Cavan", *Administration*, Journal of the Institute of Public Administration of Ireland, (1962) 10, 3, 310–17.

[8] Loomis, C. P. and Beegle, J. A., *Rural Social Systems*, Prentice Hall, 1954, 188–97.

Four other small factories have been opened since then. There are in the town four secondary schools and one vocational school, serving a large area.

Belturbet, another town within the community studied, is ten miles to the north of Cavan, just a few miles south of the border. It had two factories at the time of the survey—a shoe factory whose employment is still expanding; and a glue factory which has since transferred to Dublin. The population of the town is nearly static, being 1,093 in 1961 and 1,100 in 1966.

Killashandra, another town about twenty miles west of Cavan town and separated directly from it by the many lakelets of Lough Oughter, has a population of 397. It has one of the most thriving milk processing cooperatives in the country, plus an independent milk processing factory. For a town of its size it has good employment opportunities. The population reached 408 in 1966, a very slight gain since 1961.

Up to seventeen miles to the south of Cavan are situated the small towns of Ballyjamesduff and Virginia, the subject of some of Percy French's songs. They are both very small market towns (Virginia: 515 in 1961, 511 in 1966; Ballyjamesduff: 581 in 1961, and 630 in 1966) and fall outside the area surveyed. Virginia has a vocational school and is situated on the main road to Dublin. There is a girls' secondary school in Ballyjamesduff, and a boys' school is situated a few miles out of the town. Balieborough is situated about 30 miles almost directly east from Cavan, well out of the survey area. Its population was 1,136 in 1961 and 1,173 in 1966. In 1965 it had one vocational school.

Cootehill is situated about sixteen miles north-east of Cavan. It had a population of 1,296 in 1961 and 1,303 in 1966. It had one of the first comprehensive schools established in the country, based on an original secondary school and vocational school in the town.

There are a number of small villages within the community area of which Ballinagh, Ballyhaise, Butlersbridge and Stradone are the largest. These surround the centre, and are no more than four to six miles from it.

The rest of the community lives in open country areas, usually in individual farmhouses on their own farms. These are normally situated a little off the main roads or off small minor roads. Most of the roads are surfaced with tarmacadam, although some are still soft surfaced and are very muddy during rainy weather.

The landscape is typical of the drumlin country of which Cavan is the centre—a landscape of numerous little hills, and very varied conditions of soil and drainage. Most of the land is unsuitable for tillage farming because of the steep hillsides and poor drainage properties of the soil. In parts of the community the small farms are often interrupted by patches of bogland or by rocky outcrops and occasionally by woodland. The farming is characteristically 'mixed': primarily dairying, pigs and store cattle, and a small amount of tillage.

From an economic and social structural perspective the county is in a rather homogeneous region of the country, comprising the three counties of the province of Ulster which are in the Republic, and the province of Connaught. If the more urbanised counties of Sligo and Galway are excluded from the Connaught data, over 74 per cent of the remaining population live in open country areas, and over 60 per cent of the population are dependent on farming for a living. A comparison of several relevant statistics for the county with those for the region as a whole as well as with the total country are presented in Table II.

Over sixty per cent of the county's total population depends on farming for a living. This figure is similar to those for the other counties of Ulster and Connaught, but is almost twice that of the whole country (34.5 per cent). The farms are primarily family farms. This is clearly illustrated by the fact that less than 7 per cent of the total male labour force employed in agriculture are fully employed farm labourers: half the figure for the country as a whole, and roughly a quarter of the figure for the province of Leinster, where farms are much bigger. The farms are very small, with almost 50 per cent of the male agricultural labour force employed on farms of under 30 acres. This is about one third higher than the figure for the country as a whole, and almost twice that for Leinster. Agricultural and non-agricultural incomes are also among the lowest in the country, being almost 30 per cent lower than the average. As a result of these cumulative disadvantages, the county and the whole region, in fact, has suffered the nation's greatest rate of migration and of population decline for the past few decades. Although the emigration rates have fallen considerably since 1961, the figures for this north-western region were still more than two and a half times greater than the national average and almost ten times the rate for Leinster, which has the lowest emigration rates.

TABLE II: SOME CHARACTERISTICS OF THE POPULATION OF CO. CAVAN, THE PROVINCE OF ULSTER (3 COUNTIES) AND THE PROVINCE OF CONNAUGHT (5 COUNTIES)

AREA	% Population in towns of over 3,000. (1961)[1] %	% of the total population dependent on farming (1961)[2] %	% permanent agricultural labourers of total males employed in agriculture (1961)[3] %	% of total males engaged in farm work on holdings of under 30 acres (1960)[4] %	Income in agriculture per male engaged[5] pounds	Average annual rates of net emigration rate per 1,000 of average pop.[6]		
						1951–6	56–61	61–6
CO. CAVAN	7.0	60.2	6.5	49.2	237	18.2	21.3	13.8
ULSTER (3 Cos.)	7.4	63.3	6.2	51.1	226	19.6	20.7	14.2
CONNAUGHT (5 Cos.)	14.0	61.3	4.1	52.5	247	17.4	18.3	13.6
TOTAL COUNTRY	42.2	34.5	13.2	37.1	337	13.4	14.8	5.7

[1] *Census of Population of Ireland*, Stationery Office, Dublin, 1963, Vol. 1, 1961, Table 8, 15–19.
[2] *Census of Population of Ireland, Occupations*, Stationery Office, 1963, Vol. 3, 1961, Table 7, 120–5.
[3] *Agricultural Statistics*, Stationery Office, Dublin, 1960, Table 23, 70.
[4] *Agricultural Statistics*, 1960. Supplement to *Irish Trade Journal and Statistical Bulletin*, 1962, Central Statistics Office, Dublin, 5–10.
[5] Attwood, E. A., and Geary, R. C., *Irish County Incomes in 1960*, Economic Research Institute Paper No. 12, 1963, Table 12, 21.
[6] *Census of Population*. Stationery Office, 1967, Vol. 1, 1966, Table 12, xx.

The area in question has had a long tradition of migration, going back for well over a century. Most families have wide contacts with migrants outside the county. A decision to migrate from this area would therefore probably meet fewer barriers than in less mobile communities. The universe of effective comparative reference groups used in making such a decision is greatly enlarged by these extended migrant contacts.[9] In this situation feelings of attachment to the home community probably have less effect than they would in communities with less migration. This may be another limitation on generalising from the study and should be kept in mind.

THE COMMUNITY SELECTED

1. Delineation

Map 2 shows the boundaries, and some of the other major features of the community: the centre and its relationship to some of the smaller towns, and the location of the primary, vocational and secondary schools.

The community was delineated on the basis of a single service— secondary school education. The community's centre is the major postprimary educational centre for the county. There are four secondary schools there—two for girls, one for boys and one co-educational school, plus the county's major vocational school. Since the nearest other vocational schools are ten to fifteen miles away at Belturbet (north) and Kilnaleck (south), there is a large area surrounding Cavan town which is highly dependent on the centre's educational services.

The relationship between these secondary schools in Cavan town and the primary schools in the surrounding areas was the determining factor in delineating the community. The location of the secondary schools attended by school leavers from over a hundred primary schools in the countryside surrounding Cavan town was first determined through a survey. The majority of the pupils from fifty-two of these primary schools had gone to secondary schools in Cavan town. The pupils from the other fifty schools surveyed had in the majority gone to other secondary schools. The areas served by these

[9] Kelley, H. H., "The two functions of reference groups", reprinted in Swanson, Newcomb and Hortley, et alia, (Eds.), *Readings in Social Psychology*, Holt, NY, 1952, 410–14.

fifty-two primary schools formed a compact territory surrounding the centre. These small primary school areas usually range from approximately two to four miles in diameter. They are provided usually on a parish basis and are nearly always administered by the religious authorities of the parish, whether Catholic or Protestant.

As Map 2 shows, the boundaries of the community selected are very irregular, ranging in distance from 10 to 16 or 17 miles from the centre. It contains within its boundaries, at Belturbet, a second vocational school. A number of other vocational and secondary schools are situated some distance away from, but right around, its boundaries.

During the primary school survey a complete enumeration was obtained of all school leavers from this community who had completed their primary education in the previous five years—1960–4 inclusive. Additional data were also gathered on their social background characteristics and their postprimary educational, occupational and residence movements. Chapter 3 examines the relationship between these social factors and educational movement. Subsequently a sample of these school leavers was interviewed on their migration decisions and on the factors affecting them, and this information is analysed in Chapters 4, 5, and 6. The follow-up survey restudied a subsample of these in 1968.

Population figures are not, unfortunately, available for the small primary school areas. Since some demographic information would be useful it was decided to use the data available for the District Electoral Division Areas, as used in the census reports, within which these school areas are situated. A total of 25 Divisions were included in all, each of which contained approximately two primary school areas. The following section examines some statistics available for these districts.

2. Description of the Community Population

The District Electoral Divisions were arranged in distance bands as measured out from the centre. Since the distance of each primary school from the centre had been measured, and there were approximately two of these in each District, the average school distance per District was used as the relevant statistic here. Table III below contains some important population characteristics of these different Electoral Divisions.

As distance from the centre increases, the proportion of the population dependent on agriculture for a living also increases from about three per cent of the household heads at the centre to ninety-one per cent for districts ten miles or more from the centre. Similarly the percentage of the male labour force employed in agriculture increases from roughly four per cent to over eighty per cent. If we assume that there are approximately as many employed males in both farm and non-farm households within each distance band, the difference between the percentage of household heads who are farmers and the percentage of the total male force who are employed in agriculture should give a good indication of the proportion of males resident in farm households who hold jobs off the farm. The difference between these two percentage figures for each distance band decreases greatly with increasing distance from the centre: from approximately twenty-three per cent in the band surrounding the centre, to twelve per cent in the next band, nine per cent in the third and ten per cent in the outermost band. These figures demonstrate very clearly that off-farm opportunities decline very rapidly with increasing distance from the centre. Parellel trends appear in the data for females. The proportion of females not gainfully occupied outside the household increases from sixty-four per cent at the centre to eighty-one per cent at the periphery, while the percentage for females gainfully occupied in non-farm occupations decreases drastically from thirty-four per cent at the centre to seven per cent at the periphery. All these factors demonstrate the great importance of locational or ecological factors in the distribution of occupational opportunities in rural areas. They are equally likely to influence migration. The figures for population decline strengthen this interpretation since in the intercensal period 1951–61 population decreases were only ten per cent at the centre but rose steadily to over fifteen per cent at the periphery.

A comparison of the community figures with those for the county as a whole seems to indicate that it is a more advantaged part of the county than the more outlying areas. Approximately 10 per cent more of its male labour force is engaged in non-farm pursuits than of the county population as a whole, and nearly 4 per cent more of the female labour force. Perhaps it is partly as a result of this that there is less out-migration from this part of the county. The similarity of the county and provincial figures is also clearly revealed in the table, while comparisons with the national statistics given in the

Table III: Characteristics of the community's population by distance from the centre: population size and change in 1951–61; and occupational characteristics

	POPULATION SIZE			OCCUPATIONAL CHARACTERISTICS—1961			
	1951	1961	Percentage decrease 1951–1961	Percentage household heads who are farmers	Percentage of males gainfully occupied employed in agriculture	Percentage of females not gainfully occupied, of total females over 14 years old	Percentage of females gainfully occupied in non-farm occupations, of total females over 14 years old
			%	%	%	%	%
1. Centre	3555	3208	9.8	2.6	3.5	63.7	34.1
2. Up to 2 miles from the centre; Rural Districts surrounding the centre	2018	1784	11.6	68.3	45.7	72.8	22.0
3. Districts in band 3 to 5 miles surrounding the centre	4886	4337	11.2	82.8	71.0	79.4	12.8

4. Districts in band 6–10 miles from the centre*	5731	4927	14.0	87.5	78.7	79.0	10.5
5. Districts 10 miles and over from the centre*	2253	1913	15.1	91.1	81.4	80.6	7.2
6. Two districts including two towns of 400+ 1,000 pop. over 10 miles from the centre	2468	2288	7.3	33.0	29.3	69.1	28.2
7. TOTAL COMMUNITY	20,911	18,457	11.7	65.7	58.1	74.3	18.8
8. Co. Cavan	66,377	56,594	14.7		68.6	76.2	15.0
9. Ulster	253,252	217,524	14.1		63.3	75.3	10.4
10. Ireland	2,960,593	2,818,341	4.8		43.4	71.4	21.7

* Supplied by the Central Statistics Office from unpublished data. See Appendix I for details. Two D.E.D.'s, Corr and Larah, are excluded. One falls in band number four, the other in band five.

table show how disadvantaged this whole region is in terms of general economic and social characteristics.

THE COHORT SELECTED FOR STUDY

Since the study was focussed on migration decision-making among adolescents who had not then taken up a permanent adult occupation, the problem largely dictated the selection of the population. The group focussed upon was the cohort who had finished primary schooling in the area in the five years previous to the start of the study, i.e. primary school leavers in the 1960–4 period inclusive. This group varied in age from approximately 13 to 19 years.

Very few of a younger age had migrated, while older groups were already highly selected out by previous migration. Any information gathered on the migration motives of those older persons who had remained in the community but were essentially only a residual population could not be generalised to all adolescents growing up in the community. Since one of the major aims of the survey was to come to some conclusions about the migration motives of all local adolescents a rather specific age group was indicated: one which had not yet started to migrate on a large scale, but which had already become highly involved in migration decision making. The following sections first give some details of the total five year age group being examined and secondly describe the sample selected from this group for intensive personal interviewing.

1. The Five Year Cohort

In order to get a complete enumeration of all adolescents in the area and an overall view of their mobility, it was decided to gather limited information on all adolescents from the community who had terminated their primary education in the previous five years. Fifty-two primary schools fell within the community delineated. The areas served by these primary schools formed an intact territory surrounding the centre. Map 2 shows the boundaries of the community and the following (Table IV) sets out some characteristics of the schools.

The average number of school leavers per school was 29, but there was very wide variation as the results in Table IV clearly show. Over nine-tenths of the schools were one or two room schools. These

TABLE IV: CHARACTERISTICS OF PRIMARY SCHOOLS WITHIN
THE COMMUNITY. SIZE OF SCHOOLS, AND NUMBER OF STUDENTS
WHO FINISHED THEIR EDUCATION IN THE PERIOD 1960–1964

Size of school	Number of schools	Number of students finished there in the period 1960–4
One Teacher	21	218
Two Teachers	26	748
Three Teachers	1	33
Four Teachers	1	66
Five Teachers	1	67
Six Teachers	1	175
Thirteen Teachers	1	142
TOTAL	52	1,485

were usually located in the open country. Over two-thirds of all
school leavers came from these schools. The larger schools were
situated in the centre or in the neighbouring small towns. All but
eight were co-educational schools, and in almost all cases the exceptions were the larger schools.

Table V gives a breakdown of the population of school leavers
by fathers' occupation. The percentage of school leavers from a farm
background is much smaller (47 per cent) than the percentage of
farm households in the community (66 per cent). This may be
accounted for by (1) the lower proportion of farmers who are
married, (2) the older age of the married heads of farm households
and consequently the lower proportion of married couples with
school-going children, and (3) the fact that the area included in
Table III does not exactly correspond with the school area
delineated.

The majority of the non-farm respondents come from manual or
service backgrounds, while only a small minority come from non-
manual backgrounds.

Of all adolescents in this five year age group 37 per cent went to
secondary schools after completing their primary education, 36
per cent went to vocational schools, and the remaining 27 per cent
terminated their education at the primary level. Chapter 3 includes
an analysis of the relationships between these educational movements
and some selected social background factors.

TABLE V: PARENTAL OCCUPATIONS OF ALL ADOLESCENTS WHO HAD
GRADUATED FROM PRIMARY SCHOOLS IN THE AREA IN THE PERIOD
1960–4

Occupation of Father or Guardian	Percentage of total adolescents by occupation of parents	
	%	%
Farmer	47.0	47.0
Professional and Semi-professional	4.2	
Employers, Managers and Proprietors	8.0	
Intermediate Non-manual workers	3.0	
Total Non-manual occupations		15.2
Skilled manual workers	7.2	
Service and Sales workers	6.5	
Semiskilled manual workers	4.7	
Unskilled manual workers	16.8	
Total manual and Service Occupations		35.2
Other (non classifiable):	2.7	2.7
TOTAL (N = 1,485)		100

The selection of a sample of respondents from this group of
school leavers, for intensive interviewing about migration planning,
will be described in the next section.

2. The Sample Interviewed

While doing exploratory fieldwork in outside areas, a number of
problems was uncovered in selecting a suitable population for an
intensive interview study of migration decision-making. The
youngest members of the cohort (13–19 year olds) had given very
little consideration to occupational or migration decision-making for
at least one year after leaving primary school. This was especially
true of adolescents in their first of five years in secondary schools. It
was less true of first year students in vocational schools, which offer
a course of only two or three years. But in this case, and in the case
of similar youths who had received no postprimary education, such
decision-making was not of critical interest and they did not appear

to have entered the "tentative stage" of occupational decision-making.[10] Such decisions, however, had become much more relevant and had been much more fully considered by those youths who had left primary schools two to three years previously (except for those who had gone on to secondary schools). On the other hand, a considerable proportion of older youth who left primary schools four to five years before the study began had already migrated. It would not only be very difficult to locate these migrants but, since their major occupational and migration decisions had already been made and acted upon, their inclusion would have introduced too many problems of validity and reliability into the data as well as problems of comparability of data from migrants and non-migrants. For these reasons, although a representative sample of the total cohort had originally been considered as the best sampling plan, it was subsequently rejected. It was then decided to focus attention on that part of the age cohort whose members were seriously engaged in occupational and migration decision-making, but who had not as yet acted on these decisions.

For those not in secondary schools, this population included all adolescents who had terminated their primary education in 1962 and 1963. This population included all second and third year vocational school students, all those who had received only a primary education and had left school two to three years previously, and all 'drop-outs' from vocational and secondary schools who had finished their primary education at the same time.

The equivalent age group could not be selected from secondary schools, however. Since secondary schools offer a five to six year course, occupational decision-making does not become relevant for most of these students until they have reached at least the fourth or fifth year. The fourth, fifth, and sixth year students, where present, were the ones chosen, although it was recognised that the age difference between these and others might be important variables in themselves. Nevertheless, these secondary schools students were the only ones equivalent to the primary and vocational group in terms of their occupational and migration decisions and their selection posed fewer conceptual and operational problems than did any alternative. The sample interviewed therefore was the one which was then actively engaged in occupational planning, and generally

[10] Burchinal, L. G., *Career Choices of Rural Youth in a Changing Society*, A. E. S. Bull. 458, Minnesota, November 1962.

TABLE VI: CHARACTERISTICS AND NUMBERS OF ADOLESCENTS
SELECTED FOR INTERVIEWING

Characteristics	Numbers
a. All students from the community who had finished their primary education and were in the two final years at secondary school in the centre (in 1960–1).*	126
b. All students from the community who had finished their primary education in the years 1960 and 1961, and at secondary school elsewhere	29
c. All students from the community who had finished their primary education in 1962 and 1963, and in their second and third years at vocational school in the centre	74
d. All students from the community, who had finished their primary education in the years 1962 and 1963, and attending vocational schools elsewhere	26
e. All adolescents from the community, who had graduated from primary schools in 1962 and 1963 and working in 1965. Includes all those who did not receive any post primary education and those who had dropped out from postprimary education	250
TOTAL NUMBER TO BE INTERVIEWED	505

* There are four secondary schools in the centre. One is a Catholic diocesan school for boys, St Patrick's, one is a Protestant co-educational school, the Royal School, and there are two Catholic girls' schools, Loreto College and St Clare's. The last mentioned is a day school, while the other three have boarding facilities. There are approximately 450 pupils from the community in these schools. There is one vocational school in the centre which provided a two to three year course for 165 students from the community. There is one other vocational school within the community at Belturbet, and two others just outside its boundaries attract some students from the community.

one which had not yet become committed to a permanent occupation. Some characteristics of the population interviewed are presented in Table VI.

Unfortunately, this sample excluded a number of adolescents

who had left secondary schools between their third and fifth years. However, in the only school where this was a problem, interviews were also conducted with all third-year students. The population selected also excluded all those schools leavers who had already migrated. These numbered only 19 in all, or roughly four per cent of the total population. Despite these drawbacks, the sample selected appeared to be the best compromise available.

DATA GATHERING: PROCEDURES AND PROBLEMS

1. The Primary School Survey

A survey of all primary schools (52) within the community was completed between September and December 1964. Information was gathered on the postprimary education received by all school leavers for the period 1960–4, as well as on their basic social characteristics. The information required was supplied by the school principal, or gleaned directly from school records. The names and addresses of all schools, school managers and school principals in the area were made available by the Department of Education, whose officers gave every assistance to the survey. Because of this support the assistance of the school managers and principals was greatly facilitated, and access to the school records was ensured. A comprehensive national study of the total school system had just been completed by an OECD team working in cooperation with the Department of Education.[11] For this reason, school managers, principals, and teachers were conversant with similar types of research, and this also facilitated access to school records etc. The cooperation of the local branch of the Irish National Teachers' Organisation was also obtained, and proved helpful in many cases. As a result, out of 102 schools visited, only one refused to cooperate, and this fell outside the boundaries of the community subsequently delineated.

The following information was obtained on all students who had finished their education in these schools in the previous five years:

(a)   Name and address of each student, and the name of head of household.

(b)   Year finished in school; grade reached.

(c)   Sex and age.

[11] Department of Education, *Investment in Education*, Stationery Office, Dublin 1966.

(d)   Occupation of father.
(e)   Number of other children in the family and their birth
           orders.
(f)   Any subsequent education received after leaving primary
           school; any occupation that had been taken up.
(g)   Any residence movements that had been made by school
           leavers.

Additional data was also secured on each school: its size, distance
from Cavan, age of principal teacher and number of years of teach-
ing experience, etc. Some information was also gathered on the
community in which the school was located: number of organisations
present, type and quantity of social provisions, etc. Information on
the social characteristics of students was obtained primarily from the
school records or the school principal. Any additional data was
obtained from school children, such as sibs, friends or neighbours of
ex-students. This latter source of information proved important for
data on the educational, occupational and residence movements of
ex-students, especially where the teacher was not a resident of the
area or where he had only recently taken up a post there. If the
parents were farmers, the size and valuation of the farm was obtained
from records in the county rates office.

Much of the information secured from the primary school records
and teachers was subsequently checked against somewhat similar
information supplied by the secondary and vocational schools, or
obtained later from the school leavers themselves. The accuracy of

TABLE VII: THE ACCURACY OF INFORMATION SUPPLIED BY THE SCHOOL PRINCIPALS,
OR GATHERED FROM SCHOOL RECORDS. NUMBER OF ERRORS MADE. AN ERROR EXISTS
WHERE THERE IS A DIFFERENCE BETWEEN THE REPORT OF THE TEACHER AND
RESPONDENT

Occupation of father of respondent. Number and proportion of errors		Education of respondent. 1st year after leaving primary school. Number and proportion of errors		Occupation of respondent receiving only a primary education, 1st year of work. Number and proportion of errors	
N	Percentage Total responses compared	N	Percentage Total responses compared	N	Percentage Total responses compared
62	13.8	25	5.1	29	6.4

this initial information was tested against this later data. The last four items in the above list ((d), (e), (f), (g)) are the important ones in this respect, since the other pieces of information were available from school records. Assuming that the information obtained directly from respondents was the most accurate, for the 450 students later interviewed from this community the following errors occurred in the original data gathered in the primary school survey. (Table VII.)

In regard to educational movement, 60 per cent of the total errors occurred in the number of years of postprimary education said to have been received by the respondent, and the remainder in the type of education received. These latter errors occurred almost exclusively among students alleged to have had either a secondary or a primary education. Most of these errors were also in the conservative direction; that is, educational levels were given which were lower than was actually the case.

In regard to the occupation of respondents who had not gone on to postprimary schools, 6.4 per cent of total responses were errors. However, of all subjects who had taken a job, 15.7 per cent of these responses were errors. Forty-six per cent of these were due to errors in education, 9 who were actually in school being classified as workers, and 23 working respondents being classified as in school.

The total error level in family size and in students' birth orders was 10 per cent. There was very little gross error in birth order and the major error in family size occurred in underestimating the size.

Overall, therefore, a gross error of about 10–15 per cent can be expected in the data supplied by teachers. These errors, however, are mainly in the conservative direction, particularly for occupation of father, education of students, and size of family. They should act, therefore, to reduce the magnitude of any association between occupation of father, size of family, and education of children. If the information had been more accurate, any positive relationship would have been more pronounced. For the 450 community adolescents later interviewed, discrepancies in the information supplied by the teacher were corrected and this should reduce the error level to less than 10 per cent.

2. Interviewing Respondents

The questionnaire or interviewing schedule was pre-tested, on a similar population in outside areas, and revised several times—

first after 20 interviews in Co. Mayo, and again after interviewing 15 respondents in another part of Co. Cavan with the corrected schedule. Further corrections were then made, and the final form of the schedule was prepared.

The data collection instrument was designed both as an administered questionnaire and as an interviewing schedule. The former was used for those currently in secondary and vocational schools. The respondents in this case filled in their answers to a written series of questions in the presence of the researcher who could clarify the questions if required. Other respondents were interviewed in their homes or at their place of employment, if that proved agreeable to the employer. The same questions were used in both modes in exactly the same sequence. As a place for the interview the work setting was found to be more satisfactory than the house in many cases. This was particularly true for families who did not have a separate living room or sitting room in the house, where the interview could be carried out free from interference. If the interviewer was a female this was not a major problem, because the interview could then be carried out without embarrassment to the respondent in the open air, if the weather was favourable, or in the interviewer's car if not. In several cases, however, interviewing problems arose because of the interviewing situation. In two cases, a male interviewer attempted to interview a female respondent in a car on the public road. It quickly became obvious that this was a very embarrassing situation for female respondents, and this approach naturally resulted in very unsatisfactory interviews. In some small number of cases, other family members were present during the interview. This caused difficulties with questions about parental and family influences and about respondents' own intentions and attitudes, where these might have diverged from parental expectations. Many of these problems can be avoided by very careful attention to the structure of the interviewing situation: by adjusting the resources of the interviewing team to suit the situation, and by careful scheduling of interviews to suit weather and light conditions, etc. However, most of these problems could not be foreseen at the time.

Locating respondents in the field survey was not very difficult. The name of the head of household and the townland address had been secured from the school records. One inch Townland Index maps were used by the interviewers to locate these. With some experience, interviewers could easily locate townlands, and there was usually no difficulty in finding the household, as townlands usually contain only a small number of homes. That this approach was successful is shown by the fact that out of a total of 240 field interviews attempted, it proved impossible to locate only four households. In these cases either the family name or address was incorrect. If place of work was known, interviews were attempted there. Usually the proprietors of shops, garages, and other work places were willing to have employees interviewed while at work. Generally, this interviewing situation proved satisfactory.

In the early phase of interviewing some problems occurred in gaining access and establishing credentials. As the study had the blessing of the Department of Education, this name was used in the first few days of interviewing to help establish the legitimacy of the study. It was also explained that the names of the selected respondents had been obtained from the primary school rolls. This information and the general purposes of the study were always explained first to respondents' parents in order to get their permission to interview. On the second day of interviewing, the above procedure was adopted in one farm household, and the interviewer received the father's permission to interview his son. Since the son was not present, a tentative appointment was made for the following day. On returning for the interview, the prospective respondent was very emphatic in his refusal to cooperate, maintaining that he had no intention of returning to school, despite the wishes of the Department of Education. This misinterpretation was buttressed by the fact that the young man had previously attended vocational school for only a few weeks, although his parents would have liked him to continue. It soon became apparent also that this respondent had not kept his opinions of the survey to himself, because two neighbouring respondents were equally unwilling to cooperate for somewhat similar reasons. The relationship of the survey to any educational institution was never emphasised in subsequent interviews. Almost all the direct refusals, and a number of those who could not be contacted even after repeated return visits (in many cases an indirect refusal) were due to similar misunderstandings of the purposes of the survey despite the great care taken to avoid this.

The following table (Table VIII) sets out the number of respondents interviewed, and the number of refusals, repeated unsuccessful "callbacks", respondents who were not traceable or who had left the area. Almost 12 per cent of the total sample were not interviewed for these reasons. Nearly half of these had already migrated out of the area, bringing the total present in the community but not contacted to roughly 7 per cent of the total sample to be interviewed originally. However, 110 "extra" interviews were obtained, largely from students present in local secondary and vocational schools, who were from areas in Co. Cavan just outside the community boundaries. These additional interviews were used to test hypotheses which are not related to ecological factors.

Some disturbing ethical problems arose during the course of the interviewing, due in most cases to a glaring need for occupational

TABLE VIII: NUMBER AND CHARACTERISTICS OF THE POPULATION INTERVIEWED, AND OF PROSPECTIVE RESPONDENTS NOT CONTACTED

Situation interviewed	Numbers interviewed from the community	Numbers not contacted from the community	Numbers interviewed from areas outside the community
Secondary Schools			
St Patrick's College	47	0	20
The Royal School	6	3	2
St Clare's	42	4	6
Loreto College	24	0	19
Other Secondary Schools	19	10	0
Sub-total	138	17	47
Technical Schools	61	13	3
Cavan Technical School	10	4	3
Belturbet Technical School	10	2	53
Other Technical Schools	—	—	—
	31	19	59
Sub-total	—	—	—
Field Survey			
Major Field Survey	206	0	4
Dropouts from Technical Schools	21	23	0
Sub-total	227	23	4
TOTAL NUMBERS	446	59	110

counselling. In a number of cases, especially amongst the poorly educated farm boys, respondents were highly confused about what they could do, how they would go about obtaining a suitable job, whether or not they should migrate, and what they might expect if they did. It would have been possible, with some additional work, to help solve some of these problems. Even limited advice could have helped many respondents who were very worried and upset about their future and who were highly uninformed or misinformed about opportunities open to them. But this would, of course, have interfered with the behaviour being observed.

Problems arose also in the case of a number of parents who requested help from the interviewers for their children. In two cases, fathers sought information on what their sons wanted to do, after the interview had been carried out in private with the sons. In both cases sons worked on the home farm with an older brother, so that there was apparently no future in farming for them. In both cases, too, there was obviously no effective communication between father and son, a situation which was not at all unusual. Both fathers appeared to be very concerned with their sons' welfare, but didn't know what their sons wanted to do, or what their interests were. Both men felt, however, that their sons would have to seek work off the farm. This lack of effective communication between parents and children, especially between father and son, as observed by the interviewers, appeared to be very general and was typically accompanied by a deep, but greatly thwarted desire to help their children. It also appeared that parents and adolescents would generally have welcomed counselling. The very narrow limits of the research sociologist's responsibilities to his respondents became painfully obvious to several of the interviewers who encountered these family difficulties.

OPERATIONALISATION OF THE STUDY'S MAJOR VARIABLES

Developing the Questions

As a result of the pre-tests extensive revisions were made in the questionnaire or schedule. Problems of ambiguity, poor phrasing, use of words and phrases which were too sophisticated for the population being studied, use of symbols which triggered verbal value responses, and the sheer length of interviews were the major difficulties encountered. Some words (e.g. 'anxious') have clear regional meanings; words like 'exploited' are too sophisticated, especially for the primary educated; a straightforward question on prestige or income level of the family relative to other community families usually gets a slightly offended and highly unreliable response.

The positioning of questions also posed problems. In some of the early interviews, highly personal questions were asked too early in the interview, before rapport had been sufficiently established. Unfortunately, this was overcompensated for in the final edition and descriptive type, social background questions took up too much time in the initial questioning. As a result interviewers had some problems in stimulating the interest of the respondents. Questions on personal interests and attitudes should have come earlier in the interviews and some of the social background questions should have been postponed until the end.

Information was obtained from the respondents about the following areas, and roughly in the following sequence:

a.   General demographic and social background data on the respondent and his family.

b.   Occupation and residence of all siblings, uncles, and aunts.

c.   Communication, organizational, and recreational behaviour of his family.

d.   Educational and occupational roles (if any) of respondent after leaving primary school, up to the time of the interview.

e.   Occupational aspirations; beliefs about achieving these locally; and parental expectations about respondents' occupations.

f.   Migration intentions, and parental expectations about migration.

g.   Occupations rejected because of family prestige factors.

h.   Occupational values.

i.   Level of living aspirations, and beliefs as to whether they can be achieved locally.

j.   Income aspirations, and the extent to which it is believed they can be achieved locally.

k.   Reasons given for migrating, if thinking of doing so.

l.   Attitudes toward the home community's social provisions.
m.   Community Satisfaction.
n.   Family Obligations of the respondent.

The schedule took approximately one hour to administer. In most cases, the administered form took longer than the interviewing form, once interviewers had some experience.[12]

Procedures for Operationalising the Major Variables

The questions used were generally highly structured and, where applicable, scaling techniques were used. In the following pages the major variables utilised in the analysis are operationalised starting with the main dependent variable—migration plans.

1. *Dependent Variable: The Intention to Migrate*

Three fixed-alternative questions were used in the schedule to measure this variable, two of which most respondents were expected to answer. *Question 27 (g) or 28 (k)* (Appendix I) was asked of respondents who were already working.

"Do you think that you will stay permanently (working) at this particular job?" ____ Yes ____ No ____ Not Sure.

If respondent answered "Yes" to this particular question, he was categorized as *"not intending to migrate"*, and was not to answer Questions 35 or 64. If he answered "No" or + "Not sure" he was asked to answer *both* Questions 35 and 64.

Question 35 read:
"Do you intend to leave this part of the country to get a job, and live your life elsewhere?" ____ Yes ____ No ____ Not Sure.

Question 64 read:
"Do you intend to leave this part of the country so that you can get a better income elsewhere?"
____ Yes ____ No ____ Not Sure.

"This part of the country" was clarified to read "Co. Cavan" in the course of interviewing. If respondent answered "No" to both Question 35 and Question 64, he was categorized as *"not intending to migrate"*. If he answered "Not Sure" to Question 35 and Question

[12] See Appendix No. I for the Questionnaire used.

64, or "No" to one and "Yes" or "Not Sure" to the other, he was categorised as *"uncertain whether to go or stay"*. If he answered "Yes" to both Question 35 and Question 64, or "Not Sure" to one and "Yes" to the other, he was categorized as having a *"definite intention to migrate"*.

2. Independent Variables

(a) *Occupational aspiration level:* To measure this variable, an earlier developed self-administered instrument of Sewell and Haller[13] was used, with modifications appropriate for Irish respondents and to suit the interviewing technique. It was comprised of these questions (Questionnaire—Appendix I):

Question 29:   (a) What jobs (occupations) have you thought of
                    going into?
                    1. _____   3. _____
                    2. _____   4. _____
                (b) What job(s) would you really like to get?
                    1. _____   3. _____
                    2. _____   4. _____
                (c) What is the first job(s) that you think you will
                    get?
                    1. _____   3. _____
                    2. _____   4. _____

An external criterion, the North-Hatt Scale, was used to order the occupations in terms of their relative prestige status.[14] The applicability of this scale to conditions in Cavan was verified by showing it was highly correlated with the way local respondents ranked occupations (See Appendix II for details). The scale was divided into nine ordinal categories of occupations, ranging from Higher Professional to Unskilled Labourer. Two codes were utilized: (1) the highest status group to which the respondent aspired, and (2) the lowest status group to which he aspired. The former closely

[13] See Haller, A. O. and Miller, I. W., *The Occupational Aspiration Scale: Theory, Structure, and Correlates*, Michigan State University, A. E. S. Tech. Bull. 288, 1963, 25.

[14] North, C. C. and Hatt, P. K. "Jobs and occupations: a popular evaluation", *Public Opinion News* (1947) 3, 3–13; and reprinted in Bendix, R. and Lipset, S. M., *Class, Status and Power*, Free Press, 1957, 424–5.

conforms to what Kuvlevsky and Bealer[15] call "occupational aspiration"—occupational goals which are desired. The latter closely conforms to what they call "occupational expectations"—the probable occupational position that respondents expect to reach, whether they desire them or not. This latter variable will be the one used in this research.

(b) *Occupational Frustration:* This was operationalized in Question 33 (Appendix I) which follows soon after Question 29. It reads:

(a) "Of the jobs that you have just considered, do you think that you will be able to get any of them in or near your home community?"

_____ Yes _____ No _____ Not Sure.

If the respondent answered "Yes", he was categorized as *"not frustrated in occupational aspirations"*. If he answered "No", the respondent was categorized as *"frustrated"*, while if he answered as "Not sure" he was categorized as *"partly frustrated"*. Of course, if he was already working and did not intend to leave his job (see under "Intention to Migrate"), he was regarded as *"not frustrated"* occupationally.

(c) *Income Aspirations:* This was operationalized in Question 61, (Appendix I) as follows:

"Now, if you could get a permanent and otherwise suitable job, in a place of your own choosing, how much would the job need to pay *per week* before you would be satisfied with it?"
The responses were categorised in steps of two pound units from two pounds up to over twenty pounds.

(d) *Income Frustration:* This was operationalized in the following way in:

Question 62: "Now, for the type of income that you want to earn, do you think if you stay in or near your home community, that you will be able to earn this income?"

_____ Yes _____ No _____ Not Sure

The responses were coded in the same way as for Occupational Frustration.

[15] Kuvlevsky, W. P. and Bealer, R. C., "A clarification of the concept 'Occupational Choice' ", *Rural Sociology* (1966) 31, 3, 265–76.

(e) *Community Satisfaction:* This was operationalized by using a considerable modification of the Schulze *et al.* scale items,[16] and the Vernon Davies scale items.[17] These changes were necessitated by the differences in the cultural environment. Ten items were initially used in the pre-tests; and since they seemed to be highly relevant, and gave high item variability, they were retained for the final schedule. The ten items are given in Question 70 in Appendix I. Five responses were allowed to each item, ranging from "Strongly Agree" to "Strongly Disagree". Items varied from a positive one like "The people of this community are very friendly and helpful to one another" to a highly negative one like "Any young people worth their salt should leave this community". An item analysis of the responses was subsequently carried out on a representative sample of 100 respondents, using the Chi Square technique developed by Sharp and Ramsey et al.[18] All ten items were found to discriminate between the top and bottom quartiles. Since only nine items were required, the least discriminatory item (item 'h') was dropped, and the scale was scored from 9 to 0 (most dissatisfied to most satisfied) by dichotomizing the responses. For the first five negative items of the scale, responses of 'Disagree' or 'Strongly Disagree' were each scored as 1; while responses of 'Agree' or 'Strongly Agree' were scored as 1 for the remaining four positive items. Other responses and ones of 'Undecided' were coded as 0.

In all four of the scales used, it was clearly observed that respondents were not making any comparable meaningful distinction between 'Strongly Agree' and 'Agree' or between 'Strongly Disagree' and 'Disagree'. As a result, no attention was paid to this distinction in the scoring.

(f) *Attitudes toward the community's social provisions, or community evaluation:* This was operationalized by using a scale of similar design which measured satisfaction and dissatisfaction with ten separate social facilities and institutions in the community. (See Question 66 Appendix I). A similar item analysis yielded a nine item scale with scores ranging from 0 to 9—from most dissatisfied to most satisfied with social provisions in the home community.

[16] Schulze, et al., "The measurement of community satisfaction and the decision to migrate", *Rural Sociology* (1963) 28, 3, 279–83.
[17] Davies, V., "Development of a scale to rate attitudes of community satisfaction", *Rural Sociology* (1945) 10, 3, 246–55.
[18] Sharp, E. E. and Ramsey, C. E., "Criteria of item selection in level of living scales", *Rural Sociology* (1963) 28, 2, 146–64.

(g) *Family Obligations of the Respondents:* This was operationalized by using 3 questions in sequence—Questions 71, 72 and 73 (Appendix I):

Question 71: "Do you help out your family or some other relation in any way?" ____ Yes ____ No
If yes, please give details of what you do:

_____

_____

Question 72: "Do you think that your family or some relation depend on your help to any extent?"
—— Yes —— No
If Yes, how much? ( ) A great deal
                   ( ) Somewhat
                   ( ) Undecided
                   ( ) Not very much

Question 73: "Now, if you were to leave your community and home, could somebody else do the work that you are doing for them?"
                   ( ) Yes, very easily
                   ( ) Yes, somewhat easily
                   ( ) I don't know
                   ( ) No, not very easily
                   ( ) Not except with difficulty

Respondents were categorized as having:
  (i) *No Work-Role Obligation* if: (1) They were in boarding school; or (2) answered "No" to Question 71; or (3) if answered "Yes", obligations, as detailed, did not require that the respondent remain at home to fulfill them.
  (ii) *Very Slight Work-Role Obligations:* (1) Works evenings at home while doing other work during the day, or at school during the day; and (2) family does not depend "a great deal" or "somewhat" on his help (Question 72); and (3) somebody else could do the work "very easily", "somewhat easily", or "don't know" (Question 73).
  (iii) *Medium Work Obligations:* (1) Works evenings at home, while doing other work away from home or at school; (2) family do not depend "a great deal" or "somewhat" on his

help (Question 72); (3) but could not be replaced "very" or "somewhat easily" (Question 73).

(iv) *High Work Role Obligations:* (1) Works full time at home; (2) family depends a "great deal" or "somewhat" (Question 72); and could be replaced only "with difficulty" or "not very easily" (Question 73).

(h) *The social status or prestige level of the Respondents' families:* This variable proved to be a major problem, both conceptually and operationally. The best solution would have been to use some type of reputational technique, and to have the respondents' families placed on a relative prestige continuum. But the population was too large, and too widely scattered to allow for any small number of 'judges' to know the population, and thus to do this effectively.[19] Classifying respondents by the occupational status level of their families seemed to be the next best approach and was in fact the approach taken for the non-farm sector of the population.

Occupations were classified into nine groupings on the basis of their type of work and their loadings on the North-Hatt scale. The validity of the North-Hatt scale in this setting was established by having respondents evaluate 51 well-known occupations in terms of their local prestige level. By correlating 14 occupations which were common to the North-Hatt and Cavan scales, a Spearman rank order correlation of .87 was obtained.[20] Appendix II contains the details of this occupational classification. The occupational categories used are as follows, ordered in descending order of status;

1. Higher professional workers
2. Lower professional workers
3. Employers and proprietors of wholesale and retail shops etc.
4. Farmers
5. Intermediate non-manual workers
6. Skilled manual workers and foremen
7. Service and sales workers and other non-manual workers
8. Semiskilled manual workers and lower order service workers.
9. Unskilled manual workers

[19] Warner, W. L., Meeker, M. and Eells, K., *Social Class in America*, Harper Torchbooks, 1960, 47–71.
[20] See Hannan, D. F. and Beegle, J. A., "Evaluations of occupations on the basis of their prestige and difficulty of achievement", *Rural Sociology* (1969) 34, 3.

Occupations were coded individually using two columns. The first column represented the major occupational category, while the two columns in combination give the individual occupation. If necessary then, individual occupations could be treated separately in the analysis.

Farmers, as an occupational group, are far too heterogeneous in terms of social status and its correlates to be treated in this way.[21] It was decided to ignore this dimension of status for this category of respondents, since it could not be comparably measured. Instead, attention will be focused on the income class, or size and valuation of farms.

(i) *Father's incomes:* Fathers' incomes were reported by non-farm respondents, and estimated for farm respondents from the farm production figures they supplied (Question 16 (c) of the schedule, Appendix II). The income responses and estimates were coded as follows:

Up to £4 per week, or £208 per annum
From £5–6 per week, or £209 to £312 per annum
From £7–8 per week, or £313 to £416 per annum
From £9–10 per week, or £417 to £520 per annum
From £11–12 per week, or £521 to £624 per annum
From £13–14 per week, or £625 to £728 per annum
From £15–20 per week, or £729 to £1,040 per annum
Over £20 per week, or over £1,041 per annum.

Farm production figures were supplied by respondents from farm backgrounds, and production unit 'incomes' were calculated from figures made available for 36 farms in the county.[22] Average 'profits' per unit of livestock and crops were computed for each farm, and summed to get the family farm income, a rough equivalent of non-farm incomes. The variability of the method was estimated by comparing actual and estimated family farm incomes on these 36 farms. On 17 farms, the estimates and the actual income levels occupied the same code categories and, in 13 additional cases, the estimates were found to be within two code categories of the true one. The

[21] See Duncan, O. D. and Artis, J. W., *Social Stratification in a Pennsylvania Rural Community*, Penn. A. E. S. Bull. 543, October 1951; Vidich, A. J. and Bensman, J., *Small Town in Mass Society*, Princeton University Press, 1958, Chapter 3.

[22] From figures kindly supplied by Dr. E. A. Attwood of the Rural Economy Division, Agricultural Institute, Sandymount Avenue, Ballsbridge, Dublin.

farms used in the incomes study were very similar to the farms included in this research. Therefore, the income estimates should be correct in roughly forty per cent of the cases, and should be within two levels of the correct income category in over ninety per cent of the cases.

(j) *Birth order or position in the family cycle:* The position of the respondent in the family was measured by asking him to give the number of older and younger siblings (Appendix I, Question 8). The responses were coded in the following way.

> *Position 1* in the family indicates that the respondent is the oldest child in the family;
>
> *Position 2* indicates that the respondent is the second child in the family, where the older child is a girl;
>
> *Position 3* indicates that the respondent is the second child in the family, where the older child is a boy;
>
> *Position 4* indicates all other situations.

Focussing our attention on the time the respondent is finishing at primary school, the first position indicates a situation in a farm family in which there is the greatest proportion of young unproductive members, and the greatest pressure on family resources.[23] With, for instance, a family of five, all under fourteen years of age, there would be one worker—the father—and five young dependents. As a result the family might be more likely to keep this older child at home to help out the parents with the farm and family problems. Especially with larger families the first members of the family appear likely to get less education than others coming later in the family. Positions two and three will be aggregated in many cases in the analysis.

Other minor variables which are used throughout the analysis are operationally defined in the footnotes or in the appendix.

STATISTICAL ANALYSIS OF THE DATA

Due to the level of measurement established for the major independent variables (categorial or ordinal) and for the dependent variable (ordinal in the case of migration plans) it is obvious that an analysis of variance technique cannot be employed, although it would have been theoretically the most appropriate. Some analogue

[23] Loomis, C. P. and Beegle, J. A., *Rural Social Systems*, Prentice-Hall, NY, 1951, 77–87.

to analysis of variance would be desirable which would provide information on the independent and interactive effects of the major independent variables. Such an analogue, however, is not available given the level of measurement involved.

The next most appropriate procedure which yields approximately equivalent information seems to be the use of bivariate and multi-variate contingency tables, and this is the procedure employed.

Since we are dealing with a total population, statistical tests of significance are strictly unnecessary. However, as an aid in decision making, where relationships are weak and not very consistent, a Chi Square test of significance will be employed.[24] Where the level of significance is less than .95 (i.e. the relationship is not "significant") the specific probability associated with the result will be stated for each table. It could be argued that very weak relationships present in the data (which might lead to the confirmation of particular empirical hypotheses) could be accounted for by random factors which change from year to year, and are not due to the effect of the particular independent variable involved. This could hold particularly in the case of the two-year age group treated in Chapters 4 to 6. If one were to imagine the population interviewed to be a representative sample of the total five year cohort treated in Chapter 3 (which, in fact, it is not), random factors alone might account for some weak relationships found in the hypothesised direction. The actual probability associated with the Chi Square statistic then will be taken into consideration in the decision as to whether the trend in the table is clearcut enough to lead to the rejection of the null hypothesis in each case.

The strength of the relationship will be measured by Goodman and Kruskal's Gamma,[25] where the variables are ordinal. In such a cross-classification, Gamma measures the difference in the conditional probabilities of like and unlike order. It tells how much more probable it is to get like than unlike order in the double classification,

[24] Walker, H. M. and Lev, J., *Statistical Inference*, Holt, Rinehart and Winston NY, 1953, Chapter 4, 81–109.

$$\chi^2 = \sum_{1}^{k} \frac{(f_o - f_e)^2}{f_e}$$

[25] Goodman, L. A. and Kruskal, W. H., "Measures of association for cross-classification", *Journal of the American Statistical Association* (1954) 49, 732–64. See Zelditch, M., Jr., *A Basic Course in Sociological Statistics*, Henry Holt and Company, NY, 1959, 180–3, for the computational method.

where two individuals are chosen at random from the population. If there is independence, the order within one classification has no connection with the order of the other. In this case Gamma is 0. If there is high positive association between the two, the order on one classification would generally be the same as that of the other classification, and Gamma in this case approaches plus 1. If there is high counter-association, the order in one classification would be directly opposite to that of the other, and in this case Gamma approaches minus 1. The greater the degree of association between the two variables the larger the value of Gamma.

3. Results I—The Mobility of Primary School Leavers

Introduction

This chapter deals with the movement of primary school leavers into postprimary schools or directly into occupations. Since the educational level achieved by adolescents has such an important influence on aspirations and migration plans, this account of how educational mobility itself is structured sets the stage for the later analysis of migration planning. Sex, social status, distance from the centre, family size and birth order, were the major variables proposed as affecting educational mobility. The relationships between these variables are explored in the following sections.

EDUCATIONAL MOBILITY, SEX AND SOCIAL STATUS

Social status refers to the occupational status level of parents, as defined in the previous chapter. Although risking the danger of some confusion, these occupational status groups will, for the sake of clarity and in accordance with traditional usage, be sometimes referred to as in three main "class" groups; the middle class, farmers, and the working class. The middle class is composed of professional and semi-professional workers, all employers, proprietors, and managers, and all intermediate non-manual workers. The working class includes all the manual occupations: skilled and service workers, semiskilled and unskilled workers. Each of these three categories will sometimes be dichotomized into upper and lower levels.

Postprimary education and sex: As can be clearly seen from Table IX, both the occupational background and sex of adolescents is very closely related to postprimary educational careers. First, educational chances are obviously highly related to sex. Of the females in the

TABLE IX: The educational achievement of all adolescents from the community as related to sex and occupational background. Education received first year after leaving primary school

Level of Education Received	The Middle Class		Farmers	The Working Class				Total
	Professional, and Semi-professional Workers	Proprietors Managers and Intermediate Non-Manual Workers		Skilled Workers	Service Workers	Semiskilled Workers	Unskilled Workers	
Males	%	%	%	%	%	%	%	%
Secondary	96.6	71.1	26.2	42.4	42.4	22.2	8.9	33.4
Vocational	3.4	17.8	26.4	40.7	35.2	31.1	35.1	28.1
Primary only		10.0	46.6	16.9	20.4	46.7	55.3	37.7
TOTAL %	100.0	98.9	99.2	100.0	98.1	100.0	99.3	99.2
TOTAL N	29	90	337	59	54	45	134	748
Females								
Secondary	97.1	71.4	37.9	32.6	52.3	33.3	10.6	41.1
Vocational		15.5	42.7	38.5	27.2	39.4	37.5	35.1
Primary only	2.9	11.9	19.1	25.0	20.5	27.3	50.0	22.9
TOTAL %	100.0	98.8	99.6	96.1	100.0	100.0	98.1	99.1
TOTAL N	35	84	351	52	44	33	104	703

The percentages given here are computed from the total N given at the bottom of each column but since information on education in not available for each respondent the missing percentages are those for whom information on education is not available.

cohort, 41 per cent[1] attended secondary schools as compared with 33 per cent of the males. This difference lies mainly in the proportions of secondary school students from farm backgrounds attending the schools in Cavan town as day pupils (19 per cent males compared to 27 per cent females). Although in the total population, only 39 more females than males attend secondary schools, 46 more farm females than farm males do so. This difference may be due to the fact that a girls' secondary school in the centre offers a secondary education at lower fees than that available for boys. But, since the differences do not hold in the same degree for those from the unskilled worker category where cost should be of more importance, this is unlikely to be the explanation. On the other hand, it may be that even where equal facilities exist, farm fathers, or more probably farm mothers, will see to it that their daughters get a better education than their sons.[2]

This situation also seems to hold for farm adolescents in vocational schools. These are attended by 7 per cent more females than males, 28 per cent of males as against 35 per cent of females. Here again the same pattern holds in regard to fathers' occupations. The difference occurs solely in the farm category, with other occupational groups generally showing no great sex differences. Indeed the reverse holds in the case of skilled and service occupations, where more males than females attend vocational schools. Further analyses demonstrated that this sex difference for the farm category did not occur for the vocational school in Cavan town, but rather in the outlying vocational schools.

It appears then that farm families will generally send more of their daughters on to postprimary education, preferably to a secondary education. Where this is not available cheaply (i.e. as in the outlying areas where secondary education can only be achieved through sending children to boarding schools), they will send the excess of females to vocational schools. This sex selection exercised by farm families is probably related to the different obligations of farm girls and boys, with more boys having to stay home and work on the farm upon leaving primary school. In total 31 per cent of farm boys but only 11 per cent of farm girls remained working on the home farm after completing their primary education. And of the remainder

---

[1] Percentage figures in the text are rounded to the nearest whole number.
[2] McNabb, P., in Newman, J. (Rev.), *The Limerick Rural Survey 1958–64*, Muintir na Tire Publications, Tipperary, Ireland, 1964, 187, 204, 210.

who did not stay at home on the farm, 78 per cent of the boys but 91 per cent of the girls received a postprimary education. Even in the case of those moving off the farm, therefore, upon finishing at primary school, farm girls received a better education. However, the difference between farm boys and girls in the "opportunity" to stay on the home farm upon leaving primary school accounts for the major part of the overall sex difference in attendance at postprimary schools. The difference in percentage points between males and females receiving a postprimary education is reduced from 28 percentage points in the total farm youth population—53 per cent of all farm boys but over 81 per cent of all farm girls receiving a postprimary education—to 13 percentage points for those moving off the farm. McNabb, making a similar observation, theorizes that farm females, finding greater difficulty in "establishing" themselves in the home community, are given a better education, so that they will be able to find occupational and marriage opportunities of an acceptable status level in other areas.[3] The results found here tend confirm this explanation.

Postprimary education and social status: It is also clear from Table IX that educational life chances are very closely related to social status. The "Middle Class" almost exclusively ensure that their children get a postprimary education, and almost always a secondary education. If we ignore the Farmer category temporarily, and take the average figures for skilled and service workers, there is a clear linear relationship between the status level of fathers' occupations and (a) the proportion of adolescents getting only a primary education and (b) the proportion of adolescents getting a secondary education. The lower the occupational status of the father the greater the proportion getting only a primary education, and the smaller the proportion getting a secondary education. This relationship is closer for males than females, but it is also clearly and consistently present for females if the skilled and service worker categories are aggregated.

For vocational schools the picture is not as clear. This seems to be due to the great popularity of this form of education for the sons of skilled and service workers, and also for the daughters of skilled workers. While 31 to 35 per cent of the sons of semiskilled and unskilled workers attend vocational schools, 35 to 41 per cent of skilled and service workers' sons do so. There are no clearcut

[3] McNabb, *op. cit.*, 187 and 210.

differences among females from the same occupational groups. For both sexes, the lowest proportions attending vocational schools came from the middle class. Children of skilled and service workers who do not receive a secondary education are generally given a vocational education, and only a small proportion—less than one quarter—get only a primary education. Not only do much lower proportions of those from unskilled and semiskilled backgrounds receive a secondary education but for the boys, fewer receive a vocational education as well.

The difference between semiskilled and unskilled workers is not very great at any level of education, except that somewhat more of the unskilled receive only a primary education while more of the semiskilled receive a secondary education. Only 9–11 per cent of the unskilled worker's children are in secondary schools, compared with 22–33 per cent for the semiskilled. However, the sample sizes, in the case of semiskilled workers especially, are too small to be sure that these percentages are stable.

Because farmers are so heterogeneous in their class and status characteristics they cannot easily be fitted, as a group, into an occupational status system.[4] If farms are categorized by land valuation, however, Table X shows clearly that somewhat equivalent distinctions within the farmer category are equally important in influencing the educational chances of farm adolescents.

The pattern is very clear for females: a consistent increase in the proportions attending secondary schools and a consistent decrease in the proportions attending vocational schools is associated with increasing valuation of the family farm. The proportion in secondary school consistently increases from 29 per cent for those from farms under £15 valuation, to 74 per cent for those from the highest valuation farms. The proportion in vocational schools consistently decreases from 50 per cent to 18 per cent respectively for the same valuation categories. The pattern for males is less clear. If the two lowest and two highest valuation categories are aggregated, there is again a clear relationship between educational life chances and the valuation of the farm. The proportion in secondary schools rises

---

[4] See Duncan, O. D. and Artis, J., *Social Stratification in a Pennsylvania Community*, A.E.S. Bull., Penn., 1951, 543, and Vidich and Bensman, *Small Town in Mass Society*, Princeton University Press, 1958. Hollingshead, A. B., in *Elmtown's Youth*, also takes note of the same phenomenon in regard to large and small shopkeepers. This probably holds good for this study as well, but cannot be controlled for.

sharply from 19 to 54 per cent, although the proportion in vocational schools remains relatively constant.

TABLE X: THE EDUCATIONAL ACHIEVEMENTS OF MALE AND FEMALE FARM ADOLESCENTS, BY VALUATION OF FARM

Postprimary education received, if any		Under £15	£15–£29	£30–£44	£45 and over
Males		%	%	%	%
Secondary		21.7	17.4	53.1	55.9
Vocational		24.3	31.3	25.0	14.7
Primary only		52.2	50.7	21.9	29.4
TOTAL	%	98.2	99.4	100.0	100.0
	N	115	144	32	34
Females		%	%	%	%
Secondary		29.2	36.6	46.2	73.5
Vocational		50.0	46.2	30.8	17.6
Primary only		20.0	17.2	23.1	8.8
TOTAL	%	99.2	100.0	100.1	99.9
	N	120	145	39	34

Similarly, if the two highest and lowest valuation categories are aggregated, the relationship between valuation of farm and the proportions receiving only a primary education is very clear for males. This increases from approximately 25 per cent to 51 per cent with decreases in farm valuation. Valuation of farms then is closely related only to the type of postprimary education received by females. However, it is closely related both to the type of postprimary education received by males, and to their total prospects of receiving such education.

If Tables IX and X are compared it appears that both males and females from the highest valuation farms (over £45) exhibit educational patterns similar to those from lower middle class backgrounds (proprietors, managers, and intermediate non-manual workers). On the other hand, males from the smallest farms (under £30) have educational patterns very similar to those from an unskilled manual background. One difference, however, is that a much larger proportion of manual workers' sons go to vocational school, whereas a larger proportion of farmers' sons go to secondary school.

The pattern of educational mobility for females from small farms is very similar to that of females from skilled manual and service occupational backgrounds but much higher than unskilled. Overall, however, the poorest farmers have given their children a somewhat better education than have unskilled and semiskilled manual workers, while the better-off farmers have given their children an approximately equivalent education to that of lower middle class families.

Secondary education then is largely a middle class phenomenon, achieved by adolescents from professional, proprietorial, managerial and other non-manual occupational backgrounds; as well as the

TABLE XI: THE CLASS CHARACTERISTICS OF SECONDARY AND VOCATIONAL SCHOOL STUDENTS. PERCENTAGE OF TOTAL STUDENTS WITHIN EACH SCHOOL SYSTEM, FROM THE DIFFERENT OCCUPATIONAL CATEGORIES. (PERCENTAGES ARE COMPUTED ACROSS THE ROWS)

Educational Level Achieved by Subjects	Class Characteristics of Families				
	Middle Class (All Professional, proprietorial and Non-Manual Occupations)	Farmers		Working Class (All manual Occupations)	Total
		Large (30 plus)	Small (under 30)		
	%	%*	%*	%	%
Males					
Secondary	36.8	14.7	20.5	28.0	100.0
Vocational	8.1	6.4	36.0	49.5	100.0
Primary only	3.2	6.3	49.4	41.1	100.0
TOTAL %	15.9	9.2	35.8	39.0	99.9
N	119	(66)	(259)	292	
Females					
Secondary	32.6	15.1	30.9	21.4	100.0
Vocational	5.3	7.5	53.2	34.1	100.1
Primary only	6.7	8.2	33.4	51.6	99.9
TOTAL %	16.9	10.8	39.1	33.1	99.9
N	119	(73)	(265)	233	

* Since information on valuation is not available for a small proportion of farmers (13/351 females and 12/337 males), the percentages are computed first for the total number of farmers and then this percentage is distributed on the basis of the proportion within each valuation category, for whom such data is available.

majority of those from large farms. Vocational education on the other hand, is to a large extent confined to small farm and working class youth. Those who receive only a primary education come almost exclusively from a small farm or working class background.

This class selectivity of the two school systems is brought out clearly in Table XI. For both sexes, almost 90 per cent of all those who receive *only* a primary education (and this is only 31 per cent of all adolescents) come from a small farm background or from the working class. Much the same situation holds for those receiving a vocational education. On the other hand, of those who receive a secondary education, over half come from the middle class or from the larger farms, although persons from these groups comprise only one quarter of all adolescents. Besides their purely educational effects, the markedly different class profiles of the secondary and vocational schools must exert very different socializing influences on their students, both in terms of interaction between students and staff, and in terms of peer group interaction. These influences are likely to have major consequences for the development of aspirations and migration plans.

This completes consideration of sex and social class factors on educational mobility. Clearcut differences in educational chances have been observed amongst the different classes and between boys and girls. These are likely to have major consequences on migration chances and these consequences will be examined in Chapter 5. Besides sex and class factors, the distance of persons' homes from educational facilities was also thought to be important and this influence is next examined.

POSTPRIMARY EDUCATION AND REMOTENESS

There were no school bus services in the community studied at the time of the survey. And, except for one restricted route, the public transport system was unsuitable for getting to and from school. Only a small proportion of families had cars. Even when they had, in any case, almost no family could afford the luxury of sending their children to school by car. As a result almost all the children walked or cycled to school. Consequently, the further away from the centre families live, the more difficult it should be to attend postprimary schools in the centre. Table XII sets out this relation between distance from the centre and school attendance. Since occupation is so closely related to distance, this factor is controlled.

Restricting observation to those attending secondary schools and those receiving only a primary education it appears that, up to four miles, increasing distance from the centre has little consistent influence on educational achievement for any occupational group. Indeed for the middle class group as a whole, distance seems to have little influence on educational chances at any level, although for the lower middle class group there is a slight tendency for decreasing attendance in secondary schools to be related to increased distance. For the other occupational groups, however, there is a clear decrease in attendance at secondary schools for those beyond a four mile radius, and there is a corresponding increase in the proportions receiving only a primary education. Beyond this four mile threshold, however, there is no further consistent change with increasing distance.

A comparison of those who live near the centre with those living more than four miles away, on the level of education received by adolescents from farm and working class backgrounds, reveals a drop of approximately 45 per cent in secondary school attendance for those living more than four miles from the centre. Almost the same pattern holds in reverse for those receiving only a primary education. Farm adolescents, living more than four miles from the centre, show over a 70 per cent increase over those living nearer in the proportions receiving only a primary education. There is a similar type of increase of over 100 per cent in the proportions receiving only a primary education for the more remote adolescents from skilled and service worker backgrounds. Of those from unskilled worker backgrounds, the proportion receiving only a primary education increased by over 50 per cent for the more remote group.

For those receiving vocational education the picture is less clear, largely because alternative schools are convenient to people in the outer distance bands. There is a vocational school, for instance, located within the 8–10 mile band. And two other schools are situated just outside the community boundaries, and are very convenient to many students living over ten miles from the centre. Even when we restrict consideration to attendance at vocational schools in the centre, however, it does not fall off quite as rapidly with distance as does attendance at secondary schools in the centre.

For semiskilled and unskilled workers the break occurs at about

TABLE XII: Percentage primary school leavers attending secondary and vocational schools, and the percentage receiving only a primary education, by distance from the centre. Occupational background of subjects controlled

Education of school leavers by occupation of fathers	Distance of home community from the centre						
	Centre	Up to 2 miles	2–4 miles	4–6 miles	6–8 miles	8–10 miles	10 and over
	%	%	%	%	%	%	%
(1) Non-Manual Occupations							
Secondary schools	90.5	100.0	63.6	77.8	66.7	63.6	100.0
Vocational schools—Centre	5.3		21.2	7.4	9.5	2.3	
—Other					9.5	25.0	
Primary only	4.2		15.2	14.8	14.3	9.1	
TOTAL %	100.0	100.0	100.0	100.0	100.0	100.0	100.0
N=	95	10	33	27	21	44	6
(2) Farmers							
Secondary schools	46.7	50.0	47.5	20.5	38.7	26.3	28.4
Vocational schools—Centre	26.7	28.6	34.7	35.1	19.4	15.0	0.0
—Other			0.8	4.7	6.5	24.3	32.8
Primary only	26.7	21.4	16.9	39.8	35.5	34.4	38.8
TOTAL %	100.1	100.0	99.9	100.1	100.1	100.0	100.0
N=	30	14	118	171	124	160	67

(3) *Skilled and Service Workers*

Secondary schools	52.6	50.0	57.1	25.0	35.0	28.0	11.1
Vocational schools—Centre	35.8	37.5	23.8	32.1	30.0	4.0	0.0
—Other	0.0	0.0	0.0	0.0	10.0	40.0	55.6
Primary only	11.6	12.5	19.0	42.9	25.0	28.0	33.3
TOTAL %	100.0	100.0	99.9	100.0	100.0	100.0	100.0
N =	95	8	21	28	20	25	9

(4) *Semiskilled and Unskilled Workers*

Secondary schools	19.1	7.1	21.4	4.1	10.0	13.7	9.1
Vocational schools—Centre	41.5	57.1	40.5	28.6	13.3	2.7	0.0
—Other		0.0	0.0	14.3	20.0	21.9	0.0
Primary only	39.4	35.7	38.1	53.1	56.7	61.6	90.9
TOTAL %	100.0	100.0	100.0	100.0	100.0	100.0	100.0
N =	94	14	42	49	30	73	11

the same point for both secondary and vocational schools. For farmers, however, it occurs at six miles for vocational schools, while for skilled and service workers it does not occur until over eight miles. The population sizes, however, in both the manual categories are very small, so that these percentage differences are probably very unstable. Overall, however, the major break for vocational school attendance at the centre occurs at a greater distance than for secondary schools.

The type of postprimary school attended, whether vocational or secondary is also influenced by distance factors, up to four miles from the centre a higher proportion of those from farm, skilled, and service occupational backgrounds attend secondary schools than vocational schools, whereas beyond this point the reverse pattern holds. For the unskilled and semiskilled the relative proportions also change in favour of vocational education with increasing distance from the centre, but not quite so dramatically.

The locational factor then plays a major role in the distribution of educational opportunities. This locational factor should also influence the distribution of occupational and income opportunities, and this question will be explored in Chapter 6.

POSTPRIMARY EDUCATION, BIRTH ORDER, AND FAMILY SIZE

The family into which a person is born exerts a major influence on his educational chances, particularly in its ascribing him to a economic and social position which are here found to be of major influence on educational chances. Other aspects of the family are also likely to have major influences on educational and occupational life chances. The size of the family and the individual's position amongst his siblings are two of the most important of these.[5]

Birth order, or the ordinal position of a person amongst his siblings, has been found to be associated with achievement, with the first born being the highest achievers.[6] On the other hand researchers who had studied the family cycle—particularly of farm families— from formation at marriage, through childbearing and rearing, to final dissolution, have shown that in large families especially, at

---

[5] Blau, P. M. and Duncan, O. D., *The American Occupational Structure*, Wiley, NY, 1967, 295–330.
[6] Ibid.

the time when the oldest is finishing his primary education at 13 or 14, family pressures are at their maximum to retain him at home to help on the farm or to go out to work to supplement the farm income.[7] At this stage in the family cycle there is only one producer— the father—and the maximum number of dependents. Under this rationale, in large families especially, one might expect that the oldest would have a lower probability of receiving a postprimary education than the later born. The relationship actually found between these two variables is summarised below in Table XIII.

That this latter situation does not appear to hold for farm or non-farm youth can be clearly seen from Table XIII. In fact, with some exceptions, a slightly higher proportion of the first-born from farm and manual backgrounds received a postprimary education than those whose birth order was second or later. This holds for both males and females. However, amongst those from non-manual backgrounds the differences in birth order are minor and not very consistent.

This finding appears to support the alternative hypothesis predicting higher achievement for the first born.[8] However, since the probability of falling in the later stages of the family cycle is closely related to the size of the family, and since size of family is also likely to be related to educational chances, the tentative relationships found may be spurious. The following table (XIV) examines this relationship between family size and educational chances, controlling for occupational background and sex.

Table XIV shows clearly that family size is indeed related to educational chances for adolescents, with those from large families getting a poorer education than those from smaller families. This relationship holds for both males and females and for all occupational groups except professionals and farmers. That there is no relationship between these two variables for professionals was to be expected, but it is not immediately clear why it does not hold for farmers. Perhaps Loomis' and others' finding that family farm resources are more effectively exploited as the size of family increases, so that effective family income increases to keep pace with family size, is the answer.[9] This contrasts with the position of working class

[7] Loomis, C. P., *Studies of Rural Social Organisation*, State College Book Store, East Lansing, Michigan, 1945, 190–9.

[8] Blau and Duncan, *op. cit.*

[9] Loomis, *op. cit.*; Scully, J. J., "The influence of family size on efficiency within the farm," *Journal of Agricultural Economics*, (1962) XV, 1, 116–21.

TABLE XIII: CONTROLLING FOR SEX, THE PROPORTION OF ADOLESCENTS IN OCCUPATIONAL CLASSES RECEIVING A POSTPRIMARY EDUCATION, BY BIRTH ORDER IN THE FAMILY

Occupation of the father	Birth Order Within the Family					
	MALES			FEMALES		
	1st and oldest member of the family	2nd member of the family	3rd and other members of the family	1st and oldest member of the family	2nd member of the family	3rd and other members of the family
	The percentage figures refer to the proportions receiving postprimary education					
Professionals and Semi-Professionals	100% (3)	100% (7)	100% (18)	100% (4)	100% (9)	95% (20)
Proprietors, Managers, and Int. Non-Manual Occupations	85.7% (21)	90.5% (21)	90.0% (40)	91.7% (24)	87.5% (16)	84.2% (38)
Farmers	57.0% (79)	52.9% (68)	52.0% (173)	85.9% (71)	83.3% (72)	78.6% (196)
Skilled Manual and Service Workers	76.9% (26)	85.7% (28)	79.6% (54)	88.2% (17)	77.8% (18)	70.9% (55)
Semi skilled and Unskilled Manual Workers	62.1% (29)	48.3% (29)	43.6% (117)	63.6% (22)	73.7% (19)	50.6% (87)

families where the relatively stable income of the wage earning father cannot be similarly expanded. So, in working class families, as the number of mouths to be fed increases, income per family unit contracts until the oldest members start to work and contribute to the family. Therefore with large families where none of the children have yet started to work the family level of living may drop below the "poverty line".[10] That this may indeed be so is strongly suggested by the fact that family size has a great influence on the unskilled and semiskilled manual group, where adolescents from the smaller families (less than 3) have a 27 per cent higher probability of getting a postprimary education than those from the largest families (over 6). Similar but much smaller trends appear in the case of males from skilled and service occupations and both males and females from proprietorial, managerial and intermediate non-manual occupations.

Now, if we control for the influence of family size, what is the relationship between birth order and postprimary education? Table XV below examines this question.

An examination of the table reveals that for the total population there is no consistent relationship between birth order and educational chances for males. There is, in fact, a slight tendency for the later born in the largest families (over six), and the smallest families (less than four) to receive a better education than the first born. This position, however, is reversed for the intermediate family sizes. These percentage differences, however, are very small, and the only clearcut relationship persisting for males is between family size and educational chances. For females, the relationship with birth order is consistently reproduced for all family sizes. The first born has a somewhat higher probability of receiving a postprimary education than later born. In this case also the effect of birth order becomes more pronounced with increases in family size. The percentage difference in favour of the first over the last child for the smallest family size, is five points (79 per cent as against 74 per cent), ten points for medium sized families, and 17 points for the largest families.

For the males from farm and from semiskilled and unskilled backgrounds, the two most intriguing groups in Tables 5 and 6, there is no consistent relationship between birth order and educa-

---

[10] Loomis, op. cit.; Rowntree, B. S., Poverty, A Study of Town Life, London, 1922, is the classic study in this area.

TABLE XIV: The proportions of adolescents in different occupational classes receiving a post-primary education, by size of family, and by sex

Occupation of father	Family Size					
	Males			Females		
	1 to 3	4 to 6	7 and over	1 to 3	4 to 6	7 and over
	The Percentages Receiving a Postprimary Education					
Professional and semi-professional	100.0% (3)	100.0% (14)	100.0% (11)	100.0% (6)	94.7% (19)	97.0% (8)
Proprietors, managers and int. non-manual	95.8% (24)	94.9% (39)	68.5% (19)	94.7% (19)	87.2% (39)	80.0% (20)
Farmers	50.7% (71)	52.5% (138)	56.9% (109)	84.5% (84)	76.1% (142)	85.0% (113)
Skilled and service	82.6% (23)	87.2% (47)	71.1% (38)	68.4% (19)	85.7% (36)	69.4% (36)
Semiskilled and unskilled	68.7% (32)	44.8% (58)	41.2% (85)	75.0% (20)	59.1% (44)	48.4% (62)

TABLE XV: THE PROPORTIONS OF ADOLESCENTS RECEIVING A POST-PRIMARY EDUCATION BY BIRTH ORDER, AND FAMILY SIZE: (TOTAL POPULATION, FARMERS, AND SEMISKILLED AND UNSKILLED WORKERS)

PERCENTAGES RECEIVING A POSTPRIMARY EDUCATION

Occupation of father	Family Size								
	1–3			4–6			7 and over		
	Birth Order			Birth Order			Birth Order		
	1st	2nd	3rd and over	1st	2nd	3rd and over	1st	2nd	3rd and over
(a) Total Population									
Males	% 66.6 (65)	% 67.6 (68)	% 70.0 (20)	% 71.9 (64)	% 70.9 (55)	% 58.6 (162)	% 51.7 (29)	% 50.0 (30)	% 58.2 (205)
Females	79.2 (77)	85.1 (47)	74.2 (31)	83.2 (49)	86.0 (57)	73.3 (180)	88.2 (16)	74.3 (35)	70.9 (191)
(b) Farmers									
Males	46.0 (37)	51.7 (29)	55.6 (9)	52.6 (38)	60.0 (25)	51.7 (89)	80.0 (10)	50.0 (16)	55.8 (86)
Females	85.4 (41)	88.9 (27)	76.5 (17)	87.8 (22)	76.7 (30)	74.4 (90)	100.0 (9)	86.7 (15)	83.1 (89)
(c) Semiskilled and Unskilled Workers									
Males	75.0 (12)	64.3 (14)	66.7 (6)	85.7 (7)	85.7 (7)	40.0 (45)	30.0 (10)	25.0 (8)	44.8 (67)
Females	69.2 (13)	100.0 (4)	66.7 (3)	86.7 (15)	100 (9)	54.3 (35)	33.3 (3)	50.0 (10)	50.0 (50)

tional chances for all sizes of family. Whereas amongst farmers the first born has a poorer chance of receiving a postprimary education for those from the smallest families, the reverse is the case amongst those from the largest families. These trends are exactly reversed for those from manual backgrounds. However, in both these cases the percentage differences are not very great, and the numbers involved are too small for us to be sure of the stability of the percentages.

To summarize: Family size is definitely related to educational chances for all non-farm adolescents, both male and female. There is no relationship at all between family size and education for farm respondents. In regard to birth order in the family, there are no overall consistent relationships for males. For females, the first born appear to have a slight advantage over the later born for all sizes of family and for all occupational groups except the professional.

CONCLUSION

Educational mobility has been found to be highly related to (1) social class and occupational background, (2) sex, (3) distance of homes from the community centre and to a lesser extent to (4) family size. Almost all of these findings strongly support the hypotheses proposed in Chapter 1. Through these clearcut predicted effects on educational mobility these social structural factors should have corresponding effects on migration. Those from the upper levels of the local social class hierarchy, girls—especially farm girls, and the least remote should therefore be far more migratory than others because of their greater tendencies to receive a postprimary education. These and other social factors causing differentials in educational chances, should have corresponding effects on levels of occupational and income aspiration and consequently on migration plans and behaviour. These migration differentials will, in fact, be examined in Chapters 5, 6 and 7. Before proceeding with a study of these migration differentials, however, the following chapter examines the motives involved in these migration decisions.

4. Results II—
Personal Beliefs, Attitudes
and Obligations,
and Migration Intentions

Introduction

This chapter examines the relationship between certain beliefs, attitudes and obligations of respondents and their migration intentions.[1] This is based on an analysis af the results of interviews with 556 adolescents from Cavan—a representative cross section of the adolescent cohort there. "Migration Intentions", the dependent variable, has three values: 1. Definite intention to remain locally, 2. Indefinite whether to migrate or not, and 3. Definite intention to migrate. The major independent variables are: (1) Beliefs about the ability to fulfil economic aspirations locally—Occupational, and Income Frustration; (2) attitudes toward the community—Community Satisfaction and Community Evaluation; and (3) Family Obligations. The analysis employs bivariate and multivariate contingency tables to study the independent and joint effects of these variables on migration intentions.

A number of assumptions regarding migration decision making were implicit in the original theorising about migration. Although not verbalised at that time we attempt to spell out some of these assumptions at this point in order to indicate a time order in the relationship between independent and dependent variables. Preliminary fieldwork had shown that very little consideration had been given to occupational decision making or to migration by youths of 13 or 14 years old. The great majority of these were yet in the

[1] The phrase 'migration intentions' is used interchangeably with 'migration plans'. The word 'intentions' is technically the more correct word but its exclusive use would have made for very awkward phrasing in many places.

83

"fantasy stage" of occupational decision making, and they played a highly dependent role in the family and home community.[2] From these considerations the implicit assumption was made that the decision to migrate proceeds from a situation—at 12 to 14 years old —where very little consideration has been given to the problem and the great majority of respondents see themselves as remaining relatively permanently in the family, to a position—at 18 to 20 years old—where a definite decision has been made as to whether they will migrate or not. As a cohort moves from a position of being dependent children in a family—up to 14 years old—to one where its members first begin to assume adult or independent statuses in their occupational and family roles, the gradually cumulating "pressures" of these new roles and obligations force serious consideration of the location where they might be best carried out. In effect this means that as the cohort gradually assumes those roles and obligations they also move from a position of child dependence and its concomitant commitment to present family location, and of not considering the question of migration in any but a highly tentative way, to one where the decision grows more and more relevant and finally becomes more and more polarised between a choice of whether definitely to stay or leave. If these assumptions are valid a "not sure" answer suggests that the person has moved from the original childhood or dependent commitment to home to a position of seriously considering migration but not as yet to a final decision. In this respect it is thought that as a particular adolescent grows up and comes to assume responsibility for his own adult occupational and familial roles, if these roles are ascribed to him within the family—as on a family farm—or if they are 'naturally' and easily assumed in the local area, then that youth will never change his original commitment to remain at home. On the other hand, if obstacles to the smooth local attainment of these newly assumed roles start to appear, then migration will be seriously considered. The analysis will provide some indirect evidence on these assumptions.

That the migration decision itself is a highly relevant one for most of the adolescents interviewed in this study is shown by the fact that only 24 per cent of the 550 respondents who answered the question definitely intended to remain in the local community.

[2] Burchinal, L. G., Haller, A. O. and Taves, M., *Career Choices of Rural Youth in a Changing Society*, Univ. of Minn. Ag. Expt. Station Bull. 458, November 1962.

Of the remainder, 40 per cent were not sure whether they would migrate or not, and the remaining 36 per cent definitely intended to migrate. The following sections will examine the relationship of the various independent variables to these migration decisions. And since it was hypothesised that economic considerations were the major variables involved in migration these will be the first ones considered.

THE ECONOMIC DIMENSION:
THE FRUSTRATION OF OCCUPATIONAL AND INCOME ASPIRATIONS

Table XVI below summarises the relationship found between these two variables and migration intentions. For ease of presentation in the text the percentages given are for those who definitely

TABLE XVI: THE RELATIONSHIP BETWEEN OCCUPATIONAL AND INCOME FRUSTRATION AND MIGRATION INTENTIONS

Migration Intentions		Levels of Frustration of (1) Occupational, and (2) Income Aspirations			
		Not frustrated	Partly frustrated	Definitely frustrated	Total
(1) Occupational Frustration					
		%	%	%	N
Definite intention to stay		40.7	9.7	6.2	121
Definite intention to leave		19.1	34.5	76.1	189
TOTAL	%	100	100	100	
	N	241	165	113	519

Gamma = .640

(2) Income Frustration					
		%	%	%	N
Definite intention to stay		49.1	11.9	12.5	124
Definite intention to migrate		17.8	26.5	57.7	189
TOTAL	%	100	100	100	100
	N	163	151	208	522

Gamma = .548

intend to remain in the home community and for those definitely intending to migrate. The proportion who are indefinite in their intentions can be got by subtraction from 100 per cent.

In both cases there is a very strong association between the frustration of aspirations and intentions to migrate.

As an examination of the figures in Table XVI indicates, up to half of those not frustrated in either their occupational or income aspirations definitely intend to remain in the home community, while only roughly one tenth of those who are partly or definitely frustrated in these aspirations intend to do so. On the other hand less than one fifth (18 to 19 per cent) of those not frustrated in either of these aspirations definitely intended to migrate compared to 58 and 76 per cent respectively of those frustrated in income and occupational aspirations. Those who are partly frustrated in either of these aspirations hold an intermediate position in regard to migration in this case.

The strength of the association between income frustration and migration intention is not as great as for occupational frustration, nor is the order of the relationship reproduced as consistently. The smaller size of the Gamma statistic indicates this clearly. Although more of those who are not frustrated in their income aspirations intend to remain at home than those who are not frustrated in their occupational aspirations, (49 per cent and 41 per cent respectively), a much smaller proportion of the former definitely plan to migrate if their aspirations are frustrated, (58 and 76 per cent respectively). This indicates that a considerable number of those who intend to stay in the home community are frustrated or partly frustrated in their income aspirations—in fact 44 out of the 124 involved (34 per cent) compared to only half that number who believe that they cannot fulfill their occupational aspirations locally.

Other non-economic variables must therefore play a major role in influencing these respondents to stay at home. Much the same situation holds in regard to those intending to migrate since almost a quarter of these are not frustrated in their occupational or income aspirations when each of these is considered in isolation. However, although these two independent variables are probably highly correlated with each other it is probable that many of those intending to migrate and not frustrated in their occupational aspirations may be frustrated in their income aspirations. Table LXIII in Appendix III indicates that there is indeed a very high correlation between the two independent variables (Gamma = .595). Despite this, however, it may still be possible that if the effects of occupational frustration are partialled out, income frustration may have major additional effects on migration intentions. Appendix Table LXIV has been set out to see if this is the case and the following table (XVII) summarises the results.

By controlling for the effect of variation in occupational frustration, the table shows that income frustration does indeed have major additional effects on migration intentions. At each level of occupational frustration, variation in income frustration is highly associated with variation in migration plans, as the Gamma index indicates in each case.

Controlling for those not frustrated in their occupational aspirations, over half of those who were also not frustrated in their income aspirations intend to remain locally while this is true of only slightly over a quarter of those not frustrated in their income aspirations. At the other extreme, controlling for those frustrated in their occupational aspirations, 22 per cent of those who are not frustrated but only 6 per cent of those frustrated in their income aspirations plan to stay locally. The two independent variables therefore have major joint effects in migration plans. Where both variables act together —where both aspirations are simultaneously frustrated or not frustrated—their joint effects are much greater than where only one acts. Over eighty per cent of those who are frustrated in both aspirations plan to migrate while only six per cent plan to remain locally. On the other hand, of those who are not frustrated in both these aspirations over fifty-three per cent plan to stay and only thirteen per cent intend to migrate. The joint effects of both variables, then, on migration intentions are very pronounced despite their intercorrelation.

In conclusion, occupational and income frustration have major independent and joint effects on migration intentions. Occupational frustration has by far the greatest effect but income frustration has major additional effects when occupational frustration is controlled for.

Nevertheless, almost a fifth of those frustrated in both aspirations did not definitely intend to migrate while only slightly more than one half of those satisfied with both aspirations definitely intend to stay locally. The following section examines the effects of certain non-economic factors—specifically Community Satisfaction and

TABLE XVII: THE RELATIONSHIP BETWEEN INCOME FRUSTRATION AND MIGRATION INTENTIONS, CONTROLLING FOR THE EFFECTS OF OCCUPATIONAL FRUSTRATION

	Occupational Frustration					
	Not frustrated		Partly frustrated		Frustrated	
	Income Frustration		Income Frustration		Income Frustration	
Migration Intentions	Not frustrated	Definitely frustrated	Not frustrated	Definitely frustrated	Not frustrated	Definitely frustrated
	%	%	%	%	%	%
Definite Intention to Stay	53.3	29.8	38.1	3.4	22.2	6.2
Definite Intention to Migrate	13.1	28.1	23.8	56.9	66.7	80.2
TOTAL %	100%	100%	100%	100%	100%	100%
N	122	57	21	58	9	81
	*Gamma = .346		*Gamma = .566		*Gamma = .305	

* The Gamma index is calculated for the overall results in Table LXIV, Appendix III. In the above table figures for those "partly frustrated" in their income aspirations and those "not sure" about migrating have been excluded for ease of presentation.

Family Obligations — to see whether these variables can account for such anomalies.

THE SOLIDARITY DIMENSION: COMMUNITY SATISFACTION AND FAMILY OBLIGATIONS

1. Community Satisfaction

Is alienation from or dissatisfaction with the home community important in determining outmigration? If so, do such high levels of dissatisfaction with the home community lead to migration, irrespective of the level of satisfaction or frustration of occupational and income aspirations as hypothesised? And, if they do, what proportion of the total population are so highly alienated from the home community? These are some of the questions explored in this section. First, does high dissatisfaction with the home community lead to migration? Table LXV in Appendix III contains the complete results bearing on this question, and the following table (XVIII) summarises them.

There is a very strong relationship between Community Satisfaction and plans to migrate. Only seven per cent of those who are highly dissatisfied with the community (with scores of three or less) plan to remain there, while 35 to 43 per cent of those who are highly satisfied plan to remain. The proportions planning to migrate show

TABLE XVIII: THE RELATIONSHIP BETWEEN COMMUNITY SATISFACTION AND INTENTION TO MIGRATE

Intentions to Migrate	Levels of Community Satisfaction				
	Lowest Score — — — Highest Score				
	0 to 3	4 and 5	6 and 7	8 and 9	TOTAL
	%	%	%	%	%
Definite intention to stay	6.9	18.6	35.4	42.6	128
Definite intention to leave	50.0	40.0	29.2	23.1	191
TOTAL %	100	100	100	100	
N	144	140	130	108	522
				Gamma = −.355	

trends directly opposite to this with half of the highly dissatisfied group definitely planning to migrate compared to only a quarter of the highly satisfied. The overall association, as indexed by Gamma, is only slightly lower than that between income frustration and migration intentions.

Slightly more than one quarter of all respondents (28 per cent) are highly alienated from the community, i.e. have scores of less than three. On the other hand over 54 per cent have community satisfaction scores of less than 5, and only 13 per cent of these definitely intend to remain locally. So, a rather high proportion of respondents are highly dissatisfied with their community, and very few of them intend to remain in it. This disaffection from the community may be partly a result of occupational and income frustration, however. So, if the effects of these two variables are controlled, Community Satisfaction may show little additional relationship to migration intentions.

Community Satisfaction is indeed highly associated with both occupational and income frustration as is shown in Appendix III, Tables LXVI and LXVII. (Gamma equals — .298 for Occupational Frustration and — .387 for Income Frustration). And the results summarised in the subsequent table (Appendix III, Table LXVIII) show that both of these other variables have major joint effects on Community Satisfaction. Appendix III, Table LXIX, however, attempts to examine the effects of Community Satisfaction on migration intentions controlling for both the effects of occupational and income frustration. This table shows that there is still a strong association between these two variables even when these controls are introduced. Community Satisfaction, therefore, although highly associated with both economic frustration variables, still retains a highly significant relationship to migration intentions even when the effects of the other two independent variables have been controlled.

This means that although a considerable part of the variance in Community Satisfaction scores can be explained by variations in levels of occupational and income frustration—the frustrated tending to have highly negative attitudes toward the community while the satisfied have highly positive attitudes—there are some major additional sources of satisfaction or dissatisfaction which are not at all related to such economic type considerations. Some of these non-economic influences are having considerable effects on migration planning. Some characteristics of these additional independent effects of Community Satisfaction on migration can be examined by looking at its "partial associations". It was hypothesised that where respondents had highly negative attitudes toward the community they would plan to migrate irrespective of their beliefs about the adequacy of the local community's occupational and income opportunities. If this hypothesis were upheld, it would mean that the associations between occupational or income frustration and migration intentions are greater at higher levels of Community Satisfaction than at lower levels. In fact at the lowest level of C.S. there should be no relationship between the other variables. Appendix III, Table LXX has been set up to see if this is the case.

In terms of the overall relationship the hypothesis is clearly not confirmed. As indicated by the relative sizes of the Gamma indices the highest overall associations between Occupational or Income Frustration and Migration Intentions occurs at the lowest levels of Community Satisfaction. (Gamma equals .729 — .775 at 0–3 levels of Community Satisfaction, while it only reaches .415 to .616 at the other levels.) At low levels of Community Satisfaction there is a greater difference in migration plans between those "not frustrated" and those "frustrated" than at higher levels. A careful examination of the table to see why this unexpected result occurs, however, reveals that the main cells contributing to the high association at low levels of C.S. are the bottom six cells of each table. If we restrict observation to those who "definitely plan to migrate" and those who are "indefinite whether will stay or leave", we find the percentage differences between those "frustrated" and those "not frustrated" is much greater at lower levels of Community Satisfaction than at higher. On the other hand if we restrict observations to the proportions who "definitely intend" to remain locally (the top row of figures), the opposite is the case, and the hypothesis does receive some support. At low levels of Community Satisfaction 18 per cent of those not frustrated in their occupational aspirations definitely intended to remain at home compared to only 2 per cent of those frustrated in these aspirations—a percentage difference of 16 points. On the other hand at high levels of Community Satisfaction 54 per cent of those "not frustrated" in these aspirations intended to stay compared to only 10 per cent of those frustrated in these aspirations —a percentage difference of 44 points. In other words, the lower the level of C.S. the smaller the difference does variation in occupational frustration make to plans to stay at home. The trends for income frustration corroborate this result. So, in terms of predicting variations in the proportions who definitely intend to remain at home the hypothesis is supported. It is not supported, however, by trends in the other two categories of the migration variable. In fact for these categories there is a much greater percentage difference in migration plans between those frustrated and those not frustrated in their aspirations at low levels of Community Satisfaction than at high.

In summary: variations in attitudes toward the home community (Community Satisfaction) are highly predictive of variations in migration intentions. Variations in these attitudes, however, are highly correlated with similar variations in beliefs about one's ability to fulfill occupational and income aspirations in the home community. But, even where the effects of these two variables have been controlled, Community Satisfaction still retains a pronounced association with migration intentions. So, variations in this attitude spring from sources other than purely economic-type evaluations of the home community's opportunities, and these non-economic factors are important in migration intentions. There is also some conflicting evidence that where the individual is highly dissatisfied with the home community, variation in beliefs about the adequacy of local economic opportunities makes far less difference to intentions to remain at home than do similar variations at higher levels of satisfaction. This trend is not reproduced for all values of the migration variables, however. In any case, only slightly more than one quarter of all respondents have such highly negative attitudes toward the community, i.e. scores of less than 3. However, over one half of all respondents have C.S. scores of less than 5, and only slightly more than one tenth of these definitely intend to remain at home. Thus this attitude toward the home community is very important in migration planning, although its independent effect on migration intentions, once the effects of economic frustrations have been controlled, is much less than that of occupational or income frustration. The following section explores the assumption that variations in family obligations will have somewhat similar effects.

FAMILY OBLIGATIONS

As Arensberg and Kimball have so clearly described,[3] the obligations and duties which bind children to parents and to the support of

[3] Arensberg, C. A., *The Irish Countryman*, Peter Smith 1961, 56–68, and Arensberg and Kimball, *Family and Community in Ireland*, Peter Smith 1961, 46–70.

their younger brothers and sisters are deeply internalised and are very strongly sanctioned within the Irish rural family. And, although we can no longer assume that "the interests and desires of the individual concur in large measure with the norm, and (that) he finds reward and pleasure in it",[4] such expectations are likely to be strongly sanctioned by the family and community. In this situation, respondents who have obligations to their families which require that they stay at home and work on the farm or in the household, are not likely to intend to migrate in great proportions. Is this hypothesis supported by the data? If it is, how widespread are these obligations, and how satisfied are the respondents with their roles and their community? Do such obligations require that an individual stays at home even when his occupational and income aspirations are frustrated there? These are some of the questions that we will attempt to answer on this section. How these obligations are distributed among respondents from different positions in the home community will be explored later.

As is evident from even a cursory examination of Table LXXI in Appendix III and from the summary given below in Table XIX, the level of family obligation is strongly related to migration intentions. Almost 40 per cent of those with either no or very slight obligations definitely intend to migrate, while only about 22 to 25 per cent of those with medium or high obligations intend to do so. The presence of obligations, then, acts as a barrier to migration. However, only

TABLE XIX: THE RELATIONSHIP BETWEEN FAMILY OBLIGATIONS AND PLANS TO MIGRATE

Intentions to migrate	Family Obligations				
	None	Very Slight	Medium	High	Total
	%	%	%	%	%
Definite intention to stay	11.7	26.5	34.4	51.6	128
Definite intention to leave	45.0	34.6	25.0	22.6	194
TOTAL %	100	100	100	100	
N	180	260	64	31	535
			Gamma = −.305		

[4] Arensberg and Kimball, *op. cit.*, 47.

about one-sixth of all respondents have such pressing obligations. Even of those who have such strong obligations to their families a larger proportion definitely intend to migrate than do those who believe that their occupational and income aspirations can be fulfilled locally, as a comparison of Tables XVI and XIX indicates. While less than one fifth of those not frustrated in their occupational or income aspirations intend to migrate, nearly a quarter of those with medium to high obligations intend to do so. On the other hand approximately the same proportions of respondents who are not frustrated in these aspirations definitely intend to remain locally (40 and 49 per cent respectively) as do those with medium to high levels of family obligations (34 and 51 per cent respectively). So, as a comparison of the relative magnitudes of Gamma indicates, the overall relationship of the Family Obligation variable to migration intentions is much less than that of occupational or income frustration. Apparently such individualistic aspirations are far more important than family obligations in influencing migration decisions.

The overall relationship is weakened by the fact that only slightly more than half those with high levels of obligation to their families definitely intend to remain locally and fulfill these obligations. It should be remembered that these respondents (1) worked full-time at home—primarily on the farm or in the household, (2) felt that the family depended on their help a great deal, and (3) believed that the work currently being carried out by them could only with difficulty be done by someone else in the family. These results seem to suggest that the respondents no longer accept as legitimate the onerous family obligations which are often unevenly distributed among family members. Arensberg and Kimball reported that in the 1930s the traditional obligations of farm youth to the farm family frequently included ones which required that a son, or occasionally a daughter, should remain at home to help out the parents with the farm or with the younger children, or to look after older parents etc. These authors further maintained that such family expectations had been fully internalised by farm youth. The boys or girls concerned, therefore, regarded these obligations as rightful and "natural" and would tend to carry them out despite any personal frustrations involved.[5] If this was the case in the 1930s the results from this study indicate that it is apparently no longer the case, at least in Co. Cavan.

[5] Ibid., 47–60 and 176–180.

These results suggest that family obligations do not have the precedence in migration decisions making that was expected. In line with these expectations we had originally hypothesised that where respondents had major obligations to their family they would plan to remain in the local community despite the frustration of occupational and income aspirations. Operationally this hypothesis would therefore predict that, where the effects of family obligations had been controlled, the magnitude of the association between occupational or income frustration and migration intentions would be much less at high levels of family obligations than at low levels. Table LXXII in Appendix III contains the data relevant to this hypothesis. The hypothesis is clearly not upheld. Indeed the relationships are in a direction opposite to those predicted. The magnitude of the association between occupational or income frustration and migration intentions (Gamma) is, in fact, at its highest level at the medium to high levels of family obligations. Amongst those not frustrated in their aspirations in this subgroup although the proportion definitely intending to remain at home is the highest of all respondents, those frustrated in these aspirations plan to migrate in approximately equal proportions to those with similar beliefs from lower obligation categories. In other words, where respondents believed they could not fulfill their aspirations, locally, increasing levels of family obligations made no difference to their migration decisions. However, nearly two thirds of those with such high obligations believe they can fulfill their occupational aspirations locally, whereas only one third of those with no family obligations have such beliefs. Much the same situation holds for income frustration. The higher the level of obligation the more pronounced the relationship between income frustration and migration intentions.

On the other hand, if occupational aspirations can be fulfilled locally the presence of obligations has a major influence on migration plans. Only nineteen per cent of those with no obligations but whose occupational aspirations can be fulfilled locally definitely intend to stay, compared to over sixty per cent of those with high levels of obligations. (See Table LXXII, Appendix III.) It appears, therefore, that obligations operate to retard migration only where occupational aspirations can be fulfilled locally. The variable has no influence on the migration plans of those who believe that their occupational aspirations cannot be fulfilled locally.

A similar analysis of the table, using income frustration as the control variable, reveals a slightly different pattern. For those who are not frustrated in their income aspirations increasing levels of obligation have effects similar to those for occupational frustration: they lead to increasing proportions who plan to remain locally. But for those whose income aspirations are frustrated, increasing levels of obligation do lead to increasing percentages planning to stay at home and decreasing percentages intending to migrate. This means that many of those who have high obligations and who plan to remain at home have unsatisfied income aspirations, although very few are equally dissatisfied with their jobs. This dissatisfaction with income opportunities may, however, lead to migration at a later date.

Later analyses will show that high family obligations are, by and large, restricted to those who were working at the time of the survey (primarily on the home farm or in the farm household), and those who had received a low level of education. The above results indicate that many of these are not satisfied with their present position. In fact only 60 per cent are completely satisfied with their present job, and only 41 per cent are satisfied with income opportunities in the home community. This indicates a considerable dissatisfaction with their occupations even among those working on the home farm. There appears also to be little confidence in their prospects of achieving a satisfactory level of living by remaining there. It will be interesting to see if, in fact, they do remain at home. This is explored in the follow-up study (Part Two).

ATTITUDES TOWARD THE COMMUNITY'S SOCIAL PROVISIONS AND MIGRATION

A variable that was used in the original analysis, but subsequently dropped, was the individual's evaluation of how satisfactory his local community's social provisions were. This variable is emphasised in Ireland and in some other countries as being important in motivating migration. It has also been emphasised in some social policies introduced to control migration, such as the provision of parish halls, regional water schemes and so on. The evidence available from this study, however, suggests that this variable is only of minor importance in the migration decision. The variable had the lowest association with migration intentions of any of those employed.[6]

[6] Gamma = .137.

And when respondents' occupational or income aspirations could be satisfied locally dissatisfaction with social provisions did not lead to plans to migrate.[7]

CONCLUSIONS

The results analysed in this chapter indicate that the major factors involved in the decision to migrate from or stay in the community of origin are, broadly speaking, economic ones. The joint effects of occupational and income frustration—the two variables used to index the economic dimension—explain the major portion of the variance involved. A measure of the individual's emotional orientation toward the community—Community Satisfaction—is also very important, and makes an additional contribution to the variance explained, once the effects of occupational and income frustration have been controlled. Although C. S. is highly correlated with both occupational and income frustration, both these variables explain only part of the overall variance in C. S. scores, and the independent non-economic factors involved in producing variations in this attitude are also significant in the migration decision. However, these moderate correlations with occupational and income frustration, which show that if respondents perceive that these aspirations can be fulfilled locally they will tend to like the community better, suggest that the observed correlation with migration may be spurious even though it still retains some additional independent effects. However this relationship may equally operate in the reverse direction: respondents first coming to dislike the community, for instance, for a number of reasons unrelated to occupational planning, and as a consequence become biassed in their perception of the community's opportunity structure. At this stage it is not possible to decide finally among these alternative interpretations, i.e. whether C. S. is an important antecedent variable which influences beliefs about local opportunities, whether it is partly or completely a reflexive response to these beliefs, or indeed whether it plays a completely independent role. Its clearcut independent effects indicate the last interpretation. However the follow-up study will help resolve this further.

[7] Vercruijsse, *Shannon Hinterland Survey*, Mimeo. Leyden University, *op. cit.*, found much the same situation to hold in a rural area of Limerick. See Table LXXIII, Appendix III.

Another important variable is "Family Obligations": those requiring the person to remain and work in the home community. When people have such obligations they tend to remain at home provided they are satisfied with their jobs, or believe that the jobs they aspire to can be achieved locally. If they are not satisfied, or believe that their occupational aspirations cannot be fulfilled there, they intend to migrate to where they can fulfill these aspirations despite their family obligations. This finding is contrary to that hypothesised in the first chapter.

Some additional information gathered in the course of the interviewing generally supports some of these conclusions. This is based on data elicited by means of a series of three questions put to all respondents who either definitely intended to migrate or were indefinite whether they would or not (72.6 per cent of all respondents). The questions were phrased as follows:

> "Now supposing that you could get the sort of (1) job ____; (2) income ____; (3) community social provisions ____;— that you have just considered—(their aspirations)—in or near your home community, would you take it (i.e. job, income) and stay permanently there?"

Of the prospective migrants, 72 per cent said that they would remain at home provided they could achieve their occupational and/or income aspirations in their home community. An additional 12 per cent said that they would not remain there even if their occupational and income aspirations could be achieved locally, but would stay on if the community social provisions were brought up to expectations. The remaining 16 per cent said that they would not remain at home under any circumstances.

These figures, of course, exclude those respondents who definitely intend to remain, so that they do not give an overall picture of the factors involved in the decision to remain or leave the home community. Nevertheless, for those who have some intention of migrating, the figures indicate very clearly that the major factors involved in the decision to leave appear to be their beliefs about the adequacy of local economic opportunities. Attitudes toward community relationships—personal or institutional—and toward the community's social provisions to a lesser extent, are also involved. On the other hand one of the major factors motivating intentions to stay are family obligations, althought these only appear to be important when economic type aspirations can also be satisfied locally.

A sizeable minority (28 per cent) of all prospective migrants, however, said they would not remain in the home community even if their occupational and income aspirations could be fulfilled there. In many respects these differ from the "economic" type of migrants, and Table XX has been set up to explore some of the attitudinal differences involved. Those who didn't intend to migrate at all, the "non-migrants", have the highest levels of community satisfaction and the least negative attitude toward the community's social provisions of all respondents. On the other hand those who said they would remain only if their aspirations for the community's social provisions were satisfied, had the most negative attitudes toward the community's social provisions and the lowest community satisfaction scores of all respondents. Those who would not remain in the community under any circumstances had almost equally low Community Satisfaction levels but, with the exception of the non-migrants, they appear to have the most positive attitudes of all respondents toward the home community's social provisions. It would appear then that this latter attitude is not important in their decisions, but is highly significant in the second case. On the other hand, both the non-economic type migrants have equally low levels of Community Satisfaction, far below that of all other respondents.

TABLE XX: COMPARISON OF THE MEDIAN SCORES OF THREE TYPES OF POTENTIAL MIGRANTS ON THE COMMUNITY SATISFACTION SCALE AND IN ATTITUDES TOWARD THE COMMUNITY'S SOCIAL PROVISIONS

	(1) Economic type migrants	(2) Social Provision migrants	(3) Permanent migrants	(4) Non-migrants
Community satisfaction. Median score	5.9	4.5	4.6	6.6
Attitude toward the community's social provisions. Median score	7.6	8.5	6.7	6.5

Note: In the scale measuring attitudes toward the community's social provisions, the higher the score the more negative the attitudes. The Community Satisfaction scale runs in the opposite direction—the higher the score the more positive the attitudes.

It is obvious that these attitudinal differences between the three types of potential migrants, although important, explain only a small part of the total difference involved. The next chapter will examine other differences and make a more detailed examination of the distinctions between the different kinds of migrants.

The following chapter is concerned with some major structural factors involved in migration. It will examine how (a) the migration decision, and (b) the major motives involved in this decision which have been examined, vary with the social characteristics of the individual. This chapter has been concerned with the attitudes, beliefs and obligations of the individual as they are related to his intentions to migrate or remain in his home community. The analysis has not concerned itself at all with the background or origin of the individuals concerned—whether male or female, from farm or non-farm background, highly educated or receiving only a primary education, etc. And although beliefs held by respondents about their ability to fulfill their aspirations locally proved the most important variable in this chapter, the content of these aspirations —whether aspiring to a professional or an unskilled manual occupation, or for an income of more than £20 or less than £5 per week —has not yet been considered. Both these factors—the "content" of aspirations, and the social background of individuals—will be examined in the next chapter.

5. Results III—
Structural Constraints and Migration Intentions— Level of Aspiration, Education, Sex, and Occupational Background

The second of the research questions being investigated in this study asks: "How do migration intentions and the factors affecting them vary with the position of the individual in the social structure of his home community?" An answer is attempted here and in the next chapter. A large number of hypotheses were proposed in the first chapter as to how migration rates would vary by sex, social class, educational level, level of aspiration and so on. In these two chapters the data is examined to see to what extent the results conform to those hypothesised.

We first examine four major social structural factors: (1) Level of aspiration; (2) Educational level achieved; (3) Sex; (4) Occupational background. And the following chapter will examine the effects of remoteness, family expectations and migration systems.

Although neither the prestige level of the occupation aspired to, nor the amount of weekly wages considered to be satisfactory, are social structural variables in any strict sense, they are so closely related to the level of education received, to social class and even to sex—as the results in Tables LXXIX, LXXX, XC and XCII in Appendix IV clearly indicate—that they will be considered as such in this study. By doing this we can examine the relationship between the structure of these aspirations, beliefs about one's ability to fulfill them in the home community, and the structure of current occupational outlets in that community. In this sense the level of

101

aspiration can be more logically examined here than in the previous chapter.

The first section will examine the relationship between educational level, level of occupational and income aspiration, and migration intentions.

THE LEVEL OF OCCUPATIONAL AND INCOME ASPIRATION AND MIGRATION INTENTIONS

The rather obvious hypothesis has already been proposed that higher levels of occupational and income aspiration lead to higher levels of frustration of these aspirations, and therefore to greater tendencies to migrate. Are things, however, quite as clearcut as this? Tables LXXIV–VIII in Appendix IV contain the data relevant to this hypothesis.

The results indicate very clearly that the hypotheses are confirmed regarding the proportions of those "not frustrated" in their aspirations locally. The higher the level of occupational aspiration, the lower the proportion of respondents who believe they can fulfill their occupational and income aspirations locally. From 42 to 44 per cent of those who aspire to manual occupations definitely believe they can find such occupations locally, while only 26 to 31 per cent of those who aspire to non-manual occupations are so optimistic. And while 27 to 33 per cent of the former believe they can fulfill their income aspirations locally only 18 to 21 per cent of the latter are so optimistic. Because those who aspire to semiskilled and unskilled occupations are far more definite in these beliefs than others, however—only 14 per cent of these are "partly frustrated" in their occupational aspirations compared to over 40 per cent of those who aspire to non-manual occupations—a higher percentage of the manual are frustrated in their aspirations than would be expected. As a result, the overall association between the two variables is greatly reduced below what one would expect from considering only the proportions not frustrated. Since most of those aspiring to manual occupations have been working for some time in the home community while those aspiring to higher levels are mostly in postprimary schools, the greater polarisation of their beliefs is understandable.

There is a much more clearcut relationship between the level of income aspiration and the level of frustration of these aspirations.

(See Appendix IV, Table LXXV.) While over 52 per cent of those who aspired to incomes of £6 or less believed they could fulfill their aspirations in the home community, only 21–23 per cent of those who aspired to incomes of £15 or more are equally optimistic. The reverse situation holds in the case of those frustrated in their aspirations—25 per cent of those with aspirations of £6 or less being frustrated compared to 46 to 51 per cent of those with aspirations of £15 or more.

Probably as a result of the greater certainty of beliefs amongst the manual aspirers there is no clearcut relationship between the level of occupational aspiration and plans to migrate, as the results in Appendix IV, Table LXXVI clearly indicate. The only group showing a strong tendency to remain in the home community are those aspiring to skilled manual occupations. There is no clear or consistent difference amongst the other groups, whether they aspire to manual or non-manual occupations. Although those aspiring to semiskilled and unskilled occupations are also more definite in

TABLE XXI: THE RELATIONSHIP BETWEEN THE LEVEL OF OCCUPATIONAL ASPIRATION OR CURRENT OCCUPATIONAL ACHIEVEMENT AND INTENTIONS TO MIGRATE

Intentions to migrate	Level of Occupational Aspiration or Achievement				
	Professional and semi-professional	Farmers	Inter-mediate non-manual	Skilled and service	Unskilled and semi-skilled
	%	%	%	%	%
Definite intention to stay	8.8 (5)	88.9 (40)	10.2 (18)	26.0 (47)	28.1 (16)
Indefinite whether will stay or leave	47.4	6.7	44.6	41.4	29.8
Definite intention to leave	43.9	4.4	45.2	31.5	42.1
TOTAL %	100.1	100	100	99.9	100
N	57	45	177	181	57

$\chi^2 = 30.3$; $p > .95$

Excluding farmers: Gamma $= -.140$ (Aggregate indefinite and definitely migrating: Gamma $= -.429$).

their migration intentions than others, they still show no consistent tendency to migrate less than the non-manual aspirers.

There is a definite relationship between the level of income aspiration and plans to migrate, however. (See Appendix IV Table LXXVII.) The higher the level of income aspiration the greater the tendency to migrate. Only 18 per cent of those aspiring to incomes of £15 and over intend to remain in the home community, while 33 per cent of those with aspirations of £8 or less intend to do so.

However, only those who did not have a current job that satisfied them were asked about their occupational aspirations. Thus, those who were satisfied with their present jobs were excluded from the tables using level of occupational aspiration as an independent variable, but not from tables using the level of income aspiration as an independent variable. If these occupationally satisfied respondents are included, and if we look at the relationship between the level of occupational aspiration or current occupational achievement and intentions to migrate, the two tables are made comparable and the following position holds. (See Table XXI.)

If farmers are excluded there is a very clear relationship between the level of occupational aspiration/achievement and intentions to migrate. Between 26 and 28 per cent of those aspiring to, or achieving, manual occupations definitely intend to remain at home, while only 8 to 10 per cent of those aspiring to non-manual occupations intend to do so. As compared to Table LXXVI in Appendix IV, where the relationship between the level of occupational aspiration and migration intentions has been set out, the relationship here is much more pronounced. This is brought out very clearly by the magnitude of the statistics computed for the table. The Chi-Square statistic for the former table (Table LXXVI, Appendix IV) yields such a low probability when the Service and Skilled categories are aggregated that the relationship could easily be of chance occurrence, while in the latter case (Table XXI) the same statistic yields a highly significant relationship. Similarly, Gamma increases from a figure very close to zero to one of .140. And if those who are indefinite and those definitely planning to migrate are aggregated, Gamma is much higher. There is a clearcut relationship, therefore, between the two variables.

Of the non-farm group there is little difference in migration plans between those who aspire to, or are already occupied in, service occupations and the non-manual aspirers, (see Table LXXVIII, Appendix IV). This occurs despite the fact that their level of occupational frustration is much lower than that of the non-manual group. In fact, there is little difference between service and skilled workers in their level of occupational frustration, although the former group's level of migration intentions is much greater. (37 per cent of those aspiring to or achieving skilled manual occupations intended to remain locally, compared to only 17 per cent of those aspiring to or having achieved service occupations.) There are, however, differences in levels of income frustration, the latter being more frustrated in their income aspirations. Similar differences occur in regard to community satisfaction and attitudes toward the community's social provisions. Service workers are more negative in both these attitudes than skilled workers. All these differences, however, are not sufficient to explain why service workers should be less than half as likely as skilled workers to remain in the home community. Perhaps sex, educational and class differences between the groups may explain why this occurs. This possibility will be explored in later sections.

Except for this one exception, however, the non-manual aspirers

TABLE XXII: COMPARISON OF THE OCCUPATIONAL ASPIRATIONS AND ACHIEVEMENTS OF ADOLESCENTS WITH THE OCCUPATIONS OF THEIR FATHERS

Occupational Status	Occupational aspirations/ achievements of sons and daughters		Occupations of fathers		Ratio of youths' aspirations to the achievements of their parents
	N	%	N	%	Ratio
Professional and semi-professional, managerial, managerial and all non-manual occupations	238	45.5	109	19.7	2.18
Farmers	43	8.2	276	49.8	0.15
Skilled and service	185	35.4	72	13.0	2.57
Semiskilled and unskilled	57	10.9	97	17.5	0.59
TOTAL N	523		554		
%		100%		100%	

are far less likely to stay at home than the manual group. A comparison between the occupational aspirations of youth with the occupational backgrounds of their fathers reveals why the high aspirers might be more migratory.

A number of trends are very clear. First, there is a tremendous movement away from the parents' occupational background, and the bulk of this mobility is in an upwardly mobile direction. Less than one fifth of the respondents' fathers have non-manual jobs, whereas nearly half of their children aspire to these occupations. And although the trend is less extreme, far fewer of the adolescents aspire to or have achieved jobs at the unskilled or semiskilled level than their fathers did, while almost three times more youths than fathers aspire to or have already achieved jobs at skilled and service levels.

Secondly, there is a massive movement out of agriculture. Only 8 per cent of all respondents aspire to or have taken up jobs in the farm sector, whereas almost 50 per cent of them have come from farm backgrounds. Overall, the ratio between adolescents' aspirations and the occupational achievements of their fathers summarises this movement. The flow into the non-manual and skilled and service sectors is over twice as great as it was for the previous generation, while for farming and the unskilled and semiskilled occupations it varies from approximately one seventh in the case of farming to almost six tenths for the unskilled and semiskilled category.

The types of occupations demanded by these adolescents—non-manual and skilled manual work—and, (an equally important factor), the types of occupations rejected—farm and unskilled—have very significant consequences for the development of the community studied if the people there wish to retain its present population. At present, the structure of occupational aspirations differs considerably from that of occupational opportunities. This is leading to the migration of the "excess" aspirers.

Developments that emphasise skilled and service occupations, and those of a lower level non-manual nature should lead to a considerable diminution in migration rates. Expansion of work at the unskilled and farm level would not have any great impact, given the current lack of appreciation for these occupations.

All of this assumes that these youths are "satisfactorily" remunerated for their work. But as the results presented in Table LXXIV in Appendix IV indicate, less than 20 per cent of those aspiring to non-manual occupations believe that they can fulfill their income aspirations locally under existing conditions, while those aspiring to manual occupations are not much more optimistic. Again a comparison of youths' aspirations and fathers' achievements highlights this fact. Table XXIII below contains the relevant data.

There is again a great upward shift in aspirations over the level

TABLE XXIII: A COMPARISON OF THE INCOME ASPIRATIONS OF ADOLESCENTS WITH THE REPORTED ACTUAL INCOMES OF THEIR FATHERS

Level of income (weekly wages) aspired to	Income aspirations of sons and daughters	Estimated incomes of fathers	Ratio of youths' aspirations to fathers'
	%	%	
Less than £6 per week	13.0	30.4	0.43
£6 to £10 per week	31.8	35.5	0.90
£11 to £15 per week	22.9	20.4	1.12
Over £15 per week	32.3	13.7	2.36
TOTAL %	100%	100%	
N	507	451	

achieved by fathers. Relative to the level achieved by their fathers, proportionately more than twice as many youths aspired to incomes of over £15 per week, while less than half of them aspired to incomes of less than £6 per week, Since fathers' incomes are approximately representative of those generally available in the community,[1] even if sufficient occupational outlets were available locally to satisfy all occupational aspirations (ah ighly unrealistic expectation), the incomes available would have to be increased well beyond those now earned by its older members if this community wants to retain the labour of its young people. In both respects then—occupational status and income aspirations—the aspirations of respondents far outstrip the capacity of this community to satisfy them. Any reorganisation of the economic life of the community aimed at reducing population loss would have to take into consideration this

[1] Average reported income of fathers from wages or estimated incomes realised from the family farm came to £470 as an average. The average income in agriculture per person engaged was estimated at £423 for 1965 and of non-farm employees and independent trades at £590. Michael Ross, *Irish County Incomes in 1965*, published by the Economic and Social Research Institute in 1969.

disjuncture between the current structure of occupational and income opportunities and the corresponding aspirations of young "replacements" to the system.

To conclude: level of aspiration is closely related to one's ability to fulfil aspirations locally, and consequently about one's intention to migrate. How is level of aspiration related to the level of education received? Is the effect of education on intentions to migrate explained fully by its expected close relationship to level of aspiration and to the local frustration of these aspirations? These are some of the questions explored in the following section.

THE LEVEL OF EDUCATION RECEIVED AND MIGRATION INTENTIONS

The results presented in Tables LXXIX and LXXX in Appendix IV clearly demonstrate the very close relationship between the level of education received and one's level of aspiration. This is particularly true in regard to one's level of occupational aspiration or achievement. Almost 90 per cent of the secondary educated aspire to non-manual occupations. This is true for less than 10 per cent of the primary educated, but for 30 per cent of the vocationally educated. On the other hand less than one per cent of the secondary educated aspire to semiskilled and unskilled manual occupations, while over one third of the primary educated do so. The vocationally educated hold an intermediate position. The very high relationship between these two factors is nicely illustrated by the fact that the highest measure of association (Gamma) calculated between any two variables was found in this case (Gamma = .808).

Similarly the relationship between educational level achieved and income aspiration is very clearcut, as even a cursory examination of Appendix IV, Table LXXX indicates. While almost a quarter of the primary educated aspire to incomes of £6 or less, this is true of less than 2 per cent of the secondary educated. And, while nearly half of the secondary educated aspire to incomes of £15 or more this is true of less than a quarter of the primary educated. The vocationally educated hold an intermediate position, but are much closer to the primary than the secondary educated in their aspirations. There is then a very clearcut relationship between the level of occupational aspiration/achievement of respondents and their educational level; and, although the association is not as close, there is a similar strong relationship with income aspirations. Given those trends, one would expect a very clearcut relationship between education, occupational and income frustration and migration intentions. Is this in fact the case? The following table (XXIV) examines two of these relationships.

There are, in fact, very clear relationships between all the variables. There is no material difference in the overall strength of the

TABLE XXIV: THE RELATIONSHIP BETWEEN (1) OCCUPATIONAL FRUSTRATION, (2) INCOME FRUSTRATION, AND EDUCATIONAL LEVEL ACHIEVED

	Level of Education Achieved		
	Primary only	1 to 3 years of vocational education	3 to 5 years of secondary education
(1) *Occupational Frustration*			
	%	%	%
Not frustrated	64.6	47.9	32.8
Partly frustrated	10.8	35.6	42.1
Frustrated	24.6	16.5	25.1
TOTAL %	100	100	100
N	130	194	195

Gamma = .262

(2) *Income Frustration*			
	%	%	%
Not frustrated	49.0	30.5	18.1
Partly frustrated	12.2	29.4	41.5
Frustrated	38.8	40.1	40.4
TOTAL %	100	100	100
N	147	187	188

Gamma = .188

relationship between occupational, or income, frustration and educational level. The similarity in the strength of the relationship is clear from the great but approximately equal differences between the primary and secondary educated in the proportions not frustrated in their aspirations. While almost 65 per cent of the primary educated are not frustrated in their occupational aspirations, this is true of only 33 per cent of the secondary educated (i.e. a difference of 32 percentage points) while those receiving a vocational education hold an intermediate position. Similarly while 49 per cent of the primary educated are not frustrated in their income aspirations this is true of only 18 per cent of the secondary educated (a percentage difference of 31). On the other hand, while 65 per cent of the primary educated believe that they can fulfill their occupational aspirations locally, only 49 per cent of them believe that they can achieve their income aspirations locally. In other words, far more respondents believe that suitable occupational outlets are available locally than believe that these are satisfactorily remunerated. This is true for all levels of education as a comparison of results in sections 1 and 2 of Table XXIV clearly shows. This suggests that an improvement in incomes alone, even maintaining the current occupational structure, would have a considerable influence in reducing the frustrations that influence migration behaviour. And, as will become apparent later on, this would be especially so for those receiving only a primary or a vocational education.

Because the primary educated are far more definite in their beliefs about fulfilling their aspirations locally (so that relatively few of them are "partly frustrated"), there are no consistent differences between the various educational levels in the proportions of those whose aspirations are frustrated. However, if the "partly frustrated" and the "frustrated" cells are aggregated—as those not fully convinced they can fulfill their aspirations locally—the trends become very clear.

Now, given these relationships between the level of education and the frustration of aspirations, are there any other systematic differences between educational levels which might bring about variations in migration rates? What is the relationship between educational level and the other major motives influencing plans to migrate? The following table (XXV) examines these relationships.

The primary educated have the highest levels of Community Satisfaction, and the least negative attitude toward the community's social provisions, although there are no major differences between them and the secondary educated in these respects. Surprisingly, the vocationally educated have the most negative attitudes toward the community in both respects. It was thought that this would be

TABLE XXV: THE RELATIONSHIP BETWEEN THE LEVEL OF EDUCA-
TION AND (1) COMMUNITY SATISFACTION, (2) ATTITUDE TOWARD
COMMUNITY SOCIAL PROVISIONS, AND (3) FAMILY OBLIGATIONS

Level of education received	Community Satisfaction (median score)*	Attitude toward Community's Social Provisions (med. score)*	Family Obligations: Percentage with Medium–High obligations
Primary only	6.6	7.4	37.8
Vocational	5.8	8.0	13.4
Secondary	6.4	7.9	6.7

* The higher the C.S. score and the lower the Social Provision
score the more positive the attitude.

the case with the secondary educated because of an expected greater
degree of "modernisation" of their values. If they are distinguished
in this respect, it has had little apparent impact on these two
attitudes. Variations in reference groups or in levels of relative
deprivation[2] may be a more useful explanation here as to why the
vocationally educated have the more negative attitudes of all. In
comparison with the primary educated, those in vocational schools
are far more likely to use the secondary educated as a reference
group in assessing how satisfactory their own position is. They are
both attending school, many of them within the same town. They
are, therefore, open to more obvious and more invidious comparison
by the community with the higher status secondary educated than
happens between the primary and secondary educated. They are
also more likely to compare themselves to the secondary educated.
As a result their general feelings of satisfaction with the community
are likely to be more negative than any other group. Despite these
interesting differences, however, the variations among educational
groups in these two attitudes are hardly sufficient to make any great
differences in migration intentions.

There are major differences, on the other hand, amongst educational groups in family obligations. While almost 40 per cent
of the primary educated have medium to high obligations this is
true of only 13 per cent of the vocational, and only 7 per cent of the

[2] Merton, R., *Social Theory and Social Structure*, Free Press, 1958, 225–386.

secondary educated. This would tend to make for a major difference in migration intentions. The primary educated then have much lower levels of occupational and income frustration, and much higher levels of family obligation than have the secondary educated. They also have the highest levels of community satisfaction and the most positive attitude toward the community's social provisions. Are these differences reflected in their migration intentions? The following table examines this relationship.

TABLE XXVI: THE RELATIONSHIP BETWEEN EDUCATIONAL LEVEL ACHIEVED BY ADOLESCENTS AND THEIR MIGRATION INTENTIONS

Migration Intentions	Level of Education Achieved		
	Primary only	Vocational	Secondary
	%	%	%
Definite intention to stay	37.7	24.9	12.1
Indefinite whether will stay or migrate	31.1	41.8	44.9
Definite intention to migrate	31.1	33.3	42.9
TOTAL %	99.9	100	99.9
N	151	201	198

Gamma = .254

As expected, there is a very pronounced relationship between level of education and migration plans. Only 12 per cent of the secondary educated intend to remain locally compared to 25 per cent of the vocationally educated and 38 per cent of the primary educated. Here again, however, because the primary educated are more definite in their migration plans the corresponding difference in the proportions who intend to migrate is not as great, although they also tend strongly in the expected direction. Over 31 per cent of the primary educated definitely intend to migrate compared to almost 43 per cent of the secondary educated, the vocationally educated falling in an intermediate position.

Overall, therefore, there is a much more clearcut relationship between educational level achieved and migration intentions, than between level of occupational aspiration and migration (compare with Table XXVI). This is partly the result of the inclusion in Table XXVI of those employed on farms and of those aspiring to farming as an occupation. These were excluded from the discussion of Table XXI results because of the difficulty of ascribing them to a relative status position. Nearly all of them have received only a primary education. Most of them are highly satisfied with their job and income opportunities. Consequently very few of them plan to migrate at all. As a result of their inclusion amongst the primary educated in Table XXVI, the relationship between education and migration plans is far more pronounced than between level of aspiration and migration plans.

The secondary educated have much higher levels of occupational and income aspiration, and frustration, than others and a much greater proportion of them intends to migrate. Is the former fact sufficient to explain the latter, or are there some further effects of education which are not explained by its pronounced association with the frustration of aspirations? Tables LXXXI–LXXXIII in Appendix IV contain the data bearing on this question.

The results presented in Appendix IV, Table LXXXI show clearly that if the effects of occupational frustration have been controlled, education has little additional effect on migration intentions; except for those not frustrated in their aspirations. For this sub-category, higher levels of education do lead to higher proportions who intend to migrate and lower proportions who intend to stay. Over half the primary educated definitely intend to remain locally while only forty per cent of the vocationally educated and twenty per cent of the secondary educated intend to do so. There are no consistent relationships between educational level and migration intentions for the other two values of occupational frustration, the control variable.

Quite the opposite situation holds when income frustration is used as the control variable, as the results presented in Appendix IV, Table LXXXII clearly indicate. The only situation where increasing levels of education make any consistent difference in intentions to migrate is for the "frustrated" category of the control variable. For the frustrated in their income aspirations the proportion intending to remain locally decreases from 18 per cent for the primary educated to 7 per cent for the secondary educated; while the proportion intending to migrate increases from 42 per cent to 75 per cent, for the same categories. Although there are trends in the same direction in the other two sub-categories of the control variable regarding those who intend to stay at home, these trends are reversed for the proportions intending to migrate. Thus there is no consistent trend present.

In both cases, therefore, increasing levels of education have effects on migration intentions over and beyond that exercised by any of the control variables. Consequently, the higher educated group's greater tendency to migrate cannot be explained fully by its members' greater tendency to be frustrated in either their occupational or income aspirations. It may be, however, that the joint effects of both occupational and income frustration are greater at higher than at lower levels of education, so that the effects of the two variables acting together may explain this differential. The results presented in Appendix IV, Table LXXXIII can be used to test this hypothesis.

The results indicate that only in the case of those who are not frustrated in their occupational aspirations do increasing levels of education make any consistent difference in plans to migrate—and this is true for all values of the income frustration variable. Controlling for those not frustrated in both their occupational and income aspirations, 39 per cent of the primary educated definitely intend to migrate or are indefinite whether they will or not, whereas this is true of 50 per cent of the vocationally educated and 68 per cent of the secondary educated. The same clearcut tendency holds for the other two values of the income frustration variable. On the other hand, for those frustrated or partly frustrated in their occupational aspirations, increasing levels of education have no clearcut effect on migration intentions. So, over and beyond the effects on migration intentions produced by the intervening association between educational level received and occupational and income frustration, educational level itself has important independent effects on migration. It is noteworthy though, that this holds only in the case where occupational aspirations can be fulfilled in the local community.

It may be recalled that in this case also—where occupational aspirations can be fulfilled locally—higher levels of family obligations lead to greater proportions intending to remain locally. (See Table LXXXIV, Appendix IV.) Other results presented here also indicate that family obligations are largely confined to the primary and vocationally educated (Table XXV). The additional effects of this variable at the lower levels of education would therefore account for their higher tendency to remain in the home community. This would only hold, however, when occupational aspirations can be satisfied locally.

In summary, therefore, the higher levels of migration of the secondary and vocationally educated can be accounted for by their higher levels of occupational and income frustration and their lower level of family obligations.

It was also hypothesiscd that purely economic considerations would predominate in the migration decisions of the primary educated, while occupational status factors and other social mobility considerations would be the major ones influencing the more highly educated, or the high aspirers. A re-examination of Tables LXXXI–LXXXIII in Appendix IV gives us some relevant data bearing on this hypothesis.

An examination of Table LXXXI—by controlling for the level of education received instead of for occupational frustration—reveals that variation in occupational frustration makes a greater difference to the migration decisions of the primary educated than of any other group. Of the primary educated, 56 per cent of those not frustrated in their aspirations definitely intend to remain locally, compared to only 6.3 per cent of those frustrated (i.e. a percentage difference of almost 50 points). On the other hand, only 14 per cent of the primary educated who are not frustrated definitely intend to migrate compared to 78 per cent of those frustrated (i.e. a percentage difference of almost 64).

The corresponding differences for the vocationally and secondary educated are much smaller. The correlation between occupational frustration and migration intentions reaches a Gamma of .808 for the primary educated, .555 for the vocational group, and .556 for the secondary group. It should be emphasised again that this is due to the much greater proportions of the primary educated who plan to remain locally if their aspirations can be fulfilled there (56 per cent of the primary educated compared to 41 per cent of the vocational group and only 20 per cent of the secondary group). This situation appears to hold because of the much greater level of family obligations which tend to immobilise the primary educated when they believe that their occupational aspirations can be satisfied locally. There are no other consistent differences among educational groups where aspirations are frustrated or partly frustrated. Overall, therefore, occupational frustration is not more predictive of variations in migration intentions at the higher levels of education. In fact, if the effect of the disproportionate distribution of obligations is controlled, there are almost no consistent differences among educational levels in the effect of occupational frustration. Therefore, the hypothesis, that the frustration of occupational aspirations would have much greater effects on migration where respondents aspire to higher status occupations is not supported. It was thought that social mobility aspirations would be operative at high levels of occupational aspiration whereas purely economic considerations would predominate at the lower levels of aspiration. This is apparently not the case, or if it is, such mobility aspirations are not adequately indexed by the level of occupational aspiration.

What is the situation in regard to income frustration? The original hypothesis stated that it was not the absence of jobs as such that was important at the lower levels of aspiration, but the remuneration from those jobs that were available. There are relatively more jobs available at the lower levels of aspiration, but they are relatively poorly paid. On the other hand, both occupational and income aspirations are equally likely to be frustrated at the upper levels of aspiration. Consequently one would expect a stronger relationship between occupational and income frustration themselves at the higher levels of aspiration/education. Given that, one would also expect that the joint effects of both factors on migration intentions would be much greater at the lower levels of education/ aspiration where the two independent variables are less highly associated with each other. Is this in fact the case? Again the results presented in Appendix IV, Table LXXXIII can be used to test this hypothesis.

Firstly, occupational and income frustration are most closely associated with each other at the primary level of education, and not at the secondary level as expected. Moreover, when the effects of occupational frustration have been controlled, the additional effects of income frustration on the migration decision appear to be roughly the same at all levels of education. If respondents are frustrated or partly frustrated in both aspirations there are very small differences among educational levels, since almost all of these respondents intend to migrate. However, for those not frustrated in their occupational aspirations, being frustrated or partly frustrated in income aspirations leads to decisions to migrate for only 36 to 58 per cent of the primary educated, but for 75 to 77 per cent of the vocationally educated and 81 to 92 per cent of the secondary educated. The higher the level of education the greater the proportion migrating. Similar differences also exist, however, for those who are not frustrated in both aspirations—the higher the level of education the greater the proportion migrating. As a result, therefore, the additional effect of income frustration on migration intentions appears to be approximately the same at all levels of education. There appear to be other extraneous factors operating, for the primary and vocationally educated, which tend to retard migration if they are not frustrated in their occupational aspirations. And this trend holds for all levels of income frustration. As already mentioned family obligations are the most important of these extraneous factors. Overall, therefore, the interrelationships amongst these variables are not nearly as simple as expected. But the conclusion appears to be pretty clear: occupational and income considerations play a greater role in the migration decisions of the more highly educated and the high aspirers, while family obligations and other extraneous factors are more important for the poorly educated.

These results indicate a conclusion directly opposite to that predicted. It should, perhaps, be emphasised here however, that we have been dealing only with the "characteristics" that distinguish intended migrants from non-migrants. We have then been inferring from these the correlates of migrants and non-migrants, to the causes of migration. We have not been dealing with reasons given for migrating or staying or with any "deeper" motives. It may be, therefore, that certain uncontrolled factors highly correlated with high level of occupational aspiration, for instance, may be interfering in the relationship, as obligations are "interfering" in the case of the lower aspirers. Even where occupational and income aspirations can be satisfied locally additional factors may come into play and might prevent these high aspirers from remaining in the home community. Some additional data was collected from the respondents which enables us to see if this is, in fact, the case.

As already noted, those who did not intend to remain in the home community were asked whether they would remain if a number of separate facilities were made available there. Their answers were categorised on the basis of whether they said they would remain if: (1) their occupational and income aspirations alone could be satisfied there; (2) along with these satisfactions their unsatisfied aspirations for the community social provisions could be satisfied there;

and (3) whether they would not remain under any circumstances. Unfortunately the question asked did not sufficiently distinguish between the status and income aspects of occupational satisfaction so that it is not possible to get any meaningful distinction on this basis. However, the analysis of the answers did show up major differences among educational and aspirational levels which are very relevant here. The results are summarised in the following table (XXVII).

First there are major differences among aspiration and educational levels in the proportions who say they would remain in the home community if both their occupational and income aspirations could be satisfied there. While less than 65 per cent of potential migrants aspiring to non-manual occupations say they would remain in the home community if these economic aspirations could be satisfied there, this is true of 80 to 87 per cent of those aspiring to manual occupations. There are similar systematic differences among the remaining respondents who would not remain at home for such reasons. For some of these the poverty of social provisions available in the community is an additional important reason for migrating. This appears to be particularly true for those aspiring to non-manual occupations. What is more important, however, is that a much higher proportion of those who aspire to non-manual occupations (19 per cent) as against those aspiring to low level manual and service occupations (7 |to 8 per cent), say that they would not remain in the community under any circumstances.

When education rather than aspirational level is used as the control variable the results are even more clearcut. While only 11 per cent of the primary educated say that they would not remain in the home community if their occupational and income aspirations could be satisfied there, this is true of 23 per cent of the vocationally educated and 41 per cent of the secondary educated. The differences in the proportions stating they would not remain in the home community under any circumstances is almost as great, although here the secondary and vocationally educated groups approach each other very closely, (22 per cent of the secondary educated and 16 per cent of the vocationally educated). The corresponding figure for the primary educated is considerably lower. On the other hand, social provisions become very important for the secondary educated, with about 3 to 5 times as many of these saying they would only remain if the community social provisions were brought up to expectations.

TABLE XXVII: THE RELATIONSHIP BETWEEN THE LEVEL OF OCCUPATIONAL ASPIRATION, AND THE LEVEL OF EDUCATION ACHIEVED BY RESPONDENTS AND "CONDITIONAL MIGRATION". CONTROLLING FOR THOSE WHO DEFINITELY INTEND TO MIGRATE, OR WHO ARE INDEFINITE WHETHER THEY WILL OR NOT

(1) Level of occupational aspirations of respondents	Of those respondents considering migration, the proportions who say they would remain at home provided that			Total	
	(1) their occupational and income aspirations could be satisfied there	(2) along with the satisfaction of the foregoing, the community social provisions were brought up to their level of aspiration	or (3) say that they would not remain there under any circumstances	%	N
	%	%	%		
All non-manual occupations	64.6	16.0	19.4	100	206
Skilled manual occupations	80.9	2.4	16.7	100	42
Service occupations	84.7	7.7	7.7	100.1	78
Semiskilled and unskilled	86.8	5.3	7.9	100	38
(2) Level of education received					
Primary only	88.6	3.8	7.6	100	105
Vocational	76.9	6.8	16.2	99.9	117
Secondary	59.3	19.2	21.5	100	172

These results bear out to some extent the original hypothesis and seem to contradict the immediately preceding results. If occupational and income aspirations are satisfied, the lower occupational aspirers and the primary educated are much more likely than others to remain in the home community. On the other hand much higher proportions of the high aspirers and the secondary educated would not remain in the home community under any circumstances. Although, in terms of the magnitude of the association involved, the combined effects of occupational and income frustration are somewhat greater at the secondary level of education, nevertheless far fewer of these than of others would remain in the home community even if their aspirations could be fulfilled there. The unexpected finding that attitudes toward the home community's social provisions contribute towards explaining why such a large proportion of the high aspirers refuse to remain in the home community for purely occupational or income reasons, does not fit in with previous theorising on the question. But the fact that such a large proportion of the high aspirers and the more highly educated refuse to remain in the home community for any of the stated reasons strongly indicates that there may be a complex of aspirations and attitudes which are typical of those with high levels of occupational and income aspiration and which, in addition to the satisfaction of these economic type aspirations, also need to be satisfied before the individual would remain at home. It is highly probable, however, that these residual factors can only be satisfied in a highly urban environment. Before reaching a definite conclusion on this point we will examine some further relevant evidence in the following section.

SEX AND OCCUPATIONAL BACKGROUND AND INTENTIONS TO MIGRATE

One of the few consistent findings on rural–urban migration is that it has been highly selective by sex. Whether this occurs in this study; and if it does, why and how it occurs are questions explored in this section.

It was hypothesised that sex selectivity in migration was restricted to those from farm backgrounds. As clearly indicated by census results, off-farm occupational opportunities for adolescents or young adults are relatively evenly balanced between the sexes in Co. Cavan, while farming is highly selective of males. In a traditional rural economy this was corrected for by females remaining on in the farm household, or helping on the farm until they got married, usually at a relatively early age: as consumption patterns typical of modern urban societies diffused throughout the countryside and as farming changed from being a "way of life" to an increasingly commercially oriented occupation, the participation of farm girls in the off-farm labour force also increased greatly. As a result, unless off-farm employment within the community discriminated in favour of farm females, one would expect greater migration rates from this group than from any other. In addition to this, dissatisfaction with family and community roles should be much greater among farm females than others. This would be expected, given the relatively more advantaged position of the farm male in the farm economy and the more restricted freedom of the female from the social control of a largely traditional family and community. On the other hand, farm males have much higher levels of family obligation than farm females, or any non-farm adolescents—another reason for expecting their greater immobility. Because of these cumulative factors which discriminate between farm males and females but not between the sexes of other groups, one would expect that if sex selection occurs at all it will be restricted to those from farm backgrounds. Is this so? Tables LXXXIV and LXXXV in Appendix IV contain the relevant results and these are summarised below in Table XXVIII.

The females are indeed more highly migratory than the males. In the total population 17 per cent more males than females definitely intend to remain in the home community. (35.4 per cent males, 18.3 per cent females). This appears to be partly due to the males' lower level of occupational and income frustration. Almost 14 per cent more males than females are not frustrated in their occupational aspirations (53 per cent males compared to only 39 per cent females), and almost 10 per cent more males are not frustrated in their income aspirations (36 per cent males, 26 per cent females). Are these sex differences general throughout all occupational groups or are they restricted to the farm group as predicted?

The results summarised in Table XXVIII and presented more fully in Tables LXXXIV to LXXXIX in Appendix IV, reveal that the farm category does in fact account for most of the overall

TABLE XXVIII: THE RELATIONSHIP BETWEEN SEX, OCCUPATIONAL BACKGROUND AND THE FACTORS AFFECTING PLANS TO MIGRATE

	Occupation of Father							
	Non-manual		Farmers		Skilled and Service		Semiskilled and Unskilled	
	Sex %		Sex %		Sex %		Sex %	
	M.	F.	M.	F.	M.	F.	M.	F.
(1) Occupational Frustration								
Not frustrated	32.6	35.5	57.9	43.6	58.3	42.9	53.1	33.3
Frustrated	34.9	21.0	12.9	18.2	22.2	34.3	28.6	28.9
TOTAL %	100	100	100	100	100	100	100	100
N	43	62	140	110	36	35	49	45
(2) Income Frustration								
Not frustrated	20.5	26.2	43.3	28.0	31.4	28.6	29.8	20.0
Frustrated	45.5	34.4	34.0	40.2	34.3	48.6	51.1	46.7
TOTAL %	100	100	100	100	100	100	100	100
N	44	61	150	107	35	35	47	45

(3) *Community Satisfaction*

Percentage with highly positive scores (7-9)	24.4	23.4	32.4	25.7	26.6	44.7	38.1	35.6
TOTAL N	41	47	34	35	109	150	63	45

(4) *Family Obligations*

Percentage with medium–high obligations	18.2	14.9	14.3	16.7	15.1	27.8	4.7	13.7
TOTAL N	44	47	35	36	112	155	64	44

(5) *Attitude towards the Community's Social Provisions*

Percentage with highly positive (7–9) scores	22.2	6.5	26.5	2.7	12.3	15.1	11.1	13.6
TOTAL N	45	46	34	37	106	152	63	44

(6) *Intentions to Migrate*

Definitely intend to stay at home	17.0	24.0	11.4	24.3	19.8	39.7	10.8	13.3
Definitely intend to migrate	34.0	50.0	51.4	37.8	36.2	23.7	37.5	51.1
TOTAL N	47	50	35	37	116	156	64	45

sex difference, although there are some small but consistent differences in one other group. As an aid in deciding whether differences are "big enough" to be considered as true sex differences, and not due to chance fluctuations alone, the Chi-Square statistic has been employed, and the probability associated with the computed value of the statistics has been stated in the relevant appendix tables. Since we are not dealing with a sample, but using the statistic to exclude trends in the data which could be easily brought about by operation of chance alone it is not necessary to reach the conventional p. of less than .05 to declare the trend "significant". Thus, in Tables LXXXIV and LXXXV, only in the case of farmers does the probability associated with the computed statistic reach .90 or higher. This is a very strong indication that these sex differences are not brought about by chance alone. Such sex differences should also be consistently reproduced over all values of the dependent variable before one could consider them as "true" sex differences. Thus for the semiskilled and unskilled category in Appendix Table LXXXIV, the probability also reaches over .90, but the sex difference is not consistently reproduced. While approximately 20 per cent more males than females are not frustrated, roughly the same proportion of both sexes are frustrated. On the other hand, in the case of the skilled and service category although the sex differences could easily have occurred here by chance these differences are so consistent over all categories of the frustration variable that a true sex difference probably exists here. Overall, however, the hypothesis is supported in the case of occupational and income frustration—the only place where there are significant and consistent sex differences is for the farm category, although smaller but consistent differences also appear for the skilled and service category. Even accepting the latter as a "true" difference, however, the percentage differences involved are much smaller in size than the farm category; and in terms of the numbers involved they comprise only a quarter of the farm category.

As for Community Satisfaction, the only place where major sex differences occur is in the farm category. Other differences can very easily be explained by the operation of chance factors alone as the probabilities clearly show, (see Table LXXXVI, Appendix IV). Farm males are by far the most highly attached to their community, while farm females have the lowest attachment.

Much the same situation holds for Family Obligations as for

Community Satisfaction—the only group where a consistent sex difference occurs is amongst the farm origin group. There are no clearcut sex differences amongst the manual groups; but, surprisingly enough, non-manual males have far higher levels of obligation than females. However, this could easily be a chance occurrence, as the probability figure shows. (Table LXXXVII, Appendix IV.)

Amongst all the variables looked at so far, therefore, consistent sex differences appear only among those from a farm background. However, this pattern is disrupted in considering the next variable, attitude toward the community's social provisions. Here, surprisingly, the relative position of males and females is reversed—males in general having more negative attitudes toward the community's social provisions. Almost 5 per cent more males than females have highly negative attitudes, and 4 per cent fewer have highly positive attitudes. The breakdown by occupational groups (Table LXXXVIII, Appendix IV; and Table XXVIII above) reveals that it is not the farm but the manual worker groups that account for these sex differences. In fact, no consistent sex differences occur amongst farm or non-manual groups. Amongst all the variables studied, the largest sex differences found occur for these two manual groups on attitude toward social provisions. Over 32 per cent more males than females from skilled and service occupational backgrounds have highly negative attitudes, while 8 per cent more females than males have moderate attitudes, and almost 24 per cent more females than males have positive attitudes. The sex differences for the semiskilled and unskilled are similar: 16 per cent more males than females have negative attitudes, and 16 per cent more females than males have positive attitudes. It should also be noted that males from manual occupational groups generally tend to have more negative attitudes toward the community's social provisions than do farm or non-manual males. On the other hand, females from manual groups tend to have more positive attitudes toward these provisions than do females or even males from any other group.

This reversal of the usual trends, however, does not appear to have had any major impact on migration intentions, as can be seen in Table XXVIII above and in Table LXXXIX, Appendix IV. Here the only places where consistent and significant sex differences appear are for those from farm backgrounds, and from skilled and service backgrounds. Although there are differences in other cases, these are not consistently reproduced over all values of the migration variable. The consistent differences present in the skilled and service category are in keeping with similar differences occurring in the case of occupational and income frustrations. Almost 13 per cent more males than females from skilled and service occupational backgrounds intend to stay at home, while nearly 14 per cent more females than males intend to migrate. Much greater percentage differences occur in the case of those from a farm category, however. Almost 20 per cent more males than females intend to remain at home, while almost 13 per cent more females than males intend to migrate. Since the percentage differences are somewhat greater, and since there are almost four times as many people from a farm background as from a skilled and service background, the farm category does indeed account for the major portion of the total sex differences involved in migration plans.

In summary, therefore, the hypothesis is generally upheld. The major sex difference in migration intentions, and in the factors influencing them, occur in the farm category; although some small unexpected differences also occur in the skilled and service category.

One of the major reasons put forward to explain why we expected more girls from a farm background to migrate was that farm girls were likely to receive a better education than farm boys. They would consequently be characterised by higher levels of occupational and income aspirations. An examination of Table IX (in Chapter 3) reveals that such a sex selectivity in education does hold for those from a farm background. So, farm girls may be more prone to migrate merely because more of them receive a postprimary education. As a result it may be that the sex selectivity involved in farming operates only indirectly on migration, by first selecting out primary educated males to work on the home farm while sending a disproportionate number of females on for further education, a situation which greatly increases their chances of migrating. Such educational factors however, would not explain the sex differences in migration also observed for the skilled and service group. The following section will examine this and other questions which deal with the relationship between sex, education and migration intentions.

SEX AND EDUCATION AND INTENTIONS TO MIGRATE

It was expected that along with a tendency for secondary educated males and females to aspire almost exclusively to non-manual

occupations, vocational education would also influence a disproportionate number of females to aspire to non-manual occupations.
So, in comparison with the lower level manual type aspirations of
the males, they would be much more likely to be frustrated in their
aspirations and tend to be more migratory. Is this in fact the case?
The results presented in Table XC in Appendix IV show clearly
that it is. Both males and females receiving a secondary education
aspire almost equally and almost exclusively to non-manual occupations (87 per cent and 97 per cent respectively). Great sex differences, however, do exist in the case of those receiving a vocational
education. Over 50 per cent of the girls here aspire to non-manual
occupations, while this is true of only 5 per cent of the boys. The
remaining vocational girls are also disproportionately concentrated
in the service occupational category, while the boys are heavily
concentrated in skilled manual occupations. The same pattern of
sex differences in the kind of manual or service jobs entered is
evident even for the primary educated. Given these sex differences
in the kind and level of jobs aspired to, if these differential aspirations are the critical factors in influencing levels of frustration and
intentions to migrate, one would expect that if this factor is controlled, sex, like education, would have little independent effect on
migration behaviour. Is this the case? That it apparently is is shown
clearly by the results presented in Appendix Table XCI. The results
here show that, if the level of occupational aspiration is held constant sex has no consistent influence on migration. So, females are
more migratory not because of any idiosyncratic set of factors but
because of their greater tendency to aspire to higher status and less
available occupations than males.

Since there are such small sex differences in level of aspiration
among the secondary educated while much higher proportions of
females than males in vocational schools aspire to non-manual
occupations, one would also expect greater levels of occupational
frustration among females in vocational schools. Is this the case?
Table XXIX below summarises the results which bear on this
question. These results show clearly that there are no significant
sex differences among the secondary educated, but that clear and
consistent differences do exist for the vocationally educated as
expected. Although less clearcut, these sex differences also occur
for the primary educated. Much greater proportions of the primary
and vocationally educated males are not frustrated in their occu-

pational and income aspirations while much greater proportions of females are partly or fully frustrated in their aspirations. Since we are dealing with population characteristics here and the probability of getting trends as extreme or more extreme than these is less than one in four, we can safely accept these as "true" differences.

TABLE XXIX: THE RELATIONSHIP BETWEEN SEX, LEVEL OF EDUCATION AND (1) OCCUPATIONAL FRUSTRATION, (2) INCOME FRUSTRATION, (3) MIGRATION INTENTIONS

		Education of Respondent					
		Primary		*Vocational*		*Secondary*	
		M. %	F. %	M. %	F. %	M. %	F. %
(1) *Occupational Frustration*							
Not frustrated		68.9	56.5	54.4	34.6	31.3	33.9
Frustrated		20.8	35.5	12.7	12.8	27.7	23.2
TOTAL	%	100	100	100	100	100	100
	N	106	62	79	78	83	112
		$X^2 = 4.40$ P > .75 < .90		$X^2 = 7.02$ P > .95		$X^2 = .52$ P > .10 < .25	
(2) *Income Frustration*							
Not frustrated		49.6	45.5	32.9	20.0	18.3	18.7
Frustrated		36.4	47.0	39.7	38.7	41.5	39.3
TOTAL	%	100	100	100	100	100	100
	N	121	66	73	75	82	107
		$X^2 = 2.86$ P > .75 < .90		$X^2 = 4.40$ P > .75 < .90		$X^2 = .09$ P < .10	
(3) *Migration Intentions*							
Definitely intend to stay		41.5	32.4	32.1	10.0	14.3	10.5
Definitely intend to migrate		27.6	42.6	30.9	32.5	47.6	39.5
TOTAL	%	100	100	100	100	100	100
	N	123	68	81	80	82	107
		$X^2 = 4.46$ P > .75 < .90		$X^2 = 12.92$ P > .95		$X^2 = 2.67$ P > .50 < .75	

These sex differences in the levels of occupational and income frustration among the primary and vocationally educated are also reflected in the greater migration proneness of females from these two categories. As expected, there are very small and inconsistent sex differences in such migration plans for the secondary educated, reflecting the relatively equal levels of occupational and income frustration suffered by both sexes at this level. On the other hand the vocationally educated suffer the greatest sex differences in this regard. Here the females are very similar to those receiving a secondary education in the proportions who intend to leave the community, while the males approach the less mobile primary educated. Over 22 per cent more vocationally educated males than females intend to remain locally, while over 20 per cent of the females are indefinite whether they will migrate or not and a further 2 per cent more females than males definitely intend to leave. Although the trend is not as clearcut for the primary educated, over 9 per cent more males than females intend to remain at home and 15 per cent more females intend to migrate. In general, therefore, these results confirm the hypotheses proposed and accurately reflect previously observed sex differences in the motivating factors.

Pulling together all these diverse facts about sex selectivity in migration we find that: (1) it is primarily limited to those from a farm background, although small differences also exist for the skilled and service category; (2) far more females from a farm background receive a post-primary education; (3) the higher the level of education the higher the level of aspiration and frustration of these aspirations; (4) a higher proportions of females than males in vocational schools aspire to non-manual occupations whereas other educational groups show only limited differences in level of aspiration; (5) the only educational group where levels of occupational and income frustration for females are higher than those for males concern those receiving a vocational education, and to a much lesser extent those who are primary educated; (6) migration tendencies for females in vocational schools are much higher than for males, although smaller but similar consistent sex differences also exist among the primary educated.

Concluding, therefore, it appears that sex selectivity in migration is indeed largely restricted to farm children; that it is due primarily to the higher levels of education received by the farm females; that this education leads to much higher levels of aspiration, to frustration of these aspirations and consequently to higher levels of migration. The additional fact that females in vocational schools have occupational aspirations very close to those in secondary schools, and consequently are roughly as prone to migrate is also important. As a result, even non-farm females receiving a vocational education are being subjected to influences which are likely to influence them to migrate more than males from similar backgrounds. This is probably the main reason for the sex difference in migration for those from a skilled and service background.

The explanation of sex selectivity in migration is therefore much more complex than originally proposed. This explanation was based on the sex selectivity of farming as an occupation, and the approximately equal occupational opportunities for both sexes available off the farm. Such sex selectivity does occur, as is very obvious in the results summarised in Table XXX, but it leads primarily to more farm females getting a postprimary education, and the major part of the sex selectivity involved can be explained by the differential consequences of this on both sexes. But, perhaps, even for those who do not receive any postprimary education the rationale may hold up. Do more females than males who receive only a primary education and who are working off the farm intend to migrate? The relevant results are presented in Table XXX.

First, the results indicate very clearly the disproportionate selection of males for farming. The very limited opportunities available for females in farm areas is clearly demonstrated by the fact that only 14 out of 117 (12 per cent) farm females were working on the home farm or in the farm household, and of these only 6 intended to remain there (5 per cent). On the other hand, out of the two-year cohort of 160 farm males 48 were then working on the home farm (30 per cent), but only 26 to 30 of these planned to remain there (16 to 19 per cent). Although this is much higher than the female total it still represents a tremendous movement out of agriculture. Both for those working on the farm and for those working off it, females tend to be more migration prone than males, a situation which accurately reflects their higher levels of occupational and income frustration. The differences, however, are not very marked, particularly in the case of those working off farms, and could easily be a chance occurrence. Although there is, therefore, a tendency for males to be less migration-prone than females for those working on and off the farm, the percentage differences are very small, as are the

TABLE XXX: THE RELATIONSHIP BETWEEN SEX, TYPE OF WORK OF RESPONDENTS
THEN WORKING AND (1) OCCUPATIONAL FRUSTRATION, (2) INCOME FRUSTRATION,
AND (3) MIGRATION INTENTIONS

| | Occupation of respondents *** | | | |
| | Working on the home farm | | Others now working | |
	Males %	Females %	Males %	Females %
(1) *Occupational Frustration*				
Not frustrated	82.4	63.6	61.4	54.9
Partly frustrated	8.8	9.1	11.4	7.8
Frustrated	8.8	27.3	27.1	37.3
TOTAL %	100	100	99.9	100
N	34	11	70	51
			$X^2 = 1.54$; $P > .50 < .75$	
(2) *Income Frustration*				
Not frustrated	59.6	38.5	44.9	44.9
Partly frustrated	12.8	23.1	15.9	4.1
Frustrated	27.7	38.5	39.1	51.0
TOTAL %	100.1	100.1	99.9	100
N	47	13	69	49
			$X^2 = 4.58$; $P > .75 < .90$	
(3) *Migration Planning*				
Definite plan to stay	54.2	42.9	35.7	27.5
Indefinite whether will stay or leave	35.4	28.6	25.7	25.5
Definite plans to leave	10.4	28.6	38.6	47.1
TOTAL %	100	100	100	100
N	48	14	70	51
			$X^2 = 1.10$; $P > .25 < .50$	

*** The great majority of those now working have received only a primary
education.

numbers involved. Sex differences in migration, therefore, are primarily due to the greater proportion of farm females receiving a post-primary education, and to the greater tendency of females in vocational schools to migrate.

A comparison of the differential migration tendencies of females receiving different levels of education (see Table XXIX) reveals little difference in the migration plans of the vocationally and secondary educated, while approximately three times as many of the primary educated intend to remain at home (32 per cent compared to 10 per cent). But because the primary educated are far more definite in their plans, slightly more of them definitely intend to migrate than others (43 per cent compared to 32 to 40 per cent). However, if we combine the percentage figure for those who definitely intend to leave and those who are not sure, it is found that a far higher proportion (35 to 32 percentage difference) of the vocational and secondary educated than the primary educated have some plans to migrate.

It is rather surprising that such a low proportion of the vocationally educated girls intend to remain locally, particularly in view of the relatively lower proportions who aspire to non-manual occupations as compared to the secondary educated. However, the majority of the remainder aspire to service occupations—(See Appendix IV, Table XC)—whereas most of the vocational males aspire to skilled occupations. Since those who aspire to service occupations are even more pessimistic than the non-manual aspirers about the possibility of getting a satisfactory job locally (See Table LXXVI, Appendix IV), their equally pronounced tendency to migrate is understandable. It may be remembered from a previous section that we had left partly unresolved the reason for the greater migration tendency of the service workers, although those aspiring to service occupations were found to be more frustrated in their income aspirations than those aspiring to skilled manual occupations. Results presented in Appendix IV, Table XC clearly show that it is mainly girls who aspire to service occupations while boys aspire to manual occupations, and boys in vocational schools particularly to skilled manual occupations. Since level of occupational or income frustration does not fully explain why those aspiring to service occupations are so migratory, the fact that such a disproportionate number of them are girls may be important. There must be something about local service occupations other than their availability which make them particularly unattractive for girls. Their perceived poorer remuneration has already been remarked upon, but this does not completely explain why so many of these girls intend to migrate. Perhaps the job security of a shop assistant, the majority of service workers in this study, may be an important factor. Given the other evidence available it doesn't seem likely that there are different motives involved in the migration of female service workers than is the case for other female workers or all male respondents. The argument so far has assumed that this was not the case, but that sex differences in migration, like educational differences, could be explained by equivalent differences in levels of aspiration. If this is the case, it would mean that both sexes aspiring to the same occupations would be willing to remain at home if they could fulfill their occupational aspirations locally. This should hold equally across educational lines as across sex lines. Is this in fact the case? Table XXXI has been set up to test this hypothesis.

TABLE XXXI: THE RELATIONSHIP BETWEEN SEX, LEVEL OF EDUCATION, AND "CONDITIONAL MIGRATION"

Of those considering migration, the proportion who say they would remain if:	Level of Education Received					
	Primary		Vocational		Secondary	
	Male	Female	Male	Female	Male	Female
	%	%	%	%	%	%
(1) occupational and/or income aspirations could be satisfied there	92.1	83.3	75.5	77.9	81.9	43.0
(2) besides the satisfaction of these aspirations, the community's social provisions were brought up to expectations	1.6	7.1	6.1	7.4	8.3	27.0
(3) would not remain under any circumstances	6.3	9.5	18.4	14.7	9.7	30.0
TOTAL %	100	100	100	100	99.9	100
N	63	42	49	68	72	100

The results here are very interesting. In answer to our immediate question it appears that economic factors do indeed have equal dominance in the decisions of the primary and vocationally educated boys and girls. Much the same situation holds for the secondary educated boys, but major non-economic factors intrude in the case of the secondary educated girls. A large and approximately equal proportion of the vocational and primary educated girls would remain at home if their occupational and income aspirations could be fulfilled there (83 per cent of the primary as against 78 per cent of the vocational girls) while this is true of less than half the secondary educated (43 per cent). Furthermore, there are very small differences between the sexes within each of the former two educational classes, while major sex differences occur within the secondary educated group. While secondary educated boys are very similar in their responses to both boys and girls from the other two educational levels, the responses of the secondary educated girls deviate considerably from others. From three to four times as many of these girls place great importance on the necessity to improve local social provisions before they would be willing to remain locally, and from two to five times as many say they would not remain at home under any circumstances. Secondary educated girls then differ considerably from both boys and girls of other educational levels, as well as from secondary educated boys, in the relative importance of economic and non-economic factors in migration. While economic type factors generally predominate in migration decisions non-economic factors come strongly into play in the case of secondary educated girls. There appear to be definite sex differences in the kind of motives involved in migration, therefore, but this is limited to the secondary educated.

This finding also contradicts an earlier interpretation of the results presented in the preceding Table XXVII. There, educational level was related to "conditional migration" as above, but there was no control for sex. As a result it appeared that the non-manual aspirers or the secondary educated of both sexes were equally deviant in their migration motives. Now it appears that this is only true of secondary educated girls, not boys.[3] The sex difference in the motives of the secondary educated is not due to any equiva-

[3] This misinterpretation has unfortunately already been published in a paper presented at the Second World Congress of Rural Sociology, Drienerloo, N. L. in August 1968; and subsequently published in *Sociologia Ruralis*, (1969) IX, 3.

lent difference in the level of aspirations of both sexes. In fact, since much higher proportions of males than females attending secondary schools aspire to professional and semi-professional occupations (37 per cent as against 22 per cent) one would expect the boys to have greater objections to remaining at home than the girls. We will have to find an alternative explanation, therefore. Two things are possible: first, secondary schools may select girls already highly alienated from their community. Farm girls are, in fact, disproportionately represented among the secondary educated, and they are also those with the lowest levels of community satisfaction. However, some further tabulation of the results indicated the persistence of the above sex differences even when occupational background is controlled for. So the alternative explanation appears more likely; i.e. that for girls the experience of secondary education changed their attitudes and aspirations to such an extent that less than half of them were willing to remain in the home community even when they believed they could fulfill their occupational and income aspirations there. There are different motives involved in the migration of secondary educated girls therefore. Since, however, only a small proportion of these particular girls would be able to fulfill their occupational aspirations at home in any case, their somewhat deviant motives do not invalidate the original assumption that variation in levels of aspiration is the main explanatory variable in migration differentials.

CONCLUSIONS

The level and kind of aspiration is the crucial variable in explaining variation in beliefs about the possibility of fulfilling occupational and income aspirations locally. Although education is highly related to migration plans, when respondents' level of aspiration is held constant, additional variation levels of education has little additional influence on these plans. An exception to this occurs in the case of those who believe they can fulfill their occupational aspirations locally. For these respondents, the higher the level of education the greater the proportions intending to migrate. This result was explained by the higher levels of family obligation of the primary educated who are required to remain in the home community and who generally intend to do so when they are satisfied with occupational opportunities there. This retarding influence does not operate for the secondary educated.

Sex differences in migration are very apparent, with roughly one sixth more males than females intending to remain at home. This sex difference, however, is primarily restricted to those from farm backgrounds. It is also primarily due to the relatively higher levels of education received by farm girls, and the greater tendency of farm boys to remain at home on the farm after finishing in primary school. Girls receiving a vocational education are also far more migratory than similarly educated boys. This is due to their greater tendency to aspire to less available non-manual type occupations and to service occupations. The aspirations of vocational boys, on the other hand, are biassed in the direction of the more plentiful skilled and semiskilled manual occupations.

In conclusion, therefore, a very small number of variables or social processes explains why females are more migratory than males, and why the more highly educated are more migratory than the less well educated. The main forces determining this selection relate to educational and occupational selection processes in this home community. Because sex, education and occupational background are highly related to both processes of selection they are also related to migration. There was one discrepant result here, however, in the case of the secondary educated girls. Their migration motives appear to be somewhat different in kind from those of other groups, although in their case also the argument as to occupational selection still stood.

6.   Results IV—
Structural Constraints
and Migration Intentions:
Remoteness, Family Expectations,
and Migration Systems

In this chapter the affects on migration intentions of three other social structural factors will be examined: remoteness of respondents' homes from the centre; parental expectations in regard to their children's migration; and the extent to which respondents' sibs and other near relatives had already migrated ("migration systems"). Each of these factors will be taken in turn.

(i) REMOTENESS FROM THE CENTRE AND
INTENTIONS TO MIGRATE

It has already been clearly shown that distance from the centre has a major influence on population decline and on educational opportunity. Population decline increased by approximately 50 per cent as distance from the centre increased beyond 6 miles, (see Table III, Chapter 2). And adolescents living more than four miles from the centre had a 50 per cent lower probability of receiving a postprimary education on that account alone, (see Table XII, Chapter 3). Does this also hold true for occupational and income frustration, and consequently for migration plans? Do those living in more remote districts have more negative attitudes toward their actually poorer social provisions? And have they also more negative attitudes toward their community relationships? These questions will be explored in this section.

TABLE XXXII

Level of Remoteness from the Centre

	Centre, plus area within two miles of centre		All large towns in the community plus country areas within four miles of centre		All others, mostly open country areas more than four miles from the centre	
	Males	Females	Males	Females	Males	Females
	%	%	%	%	%	%
A. Occupational Frustration I						
Not frustrated	46.7	37.3	51.0	39.5	65.5	41.8
Frustrated	31.1	21.1	26.5	23.3	14.3	27.3
TOTAL %	100	100	100	100	100	100
N	(46)	(52)	(49)	(43)	(119)	(110)
B. Occupational Frustration II						
Have job at present and satisfied (% of total respondents)	17.4	1.9	24.5	11.6	40.3	13.6
TOTAL N	(46)	(52)	(49)	(43)	(119)	(110)

	% who def. plan to stay	% who def. plan to leave	% who def. plan to stay	% who def. plan to leave	% who def. plan to stay	% who def. plan to leave
Of remainder (1) Not occupationally frustrated (2) Occupationally frustrated	35.1 37.8	36.0 22.0	35.1 35.1	31.6 26.3	45.3 22.7	33.3 31.3
TOTAL N	(37)	(50)	(37)	(38)	(75)	(96)
C. % *Aspiring to incomes of more than £15 per week*	61.0	13.0	40.0	12.8	43.0	8.3
TOTAL N	(41)	(46)	(48)	(39)	(128)	(109)
D. *Percentage of all adolescents aspiring to non-manual occupations*	31.3	65.4	22.0	67.4	17.7	53.4
TOTAL N	(46)	(52)	(50)	(43)	(135)	(118)
E. *Income Frustration* (1) Not frustrated	20.0	27.5	29.8	22.5	49.6	30.9
TOTAL N	(45)	(51)	(47)	(40)	(129)	(110)
F. *Occupation of Respondents by plans to migrate*	% who def. plan to stay	% who def. plan to leave	% who def. plan to stay	% who def. plan to leave	% who def. plan to stay	% who def. plan to leave
Working on farm M F	50.0	0.0 (2)	80.0	0.0 (5)	61.4 43.8	6.8 (44) 31.3 (16)
Working off farm M F	53.8 37.5	30.8 (13) 37.5 (8)	16.0 38.5	60.0 (25) 38.5 (13)	48.8 23.7	30.1 (43) 42.1 (38)

Both occupational and income frustration are indeed highly related to remoteness as the results presented in Table XXXII above clearly indicate. The table yields a more complex picture of this relationship than expected, however. The trend for males is, in fact, directly opposite to that predicted, since frustration of both occupational and income aspirations actually decreases with increasing distance from the centre. Over 31 per cent of the males from the centre are frustrated in their occupational aspirations (see Section A of the table), compared with 27 per cent frustrated in intermediate areas, and only 14 per cent in the most remote areas. Income frustration levels decrease similarly for males from 80 per cent frustrated or partly frustrated at the centre to 70 per cent in intermediate areas and only 50 per cent in the most remote areas.

However, since the proportion of farm adolescents increases very rapidly with distance from the centre, the proportion of males ascribed full time occupational roles on the family farm also increases, as shown by the results on Section B of the table. Only 17 per cent of the males from the centre have satisfactory jobs and none of these work on the home farm, while 25 per cent of males from intermediate areas and 40 per cent of those from the most remote areas have satisfactory jobs, and most of these work on the home farm. Table XXXIV below shows similar differentials in regard to family obligations. Only 13 per cent of males from the centre have medium to high obligations, whereas 21 per cent of those from intermediate areas and 30 per cent of those from the most remote areas have such obligations. This increasing tendency of males to hold ascribed occupational roles on the home farm, and to have pressing family obligations, may explain the unexpected decrease in rates of occupational and income frustration with remoteness. This factor has been controlled in Section B of Table XXXII. The results here indicate that for those males who *do not* have occupations that satisfy them—largely those who are at school or work at off-farm occupations—occupational frustration levels are relatively equal in the two least remote areas but *decrease* again for the most remote area. Almost 65 per cent of the males from the centre and the next least remote area are frustrated or partly frustrated in their occupational aspirations, compared to only 55 per cent of those from the most remote areas. Hence, although the differences are much reduced, they are still in a direction opposite to those predicted.

Perhaps the more remote males, having lower levels of occupational and income aspiration, (as indicated by Sections C and D of Table XXXII), are better able to fulfill these aspirations locally. Occupational opportunities, however, are not distributed evenly throughout the community, but are concentrated at the centre. As a result, unless a considerable proportion of the more remote respondents commute to the centre, and unless employers in the centre discriminate in their favour, the influence of their lower aspiration levels would be offset by the relatively sparse occupational opportunities available near their homes. Arensberg observed a very similar type of job recruitment in County Clare towns in the 1930s. The commodity or labour market did not operate on the basis of purely economic criteria. Relationships involved in the market formed part of a wider enveloping system of kinship and friendship ties. Business follows these ties. Employing working class youth from the town in the shops, garages and other businesses which primarily depend for their livelihood on the farm trade, would be dysfunctional in this kind of market system. As Arensberg notes, "the town-bred lad is seldom hired, he brings no rural kindred with him".[1] Nor indeed is the "town-bred lad" so impressionable, so easy to control, nor so likely to be satisfied with the wages and conditions of work offered. However, these relationships have changed since the 1930s. Farming has become more specialised, more mechanised, more involved in the market economy, and has become less and less an autonomous self-sufficient "way of life". Market town businesses have also changed, especially in latter years, with the introduction of supermarkets and larger, less familial concerns. Can we still expect the patterns of the 1930s to persist? The results presented in Table XXXIII below appear to suggest so. Adolescents from the more remote areas of the community have taken up a disproportionate number of jobs in the centre.

Over 50 per cent of the males and 47 per cent of the females from the most remote areas have jobs in the centre. Adolescents from the two more remote areas, in fact, comprise almost three quarters of the 78 respondents then working in the centre, while those from the most remote areas comprise over one half. These more remote youth, having lower levels of occupational aspiration, fill lower level service and manual jobs in the centre. Those nearer the centre, having higher levels of education and aspiration, also have higher

[1] Arensberg, C. M., *The Irish Countryman*, Peter Smith, 1961, 157.

levels of frustration. Whether this fact alone accounts for the results found, or whether employers also are biassed in favour of those from a farm background in their employment practices cannot be determined from the present survey. It appears, in any case, that at least in the area studied, distance does not act as a major barrier to participation in the centre's labour market. The uneven distribution of occupational opportunities by distance is compensated for by the easy mobility of the participants involved. This may not be true, of course, for areas outside this community's boundaries.

TABLE XXXIII: THE RELATIONSHIP OF PLACE OF WORK TO THE REMOTENESS OF RESPONDENTS' HOMES, FOR RESPONDENTS NOW WORKING

Remoteness of place of work	Remoteness of homes of Respondents now working					
	Centre and up to 2 miles from centre		All small towns and all open country areas up to 4 miles from the centre		All open country areas more than 4 miles from the centre	
	Males %	Females %	Males %	Females %	Males %	Females %
Centre and up to 2 miles from the centre	100	100	40	28.6	51.0	47.4
Small towns and open country areas up to 4 miles from the centre			60	64.3	12.2	23.7
Open country areas more than 4 miles from the centre				7.1	36.7	28.9
Total Number of cases	13	8	25	14	49	38

Because of these characteristics of the labour market, and the lower levels of aspiration of the more remote respondents, fewer of them, relatively, are frustrated in their occupational and income aspirations. But before coming to a final conclusion on this, another fact needs to be taken into consideration: 36 prospective respondents had already migrated by the time the survey had started. Thirteen of these were males, of whom 12 came from the most remote areas. If we assume that these were occupationally frustrated, their addition to the relevant cells in Table XXXII alters the distribution there. Of the centre males, 31 per cent would be frustrated, compared to 28 per cent from the intermediate area, and 22 per cent from the most remote areas. The differences are considerably reduced. But even with these additions, the relative proportion of males from the centre frustrated in their occupational aspirations is almost one half more than those from the most remote areas. Overall, then, the results clearly indicate that the more remote males have lower levels of income and occupational frustration than have others nearer the centre.

At first sight, the position is not very different for females. Although there is an increase in the proportions frustrated in occupational and income aspirations, with increasing distance from the centre, there is also a similar slight increase in the proportion not frustrated. This is accounted for by the fact that those near the centre are much more indefinite in their beliefs about the possible fulfillment of occupational and income aspirations locally. For those not now satisfactorily employed, however, (Section B, Table XXXII), there is a definite increase in occupational frustration with increasing remoteness. Twenty-two per cent of those nearest the centre are frustrated in their occupational aspirations, compared to 26 per cent of those in the intermediate areas, and to 31 per cent of those in the most remote areas.

In addition, 23 prospective female respondents from the community had already migrated by the time the study had started. Eighteen of these came from the most remote area, two from intermediate areas, and three from the centre. If we assume that these were occupationally frustrated, their addition to the relevant cells in Table XXXII strengthens the trends there in the direction predicted. At the centre, 26 per cent of females would be frustrated, compared to 27 per cent of those from intermediate areas, and 38 per cent of those from the most remote areas. The original hypothesis, therefore, is confirmed as regards females.

By way of summary, the relationship between occupational and income frustration is directly opposite to that predicted for males, while for females there is some evidence for the hypothesis—although not as strong as expected.

How are sex differentials related to remoteness? The figures presented in Table XXXII, section A, show that in relative proportions 9 per cent more males than females from the centre are not frustrated in their occupational aspirations. This sex difference increases to 12 percentage points at the intermediate area, and to 23 percentage points at the most remote area. Section B of Table XXXII shows that, of those not presently satisfactorily employed, approximately the same proportion of females and males from the centre are not occupationally frustrated. This changes to a percentage difference of 4 points in favour of males in the intermediate areas, and to 12 points in favour of males in the most remote areas. The more remote the area, the more the males have the advantage. The figures for those occupationally frustrated or partly frustrated give corroborating results, with females becoming relatively more frustrated in their aspirations than males, as remoteness increases. Not only then do progressively greater proportions of males relative to females enjoy ascribed occupational roles on the family farm as remoteness increases, but even for those seeking off-farm jobs, increasingly greater proportions of males, relative to females, can find acceptable jobs locally.

The trends for income frustration are similar as a glance at Section E of Table XXXII clearly shows. In relative proportions, 8 per cent more females than males from the centre are not frustrated, whereas 7 per cent more males than females are not frustrated in intermediate areas, and 19 per cent more males than females are not frustrated at the more remote areas. The figures for those frustrated corroborate these results. Does the same relationship exist between remoteness and Community Satisfaction? Because of the increasing proportions of males who come from farm backgrounds and their well known tendency to hold more traditional values, their greater tendency to have more binding family obligations and to be ascribed occupational roles within the family farm system, it was argued that males would become more satisfied with the community as remoteness increased. The level of Community Satisfaction for females, on the other hand, should decrease with remoteness. Is this in fact the case? The results pertinent to these questions are presented in Table XXXIV.

The results for females are as expected. As the distance of homes from the centre increases, the proportion of females with low Community Satisfaction scores progressively increases from 20 per cent in the centre to 32 per cent in the most remote areas. The

TABLE XXXIV: THE RELATIONSHIP BETWEEN REMOTENESS AND (A) COMMUNITY
SATISFACTION, (B) COMMUNITY EVALUATION, AND (C) FAMILY OBLIGATIONS

	Level of remoteness from the Centre					
	Centre		Towns and areas 1 to 4 miles		4 miles plus	
	Males %	Females %	Males %	Females %	Males %	Females %
(A) Community Satisfaction						
Alienated (0–3)	40.0	19.6	34.0	27.5	15.6	32.4
Highly satisfied (7–9)	26.7	39.2	38.0	20.0	40.6	27.9
TOTAL N	45	51	50	40	128	111
(B) Attitude towards the Community's social provisions						
Negative (7–9)	76.0	40.8	51.0	60.0	57.3	56.8
Positive (0–3)	4.3	26.5	14.3	15.0	13.7	11.7
TOTAL N	46	49	49	40	131	111
(C) Family Obligations Percentage with medium–high family obligations	13.0	9.6	20.8	17.1	30.0	15.9
TOTAL N	46	52	48	41	130	113

proportion who are highly satisfied correspondingly decreases from
39 per cent to 28 per cent.

For males, however, the proportion with low Community
Satisfaction scores decreases with distance and at a much greater
rate. The proportion with low scores decreases from 40 per cent
at the centre to only 16 per cent in the most remote areas. The
proportion of males with highly satisfied scores, on the other hand,
increases from 21 per cent at the centre, to 41 per cent for those from
the most remote areas. The results then are as expected, and strongly
confirm the proposed hypothesis.

What is the position, however, in regard to attitudes toward the
community's social provisions? Do the same trends occur? The
results presented in Table XXXIV indicate that they do. The

proportion of females with negative attitudes toward the community's social provisions increases greatly with remoteness, while that of males decreases. Over 40 per cent of females near the centre have highly negative attitudes, compared to 60 per cent with negative attitudes in intermediate areas, and 57 per cent with negative attitudes in the most remote areas. The proportion with highly positive attitudes similarly declines for females from 27 per cent at the centre to 12 per cent in the most remote areas. The hypothesis, therefore, is clearly confirmed in this case.

In line with our hypothesis also, the trends for males are directly opposite to those for females. The proportion with highly negative attitudes decreases from 76 per cent at the centre to 57 per cent in the most remote areas. The proportion with highly positive attitudes correspondingly increases from 4 per cent to 14 per cent. Both trends, then, are in the expected direction. Although there is actually an improvement in the adequacy of social provisions nearer the centre, males from the centre have more negative attitudes toward these provisions than have more remote males.

The rationale on which these hypotheses were based is not confirmed by these results, however. It was assumed that there would be an increasing difference between males and females in their attitudes toward the community's social provisions, as remoteness increased: the proportion of males with positive attitudes increasing with remoteness, while that of females decreased with remoteness. It was expected that the more remote females, living in largely male-centred communities, with very limited leisure, sport, and entertainment facilities (5 out of 9 items in the scale) for girls, would have much more negative attitudes toward these facilities, than would the relatively more advantaged males in that community. Females from less remote areas of the community, where facilities are better, were expected to have more positive attitudes. Males from the centre were expected to have less positive attitudes than those from more remote areas, because of the more traditional values and attitudes of the latter. However, no major differences were expected in attitudes between males and females from the centre.

This rationale seems to hold up in the case of Community Satisfaction, at least in regard to differences between the sexes from the more remote areas. But the results completely contradict the rationale in the case of attitudes toward the community's social provisions. There are no important differences between the more remote males and females in their attitudes toward these social provisions, whereas there are major differences between the sexes at the centre. It is, in fact, these differences between the sexes near the centre that have led to the confirmation of the second part of the hypothesis. Females from the centre have the most positive attitudes of all respondents, male or female, and males from the centre have the most negative attitudes of all respondents, male or female.

Some previous results indicate why this might be so. The results set out in Table XXVIII of Chapter 5 have shown that males from manual backgrounds have, of all occupational groups, the most negative attitudes toward the community's social provisions. And, the same table also shows that the females from manual backgrounds have, by far, the most positive attitudes toward the community's social provisions—far more so than is true of females from any other occupational group. Since these manual groups are concentrated in the centre, these previous results account for the unexpected findings in Table XXXIV above. The centre males are the most negative because they contain a much higher proportion of highly dissatisfied manual males. The centre females are the most satisfied because they contain such a high proportion of the highly satisfied manual females. Of course, why these differences should exist between males and females from manual backgrounds, or why there should be such a great difference between the manual group and others in their attitude toward these provisions, has not been explained. This will have to await further research.

The cumulative effect of all these results is to throw considerable doubt on the validity of the derived hypothesis that migration tendencies increase with distance from the centre. This is particularly true for males; one would, indeed, expect here a decline in migration tendencies with distance from the centre. For females, on the other hand, if those who had already migrated were included with those who intended to migrate, there would possibly be a slight trend in the originally expected direction. Table XXXV contains the relevant results.

In keeping with the previous results, the trends are indeed in a direction opposite to that originally predicted. In general, the more remote the homes of respondents, the lesser the tendency to migrate. This holds for both males and females. The differences between the centre population and that of the next most remote areas are not very great or consistent. However, compared to these two groups, the most remote respondents plan to stay in the home community in much greater proportions. For males, 23 to 26 per cent from the two least remote areas plan to stay, compared to 44 per cent of those from the most remote areas. The differences for females are much smaller, but the trend is in the same direction. 9 to 16 per cent of females from the centre and the next most remote area plan to stay in the home community, compared to 20 per cent of those from the most remote areas. Over 48 per cent of those from the centre intend to migrate, while only 39 per cent of those from the most remote areas intend to do so. Overall, then, the trends for both sexes run directly opposite to those originally predicted.

However, most of those who had already migrated came from the most remote areas, and if these are included with the cases who now definitely intend to migrate, they may alter this conclusion. When included, 39 per cent of the males from the centre intend to migrate, or have migrated. This increases to just over 45 per cent for those from intermediate areas, but decreases again to only 28 per cent for those from the most remote areas. The respective figures for females indicate that 49 per cent of those from the centre have already migrated, or plan to migrate, whereas 38 per cent of the females from intermediate areas, and 47 per cent from the most remote areas are equally prone to migration. Hence, even with this correction, the trends run counter to those predicted in the case of males, and show very small and inconsistent trends in the case of females.

Instituting controls for educational level achieved by respondents gives similar results, as indicated in Table XXXV. Of those who are primary educated and presently working, those who live further from the centre plan to migrate in smaller proportions than do those nearer the centre. This holds true for both males and females. If the numbers who had already migrated are added to the figures for the primary educated, the results are altered to some extent. 60 per cent of females from the two least remote areas plan to migrate or have already migrated, compared to 56 per cent in the most remote areas. These differences are not very important. In the case of males, only 29 per cent from the most remote areas plan to migrate or have already migrated, compared to 51 per cent from the two least remote areas combined. The same pattern persists for both males and females who have received a vocational or secondary education. The greater the distance from the centre,

Remoteness of respondents' homes from the centre

Plans to migrate	Centre plus open country area within 2 miles of the centre		All small towns plus open country areas within 4 miles of the centre		Open country areas over 4 miles from the centre	
	Males %	*Females* %	*Males* %	*Females* %	*Males* %	*Females* %
Definite plans to stay	23.9	9.6	26.0	16.3	44.4	19.7
Indefinite whether will stay or leave	37.0	42.3	30.0	51.2	34.6	41.9
Definite plans to leave	39.1	48.1	44.0	32.6	21.1	38.5
TOTAL %	100	100	100	100	100.1	100.1
N	46	52	50	43	133	117

Education of Respondents by plans to migrate		Percentage who def. plan to stay	Percentage who def. plan to migrate	Percentage who def. plan to stay	Percentage who def. plan to migrate	Percentage who def. plan to migrate	Percentage who def. plan to migrate
Primary only and presently working	M	37.5	50.0 (16)	26.1	47.8 (23)	48.1	18.5 (81)
	F	28.6	57.1 (7)	38.5	46.2 (13)	31.3	39.6 (48)
Vocational	M	36.4	18.2 (11)	31.3	31.3 (16)	60.9	8.7 (23)
	F	25.0	50.0 (12)	0.0	30.0 (10)	5.9	29.4 (34)
Secondary	M	5.3	52.6 (19)	18.2	54.5 (11)	20.7	37.9 (29)
	F	0.0	45.5 (33)	10.0	25.0 (20)	17.1	45.7 (35)
TOTAL N			(98)		(93)		(250)

the lower the tendency to plan to migrate, and the greater the tendency to plan to stay in the home community.

The fact that the more remote respondents have lower levels of aspirations, and, in the case of males, are (1) more attached to the home community, (2) have higher levels of family obligation, and (3) are less dissatisfied with the community's social provisions, all account for part of these unexpected findings. It also appears that increasing distance from the centre does not act as a barrier to participation in the centre's labour market. It may also be true that, as already proposed, the sons and daughters of farmers from areas outside the centre are being given preference by employers of manual and service workers there. In any case, it appears that adolescents from these more remote areas are contributing a disproportionate share to the young manual and service labour force in the centre. It may be, of course, that these will migrate from the area at a later date, although they seemed determined to stay at the time.

Another factor may be operating here, however. The more optimistic beliefs about local opportunities that characterise the more remote respondents may be due to their less adequate knowledge of opportunities in the community. They may, in other words, be over-optimistic and may have to alter their opinion later on. However, since more of them are already working than others, this ought not to be the case, though the more positive attitudes of the more remote males toward the community may well have influenced their views of the opportunities available there. In any case, unless trends have reversed in very recent periods, in the long run we can expect greater migration out of the more remote areas of the community (see Chapter 2).

However, it may be that these more remote adolescents migrate, or move their residence, only into the centre; while those from the centre migrate out of the area entirely. It may indeed be, as Arensberg remarks, that "the country people flock into the towns and the townspeople all die out of them".[2] This, he believed, was caused by the increasing urbanisation of values and attitudes of those born and raised in the towns. Their adaptation to a traditional social order, which still persists, is thus made more difficult. Whether this is a true statement of the case and of the manner in which it occurs, however, will have to be left for later research to answer.

[2] Arensberg, *op. cit.*, 167.

Regarding sex differentials in migration intentions, it was expected that there would be little difference in migration intentions for those from the centre, but that these differences would increase with increasing remoteness. The results already dealt with in regard to occupational and income frustration tend to strengthen this expectation. The actual results indeed do correspond to expectations, but not as strongly as expected. In relative proportions, 14 per cent more males than females from the centre definitely intend to remain locally. This declines to 10 per cent more males than females at the intermediate levels but increases to 25 per cent more males than females at the most remote areas. The figures for those intending to migrate support these trends. If those who had already migrated were included, the trends would be strengthened. Overall, sex selectivity does increase with remoteness, but not as significantly as expected.

In conclusion, remoteness is strongly related to migration, but not as originally hypothesised. The further the respondents' homes are from the centre, the lower the tendency to migrate—especially in the case of males. The trends for females are not as clearcut, but they do not consistently support the hypothesis of increasing migration with distance from the centre. These results on migration plans conform with trends in occupational and income frustration levels. However, for females they contradict trends in attitudes toward community relationships and social provisions. These become progressively more negative as distance from the centre increases, in striking contrast to the trends for males where attitudes become more positive with distance. It may be, however, that as time passes, migration plans will change into conformity with these attitudes for females.

(ii) PERCEIVED PARENTAL EXPECTATIONS AND MIGRATION PLANS[3]

The notion is frequently encountered in relevant literature that the only function the family performs in migration is to hold back po-

[3] "Parental Expectations" in this case means perceived parental expectations' since the relevant questions were asked only from the respondents themselves. Three questions were asked relating to: (1) whether parents expected them to stay locally; (2) whether they would be disappointed if they went away; (3) whether they expected them to leave. Responses were coded in terms of the categories given in Table XXXVI.

tential migrants. As early as the 'thirties however, Arensberg and Kimball had proposed a rather different idea: that for those youth who could not be satisfactorily placed locally, the family facilitated and encouraged migration, and that through its contacts with some of its members in foreign communities who had previously migrated, it facilitated the whole process.[4] To what extent does this situation still hold? It was thought that parental support for migration would be fairly widespread and would hold throughout all occupational groups. Is this so? The results presented in Table XXXVI below suggest that it is, although it should be remembered that the relevant

TABLE XXXVI: VARIATIONS IN PERCEIVED PARENTAL SUPPORT FOR MIGRATION IN GENERAL AND BY OCCUPATIONAL BACKGROUND

Parental Support		Occupational Background			
	Total population	All Non-manual	Farmers	Skilled and service	Semiskilled and unskilled
	%	%	%	%	%
(1) Question not asked, respondent is satisfied with his current occupation and is staying at home	16.5	4.6	22.5	16.9	13.5
(2) High and moderate expectations to remain at home	20.1	9.2	19.9	23.9	31.3
(3) No clear parental preference	24.1	29.4	22.5	19.8	28.2
(4) High expectations to migrate	29.0	48.6	22.1	33.8	24.0
(5) Question not answered	10.3	8.3	13.0	5.6	3.1
TOTAL %	100	100.1	100	100	100.1
N	556	109	276	71	96

[4] Arensberg, C. A. and Kimball, S. T., *Family and Community in Ireland*, Peter Smith, 1961, 145–57.

questions were put to respondents and not to parents, and there may be an element of rationalisation involved.

Of the total population, 17 per cent were already working on occupations that satisfied them and from which they did not intend to move. As shown previously, the majority of these had major obligations to their families which required them to remain at home —over two thirds of them being from farm backgrounds. In general, we can assume that parents expected them to remain at home, although they were not examined on this question. On the other hand, however, 29 per cent said that their parents definitely expected them to migrate. Another 24 per cent said that their parents had no clearcut attitudes on the subject, and only 20 per cent of the total said that their parents actually expected them to stay. In total, therefore, 37 per cent of respondents were currently working in occupations that satisfied them and did not intend to migrate or had perceived strong parental expectations to restrain them from migrating, and 53 per cent had parents who were perceived to actively encourage migration or had expressed no clear preference on the matter. We cannot, then, accept the notion of migration as a youthful rebellion against parental and community controls, since less than half the parents definitely want their children to remain at home — at least as this is perceived by potential migrants.

Does such parental support vary by occupational background, or is it general throughout all occupational groups? The findings again indicate that there is considerable variation among classes in this respect. Less than 10 per cent of the non-manual respondents perceived that their parents expected them to remain in the home community, while this was true of from 24 to 31 per cent of those from manual backgrounds and 20 per cent of those from farms. On the other hand, almost half (48.6 per cent) the respondents from non-manual backgrounds thought that their parents expected them to migrate, whereas this was true of only 22 to 34 per cent of those from manual and farm backgrounds. There appear to be very small differences among the manual or farm occupational groups in this respect. Although slightly more of those from manual backgrounds perceived that their parents expected them to remain locally than did those from farms—24 to 31 per cent as against 20 per cent— many more of the latter had current jobs that satisfied them and intended to remain locally, and had family obligations which required them to remain.

TABLE XXXVII: THE RELATIONSHIP BETWEEN PARENTAL EXPECTATIONS ON MIGRATION AND ADOLESCENTS' ACTUAL INTENTIONS

Migration Intentions	Question not asked: Respondent satisfied with current job and is staying at home	Parental Expectations			
		High and Moderate Expectations for children to stay at home	No clear parental preference	High expectations to migrate	No Answer
Definitely intend to stay	% 80.4	% 25.5	% 14.1	% 4.3	% 7.8
Indefinite whether will stay or leave	19.6	47.3	49.6	32.3	58.8
Definitely intend to leave		27.3	36.3	63.4	33.3
TOTAL % N	100 92	100.1 110	100 135	100 161	99.9 51

Gamma = .471

Although the extent of perceived parental support for migration is less than the percentage of youth who intend to migrate (29 per cent as against the 36 per cent of the children who definitely intend to migrate), the picture that emerges is of considerable parental encouragement for migration, at least as perceived by their children. This is particularly true of the middle class parent, while parents from manual worker backgrounds or from farms are much more conservative in this respect.

Do perceived parental expectations in general correspond with the intentions of their children? An examination of the results presented in Table XXXVII opposite can answer this question.

There is a marked association between the two variables as the results clearly indicate. Very few respondents who thought they were expected to migrate intend to stay. Similarly, respondents who are expected to stay tend to do so to a much greater extent than others. Nevertheless over a quarter of those expected to stay at home intend to migrate, despite their parents' wishes. There is a major conflict involved here, therefore, between parents and off-spring. However, this is only a small minority of the total—of the 181 respondents who answered this question and who definitely intended to migrate, only 30 definitely clashed with their parents on this decision. A further 52 respondents, however, had not com-pletely corresponded in their migration plans with their parental wishes, having some intentions of migrating, despite the fact that they perceived that parents wanted them to stay at home. Although migration intentions and perceived parental support are highly re-lated, they do not exactly correspond.

What function does such parental support play in the decision to migrate? It was expected that one important way in which it functioned was in overcoming the strain of breaking the bonds of attachment to the family and community. It has been demonstrated that high levels of attachment to one's community does retard migration tendencies, while alienation from it increases them. It is easily seen how those with low attachment to the community can migrate without any serious emotional upsets. Indeed, for many of these migration must be liberating, an escape from unsatisfying relationships. But for those who are highly attached migration must be a highly wrenching experience emotionally, since it requires the breaking off of highly satisfying day-to-day relationships with one's family and community. In this situation, it was hypothesised that parental encouragement for migration would help overcome these inhibiting tendencies.[5] Is this so? Table XXXVIII below contains the relevant results.

TABLE XXXVIII: THE RELATIONSHIP BETWEEN PARENTAL SUPPORT FOR MIGRA-
TION AND MIGRATION INTENTIONS, CONTROLLING FOR LEVELS OF COMMUNITY
SATISFACTION

Migration Intentions	Parental Encouragement for the migration of offspring					
	Parents expect respondent to stay at home or they have no clear preference on the matter			Parents definitely expect respondents to migrate		
	Community Satisfaction			Community Satisfaction		
	Low levels 0–3	Mod. levels 4–6	High levels 7–9	Low levels 0–3	Mod. levels 4–6	High levels 7–9
	%	%	%	%	%	%
Definitely intend to stay	12.9	14.7	24.8	—	9.8	5.6
Indefinite whether will stay or leave	54.3	47.1	46.7	31.8	31.7	33.3
Definitely intend to migrate	32.9	38.2	28.6	68.2	58.5	61.1
TOTAL %	100.1	100	100	100	100	100
N	70	68	105	66	41	54

$X^2 = 5.718$; $p > .75 < .90$ Gamma = .145	$X^2 = 6.27$; $p > .75 < .90$ Gamma = .135

The results strongly support the hypothesis. For those with perceived parental support for migration, variations in levels of Community Satisfaction make very little difference in migration intentions—as an examination of the percentage differences and computed statistics clearly indicate. Over 68 per cent of those with

[5] Crawford, C. O., "Family Attachments and Support for Migration of young people", *Rural Sociology*, 1966, 37, 1, 293–301.

perceived parental support for migration and with low levels of community satisfaction definitely intend to migrate, while 61 per cent of those with such support but with high levels of Community Satisfaction intend to do so. Although there is a slight tendency for those with high levels of Community Satisfaction to be less migratory than the highly alienated, if the parents are thought to give their support to migration the differences are reduced to a very small level indeed. In fact, those with high levels of Community Satisfaction but with perceived support for migration are far more migratory than those with low levels of Community Satisfaction but without such support. Perceived parental support, therefore, appears to be very important in overcoming the inhibiting effects of familial and community attachments on migration plans. This conclusion is corroborated by the differences in proportions who intend to remain in the home community for those with varying levels of Community Satisfaction, but with no perceived support for migration. Here, increasing levels of Community Satisfaction lead to increasing percentages who intend to remain locally. Only 13 per cent of those with low levels of Community Satisfaction intend to remain locally, while 15 per cent of those with moderate, and 25 per cent of those with high levels of satisfaction intend to do so. Family support, therefore, appears to play a very important role in migration where people are highly attached to the home community and presumably also to the family. Family expectations and their emotional and probably financial support can greatly facilitate migration. The early, rather naive idea, that migration had a major disruptive effect on family attachments and relationships, has been shown to be in error by some studies.[6] The fear of such a suspected disruption did not appear to play any role in migration planning in this study, however. Over a third of those with high levels of attachment to their community were expected by their parents to migrate. If such a fear existed, one could not expect this support.

This section has shown that the perceived support of the home family is very important in migration. What about the situation of those family members who have already migrated? Are they equally important in migration? The following section examines this question.

[6] See Litwak, E., "Geographic Mobility and Extended Family Cohesion", *American Sociological Review*, 1960, 25, 385–94.

(iii) INVOLVEMENT IN MIGRATION SYSTEMS AND MIGRATION

We assumed that most adolescents growing up in rural Ireland, where migration has been traditional for many generations, would have many uncles and aunts living in "foreign" communities: in other parts of Ireland, but particularly in Great Britain and the

TABLE XXXIX: LOCATION OF RESPONDENTS' UNCLES AND AUNTS—IN TOTAL AND BY OCCUPATIONAL BACKGROUND

Number of uncles and aunts alive, and proportion living outside the community	Total population	Occupational background of Respondents			
		All non-manual	Farmers	Skilled and Service	Semiskilled and unskilled
Information not available: N=	11		10		1
2. *1–3 alive*	%	%	%	%	%
(a) all at home:	36.8	12.5	40.7	60.0	25.0
(b) 1 away:	26.3		25.9	30.0	41.7
(c) 2–3 away:	36.8	87.5	33.3	10.0	33.3
TOTAL %	99.9	100	99.9	100	100
N	57	8	27	10	12
3. *4–6 alive*					
(a) all at home or just one away:	32.0	26.3	35.1	21.7	33.3
(b) 2–3 away:	44.4	42.1	44.7	39.1	48.5
(c) 4–6 away:	23.7	31.6	20.2	39.1	18.2
TOTAL %	100.1	100	100	99.9	100
N	169	19	94	23	33
4. *Over 6 alive*					
(a) All at home or less than 2 away:	20.4	14.6	25.3	10.3	23.1
(b) 3–4 away:	18.5	13.4	21.9	15.4	19.2
(c) over 4 away:	61.1	72.0	52.7	74.4	57.7
TOTAL %	100.1	100	99.9	100.1	100
N	319	82	146	39	52
TOTAL N	555	109	277	72	97

United States. To what extent is this so? Some data gathered in the course of the survey throws light on this question and is presented above in Table XXXIX.

Firstly, the great majority of respondents have some close relations in foreign communities. Only in less than 4 per cent of the cases had respondents no uncles and aunts outside the community, whereas 54 per cent of the respondents had more than three of these relatives living outside the home community. The great majority of adolescents, therefore, are members of very widely scattered extended kinship groups. Indeed, as the figures in Table XXXIX clearly indicate, only in a small minority of cases are most of respondents' uncles and aunts concentrated within the boundaries of the community.

Although no data was collected on this point, we can assume that interaction between most of these migrant families and the home family persists through letters, visits, gifts, and so on; especially at times of religious and family feasts and crises. And, as Arensberg and Kimball have noted, they are bound together through bonds of affection and obligation—bonds which may be activated particularly when adolescents' future careers are being decided upon.[7] Through this interaction, the relationships between the home family and these migrant families form what has been called a "migration system".[8] The great majority of adolescents in this community are deeply involved in these systems.

The results also indicate that this involvement is highly related to occupational background. Those from non-manual and skilled and service backgrounds are far more highly involved in these systems than are those from farm, semiskilled and unskilled manual backgrounds. In the case of respondents with 4 to 6 relatives alive, from 31 to 39 per cent of those from non-manual and skilled and service backgrounds have more than 4 of these relatives living in outside communities, whereas this is true of only 18 to 20 per cent of those from semiskilled, unskilled and farm backgrounds. Much the same situation holds good for those with more than 6 relatives alive. Here, from 72 to 74 per cent of those from the former cate-

[7] Arensberg and Kimball, op. cit., 148–150.
[8] See Hillary, G. A., et. al, "Migration Systems of the Southern Appalachians: Some Demographic Observations", Rural Sociology, 1965, 30:1; 33ff and Brown, J. S., et. al., "Kentucky Mountain Migration and the Stem Family: An American Variation on a Theme by LePlay", Rural Sociology, 1963, 28, 1, 48–69.

gories have more than 4 relatives living in outside communities, compared with only 52 to 58 per cent of the latter. It may well be that much larger proportions of those from non-manual backgrounds are immigrants to the community. If so, this would explain their higher rates of family contact outside the community, but this should not also hold good in the case of those from skilled and service backgrounds. Whatever the explanation, emigration in the previous generation appears to have been much greater among those whose non-migrant brothers now occupy non-manual and service and skilled trades, than among those occupying farm or lower status manual occupations.

What is the situation in regard to the more immediate family members: the brothers and sisters of the respondents who are not working? The following table (Table XL) gives the results for these.

Firstly, the majority of sibs who were then working and for whom information was available were working outside the community. Because families are in different stages of the family cycle, the results for those with less than three sibs working may be misleading. The first category—none working or all working at home—includes respondents who have only one sib working and those who have three but all are working in the home community.

For those with more than three sibs working, only 17 per cent had all of these working in the home community, and for those with fewer than three sibs working, less than 50 per cent had all of these sibs working at home. In total, for all respondents answering the question, only slightly more than one third had no sibs working outside the community at the time of the survey.

Here again, the migration of sibs appears to be closely related to occupational background. And as in the case of respondents' uncles and aunts, those from non-manual and service and skilled backgrounds appear to be more migratory than do those from farm or semiskilled and unskilled manual backgrounds. For those with more than three sibs working, just half of those from non-manual and service and skilled backgrounds have more than three of their sibs working outside the home community, while this is true of less than 40 per cent of those from farm, semiskilled and unskilled manual backgrounds. The figures for those with less than three sibs working appear to corroborate these conclusions.

How is this varying involvement in migration systems related to respondents' evaluation of local economic opportunities? Do the

TABLE XL: LOCATION OF RESPONDENTS' SIBS WHO WERE WORKING AT THE TIME
OF THE SURVEY

Number of sibs then working, and proportions working outside the community	Total population	Occupational background of respondent			
		All non-manual	Farmers	Skilled and Service	Semiskilled and Unskilled
1. *No sibs working as yet* N	136	49	63	12	12
2. *1–3 sibs working*	%	%	%	%	%
(a) none working or all working at home:	46.1	42.6	52.6	35.1	49.6
(b) 1 working outside:	33.5	29.8	32.8	35.1	27.5
(c) 2–3 working outside:	20.4	27.7	14.6	29.7	22.9
TOTAL %	100	100.1	100	99.9	100
N	269	47	137	37	48
3. *Over 3 sibs working*					
(a) all working at home or just one working away:	17.0	8.3	16.9	18.2	19.4
(b) 2–3 working away:	41.8	41.7	45.1	31.8	41.7
(c) 4+ working away:	41.1	50.0	38.0	50.0	38.9
TOTAL %	99.9	100	100	100	100
N	141	12	71	22	36

more highly involved have higher levels of income aspiration as predicted—especially among those who have received only a primary and vocational education? And do they also have less sanguine attitudes toward the local community's opportunities, as one would expect if they have higher levels of aspiration and if their greater levels of contact with the home and foreign labour markets biasses their view of local structure?

Table XCIII in Appendix IV shows that, for those from farm and working class backgrounds, variations in contact with foreign labour markets, as mediated through their uncles and aunts who are abroad, have apparently little consistent influence on the level of income aspiration. Although the population sizes are too small to be sure of their representativeness, the figures show no clearcut relationship between these two variables. Those who have many uncles and aunts abroad appear to have no higher levels of aspiration than those who have few.

Much the same situation holds in regard to occupational and income frustration, as the results presented in Appendix IV, Table XCIV clearly show. Indeed, for those with less than 6 relatives there is a slight trend in the opposite direction, those with the larger proportion of relatives abroad having slightly lower levels of frustration. For those with more than six relatives alive there is a slight trend in the hypothesised direction, but the population numbers involved here are very small and these results could easily have occurred by chance alone, as the probability levels quoted clearly show.

Tables XCV–XCVI in Appendix IV examine the corresponding influence of variations in migration rates amongst sibs on respondents' aspirations and frustrations. These show no consistent relationship with income aspirations, as is evident from the results presented in Table XCV. There is, however, a consistent tendency for those with more migratory sibs to have higher levels of occupational and income frustration (see Table XCVI, Sections A and B respectively). Of those with 1–3 sibs, all of whom are working within the Community, from 65 to 73 per cent of respondents are not frustrated in their occupational aspirations. The corresponding figures for those with two or more working outside the Community are 53 to 62 per cent respectively. Similar trends appear for those with more than three sibs working. The percentage differences involved here are not very great, but they are consistently reproduced in all cases. Much the same situation holds in regard to income frustration (see Appendix IV, Table XCVI, Section B). The hypothesis then appears to be upheld in these cases, although not for the reasons proposed. It seems to be just as likely that respondents with a small proportion of migratory sibs will have equal levels of income aspiration as will those whose sibs are far more migratory. But despite this, the latter have consistently higher levels of occupational and income frustration. So, respondents' beliefs about local economic opportunities appear to be influenced not only by their level of aspiration, vis-à-vis these opportunities—(by an objective matching of their aspirations against the community's opportunities)—but also by their degree of involvement in "migration systems". This, however, holds only in the case of sibs and not for more remote relationships. The more contacts respondents have with "outside" opportunity structures, the more negative their evaluations of the local scene. It must be emphasised here, however, that these conclusions are very tentative, since the numbers involved are so small.

Appendix IV, Table XCVII sets out the relationship between variation in the migration rates of respondents' sibs and the respondents' own intention to migrate. These show a definite and consistent tendency for those with less migratory sibs to remain at home in greater proportion than do those with more migratory sibs. Here again, although our conclusions must be tentative because of the small number of respondents involved, the trends are very clearcut and are consistently reproduced in each sub-table. These results are what one would expect, given the results of Table XCVI.

Given these relationships for the primary and vocationally educated farm and working class respondents, is there any clearcut relationship between involvement in sib migration systems and the actual migration intentions of the total population of respondents? Appendix IV, Table XCVIII contains the relevant results.

There is a consistent relationship between respondents' involvement in sib migration systems and their own migration intentions. From 33 to 36 per cent of respondents whose sibs are least migratory, definitely intend to remain at home. This is true, however, of only 18 to 22 per cent of those whose sibs are most migratory. The trends for those intending to migrate consistently support this conclusion. From 25 to 28 per cent of the former definitely intend to migrate, compared with 44 to 46 per cent of the latter.

The variant relationship between the previous migration behaviour of uncles and aunts and respondents' current migration intentions is presented in Appendix IV, Table XCIX. This shows no consistent relationship, except for those respondents with more than five relatives alive. In this case, the more migratory these relatives have been in the past the greater the proportion of respondents who now intend to migrate. This supports the results presented in Table XCIV, where only in the case of those with more than five relatives do those respondents with the more migratory relatives have higher levels of occupational and income frustration.

What does this association between the past migratory behaviour of sibs and the current migration intentions of adolescents mean? It shows that respondents' chances of migrating appear to be closely related to their families' previous migration history. This does not seem, however, to have affected levels of income aspiration—at least among those respondents where it would show its greatest influence, if present. It does appear to affect respondent's beliefs about local opportunities: the more one's sibs have migrated, the less optimistic one's views of these structures. And it does very clearly affect one's own chances of migrating. So, beliefs about local opportunity structures and 'general orientations or attitudes toward migration appear to be partly a family affair. Why this should be, and how it occurs will, however, have to await further research.

These results, then, demand some modification of the previous argument that variation in levels of occupational and income aspirations are the major causes of variations in beliefs about the adequacy of local occupational and income opportunities. This argument had been based on the assumption that knowledge of local occupational and income opportunities was very general, and that one would find few structural "blindnesses". The fact that it was possible to explain so much of the variation in levels of occupational and income frustration on the basis of this assumption appeared to strengthen its validity. However, these latter results suggest that beliefs about opportunities, whether local or not, are somewhat biassed in terms of one's kinship contacts with places outside the community. If one lives in a highly migratory family, it appears that beliefs about the satisfaction of local occupational opportunities will be much more pessimistic than the beliefs of others with the same level of aspiration who come from less migratory families. Since knowledge of, or beliefs about opportunities held by rural–urban migrants depend primarily on informal sources of information,[9] and since kinship and probably other informal communication networks vary in the extent to which they include migrant contacts, knowledge and beliefs about local and "foreign" labour markets will also vary. This has also been remarked upon by Vercruijsse and McNabb in their

[9] Smith, E. D., "Non farm employment information for rural people", *Journal of Farm Economics*, 1956, 38, 813–27, and Luebkre, B. H. and Hart, J. F., "Migration from a Southern Appalachian Community", *Land Economics*, February, 1958, 34, 1.

Limerick studies.[10] Overall, then, although there is a strong relationship between level of aspiration and beliefs as to one's ability to fulfill these aspirations locally, other variables are also of importance —and the previous migration history of one's family is among these. There may be other variables which have not been touched upon here, such as the collapse of public confidence which might accompany the failure of a new local factory or enterprise where its potential had been exaggerated. Although the original hypothesis has been confirmed in general terms, level of aspiration is not the only variable affecting one's level of confidence in local opportunities. It is perhaps appropriate to conclude this section, therefore, with the conventional exhortation that more research is needed on this problem.

This also concludes this chapter and the presentation of the results of the initial study. The following chapter summarises these results, and discusses their implications for the theory proposed. The final 3 chapters provide a brief summary of a follow up study done in 1968. It is concerned with (1) the extent to which migration intentions predicted subsequent behaviour; (2) the extent to which the motives found to be important in migration intentions were also important in actual behaviour as well as the extent to which new motives intervened; and (3) the extent to which the conclusions about the magnitude and causes of differentials in migration rates hold good in the case of actual migration.

[10] Vercruijsse E. V. W., *Shannon Hinterland Survey*, 1961, Leyden University Mimeo, 1962; McNabb, *op. cit.*

7. Summary and Conclusions to Part One

This chapter will summarise the results of the first study and evaluate them in terms of their consequences for the theoretical rationale proposed. It is presented in two parts. The first deals with the relationship of five major motivational variables to the migration plans of individuals, and the second deals with how these mediate the effects of some major social structural factors on migration planning.

(i) MIGRATION MOTIVES

Of the five variables proposed, beliefs about one's ability to fulfill occupational and income aspirations in the home community, (occupational and income frustration) were the most closely associated with migration intentions. Their joint effects on migration plans were much greater than those of any other variables. These results strongly support the hypotheses proposed.

Community Satisfaction was the next most predictive variable. If respondents had a low regard for their community, they planned to migrate in much greater proportions than others. There was some tentative evidence, also, where respondents were highly alienated from the community, that whether occupational or income aspirations could or could not be fulfilled made very little difference to plans to stay locally, whereas it made a much greater difference at higher levels. In general, however, only about one quarter of all respondents were so highly alienated from the community. On the other hand, high attachment to the community did not retard migration where parents supported the migration of their children. Respondents with such parental support were able to overcome the inhibiting effects of strong bonds of attachment to the family and the local community. As a result, they migrated in roughly equal

166

proportions to those who were highly alienated from the community.

The results, in general, strongly supported the hypotheses proposed in Chapter One. Community Satisfaction did appear to play an important independent role in migration planning. Whether, of course, these intentions lead to actual migration, and whether such attitudes are as important in actual migration behaviour as they appear to be in intended behaviour, can only be answered by the follow up study.

The fourth variable examined referred to respondents' work obligations within the family. If respondents perceived that their families had work expectations for them which they could only fulfill by remaining in the home community, they planned to remain in the home community to a much greater extent than others. Of the five variables, it was the fourth most predictive of migration plans. It was hypothesised that such obligations would have such a strong influence on migration decisions that it would lead to plans to remain at home irrespective of the level of frustration of occupational and income aspirations. This did not prove to be so, however. On the contrary, if respondents were frustrated in their occupational aspirations, they generally planned to migrate, irrespective of their level of family obligations. High levels of obligation, therefore, did not counteract the effects of occupational or income frustration. On the other hand, when occupational and income aspirations were satisfied, those with high levels of obligation planned to remain in the home community in much greater proportions than others. Whether, in fact, those respondents with strong family obligations who intended to migrate were able to do so is another question which will also be examined in the follow up study. A considerable proportion of them certainly did not want to stay.

The fifth variable, one's attitude toward the community's social provisions, or Community Evaluation, is so poorly predictive of migration plans that it can be ignored.

In general, therefore, beliefs about the ability to fulfill occupational and income aspirations predominate in the migration decisions of rural adolescents. Additional support for this conclusion came from answers to questions asked of all respondents who were definitely planning to migrate, or who were not sure whether they would migrate or not (76 per cent of all respondents). Of these, 72 per cent said that they would remain in the home community, provided that they could achieve their occupational and income aspirations there.

An additional 12 per cent said that they would remain only if, besides their ability to fulfill occupational and income aspirations locally, the local community social provisions were improved considerably. The remaining 16 per cent said that they would not remain in the home community under any circumstances.

Those who said that they would remain only if the community's social provisions were improved had lower levels of Community Satisfaction and Community Evaluation than others. However, these two variables did not distinguish between those who would remain only for social provision reasons, and those who would not remain in the home community under any conditions.

(ii) STRUCTURAL FACTORS

The major structural variables employed were: sex, education, level of occupational and income aspiration, occupational background of respondents, remoteness of respondents' homes from the centre, perceived parental support for migration, and the involvement of respondents in kinship networks which embrace some migrant members.

Level of Aspiration and Education

Excluding the farm category, the level of occupational aspiration, although clearly related to the level of occupational frustration, had a rather low relationship with migration intentions. However, farm employees were excluded from this table because of the difficulty of assigning them to a relative status level. When included, and when level of education received was used as the major independent variable, the relationship between education level and migration plans was very pronounced. Only 12 per cent of the secondary educated definitely intended to remain in the home community, whereas 21 per cent of the vocationally educated and 38 per cent of the primary educated intended to do so.

When the level of education of respondents was used as a control variable, occupational frustration was most predictive of migration plans at the primary level of education, whereas income frustration was most predictive of migration plans at the secondary level. But the joint effects of occupational and income frustration on migration plans were greatest at the secondary level of education, and least at the primary level. The major reason for this appeared to be that family obligations, being most onerous at the lowest levels of education, were intervening in the relationships at these levels.

However, when we asked respondents who intended to migrate, or who were indefinite whether they would or not, whether they would remain in the home community if their occupational and income aspirations could be fulfilled there, the answers conflicted with the above results. Only 11 per cent of the primary educated said that they would not remain there, whereas 23 per cent of the vocationally educated, and 41 per cent of the secondary educated made similar statements. Therefore, although the joints effects of occupational and income frustration on migration plans was greatest for the secondary educated, these were also the least likely to remain in the home community even if occupational and income aspirations satisfied them. A number of other variables, apparently highly correlated with high levels of education and high levels of occupational aspiration, interfered here.

Attitudes toward the community's social provisions was one of these factors. Of those who said that they would not remain in the community even if occupational and income aspirations could be satisfied there, considerably more of the secondary educated than others said that they would remain if, besides these aspirations, the community social provisions were brought up to their expectations. The remaining respondents said that they would not stay at home under any circumstances. This group comprised almost three times as many secondary educated respondents as primary educated respondents (22 per cent of the secondary educated, and only 8 per cent of the primary educated). The vocationally educated occupied an intermediate position. So, non-economic factors became increasingly more important in migration as the respondents' level of education, and their level of occupational aspirations, increased.

Later analysis showed, however, that these non-economic variables appeared to be important only in the case of females. There were very small differences among educational levels for males in these respects. Secondary educated females were the major deviant group here—only 43 per cent of them being willing to remain locally if their occupational and income aspirations could be satisfied there—whereas almost twice as many secondary educated males were willing to do so (82 per cent). There were very small differences between the other two educational levels or between the sexes within each level. Before controlling for the effects of sex, it appeared that social mobility aspirations, as indexed by high levels of occupational aspiration, included a complex of attitudes and aspirations. This would explain the greater reluctance of the more highly educated to stay, even when they could get a satisfactory job locally. If this were so, however, the argument should hold good for males and females equally. Since it did not, it appeared that the secondary educational experience brought about such changes in girls' aspirations and attitudes—the content of which were not explored in this study—that considerably fewer of them than others were willing to remain at home, even if they could fulfill their economic aspirations there. However, since it is very unlikely that their rather high occupational aspirations could be fulfilled locally on any large-scale basis, even if the community were to develop rapidly, this question of the deviant migration motives of the secondary educated girls is only of academic interest to the community itself.

It was clearly demonstrated throughout the analysis that it is useful to view migration as the result of a matching of adolescents' aspirations with the opportunities available in the home community to satisfy these aspirations. A simple matching of the *number* of adolescent entrants to the labour force, and the *number* of local job opportunities available for them, gives an incorrect estimate of migration levels. The *level* of aspirations and the *level* of opportunities must also be taken into consideration. Both can vary, depending on the level of education attained by adolescents and the structure of the local labour demand.

The simple assumption guiding this research, that the prestige level of the occupational category aspired to or achieved was the major variable determining occupational frustration levels and migration rates, has not been fully confirmed. Although there is a moderate correlation with occupational frustration levels, the relationship to migration plans is rather slight. (See Table LXXVIII, Appendix IV). Service workers in particular deviate considerably from the expected pattern, since they are almost as prone to migrate as the non-manual, and almost twice as migratory as the more prestigious skilled manual workers. Similarly, unskilled manual workers appeared to be slightly more likely to migrate than the skilled. The degree of "over-subscription" to any particular occupational category is therefore influenced by many factors other than their status or prestige level alone. Sex, educational limitations, and

cultural definitions of acceptable and unacceptable jobs for particular classes of respondents are other factors that intervene. Service
work, for instance, is dominated by girls who have received a
primary or a vocational education, whereas skilled manual work is
equally dominated by vocationally educated boys. Since there
are relatively far more girls looking for service jobs locally than
there are boys seeking skilled manual ones, more of them would tend
to migrate. Similarly, service jobs are far more likely to be "dead-
end" jobs than skilled manual ones, and are likely to be seen as such.
All of these other factors bearing on the relationship between occupational aspiration and occupational frustration and migration have
not been explored in this study and need to be examined in greater
depth. The follow up study attempts to do this to some extent.
Similarly, there appear to be certain "structural blindnesses" built
into people's perceptions of local opportunity structures, and these
"blindnesses" are not necessarily related to the actual situation at
all. The degree of involvement in migration systems is one of these.
Those more highly involved tend to have more pessimistic views
about local opportunities than others with the same aspirations.

Despite these strictures, however, level of aspiration did prove to
be a very useful variable in explaining migration, especially the
break between non-manual and manual aspirers. Communities,
however, can vary widely in terms of the structure of job opportunities and also in terms of the aspirations of its new entrants to the
labour force. A comparative study of a number of rural communities varying along the dimension of job opportunity structure, and
along the dimension of the occupational aspiration structure of the
local adolescent "replacements", would lead to very fruitful findings about the dimensions on which migrants are selected.

These conclusions may tend to overestimate the importance of
economic explanations of migration, by emphasising the inability
of local economic structures to satisfy the aspirations of potential
young replacements to the system. In this conclusion, we have taken
the adolescents' aspirations as given. When these aspirations are
examined, however, it quickly becomes clear that massive cultural
and structural changes are occurring in the community. Adolescents'
occupational aspirations show a massive departure from identification with the traditional occupational roles present within the family
or even within the community. This is particularly remarkable
among those from a farm background. Only 5 per cent of farm

females intended to remain on the farm, and only 16 to 19 per cent of farm males intended to do so. No evidence appeared of a major conflict between parents and youth on this devaluation of farming. A similar movement away from unskilled manual occupations also occurred. The "revolution of rising expectations" brought about by the intrusion of modern industrial values has, more than the actual achievements of their parents, transformed the aspirations of the youth of this farm community so that they closely approach those of their urban counterparts. This research did not examine the characteristics of these changes in aspirations over the generation, but an explanation which took only the relative remuneration of different occupations into consideration would appear to be highly inadequate. On the other hand, there was some evidence that far too many adolescents, especially girls, were going into traditional service employment, such as shop assistants, etc. These were far more migratory than others in manual employment — even in higher status skilled manual employment. This initial occupational choice appears to be highly dysfunctional from a long term perspective.

Sex Differentials

Sex differentials in migration planning occurred almost exclusively in the farm category. In all, almost 20 per cent more farm males than females intended to remain in the home community. Except for much smaller differences in the skilled and service category, there were no other consistent sex differences in groups from other occupational backgrounds. These sex differentials in the farm category were primarily due to the much greater proportion of farm males receiving only a primary education or employed on farms, and to the consequent lower levels of frustration of their aspirations. No consistent sex differences in occupational and income frustration levels occurred for any other group except, again, for those from a skilled and service background. Farm females also had much lower levels of Community Satisfaction and family obligations than farm males, while no such sex differences occurred for other groups.

Sex differentials in occupational and income frustration and migration plans were also limited to the primary and vocationally educated groups. There were no consistent sex differences in these variables for the secondary educated. Proportionately more females than males who had received only a primary level of education, or a vocational education, were frustrated in their occupational and income aspirations, and proportionately more of them planned to migrate. These sex differentials were partly explained by the relatively greater proportions of primary educated farm males who remained working on the home farm. In addition, for those not receiving a secondary education and not staying on the home farm, there were relatively more opportunities available locally for males than for females. This was particularly true for those receiving a vocational education. There were minor differences between nonfarm males and females in this respect. In total, sex differentials in the structure of off-farm occupational opportunities were greatest for the vocationally educated, moderate for the primary educated, and least for the secondary educated where opportunities for both sexes were minimal.

Unexpectedly, there were no major differences between secondary and vocationally educated females in their migration plans. On the other hand, on a percentage basis, over three times as many primary educated than secondary or vocationally educated females planned to remain in the home community. These migration differences were explained by almost exactly corresponding differences in occupational and income frustration. This unexpected similarity between secondary and vocationally educated females was explained by the high proportion of vocationally educated females who aspired to non-manual occupations and to service occupations. The vocational males, on the other hand, generally aspired to the more plentiful skilled and semiskilled jobs. There were, therefore, much greater differences in occupational aspirations between the secondary and vocationally educated males and females. On a percentage basis, over twice as many vocational as secondary educated males planned to remain in the home community, and approximately 10 per cent more of the primary than the vocationally educated males planned to remain. If these sex differences in migration plans are carried over into actual migration behaviour, it will lead to a considerable imbalance in the local sex ratios.

Remoteness

Contrary to expectations, the more remote male respondents were less frustrated in their occupational and income aspirations than were those nearer the centre. The hypothesis of increasing levels of frustration, however, received some support in the case of females, but only where those females who have already migrated were included as frustrated.

As expected, the level of Community Satisfaction of males increased with remoteness from the centre, whereas that of females decreased. And, also as expected, the proportions of males employed on farms increased greatly with remoteness from the centre.

Despite the fact of the higher levels of occupational and income frustration and of the lower levels of Community Satisfaction of females from the most remote areas of the community, *both* male and female respondents from the most remote areas of the community planned to remain there in greater proportions than those from less remote areas. In contrast to the clear differentials present for males, the differentials for females were, however, minimal.

A number of factors accounted for this unexpected finding. First, as the remoteness of the home community increased, increasing proportions of males were satisfactorily employed on home farms and had higher levels of family obligations. Secondly, the more remote respondents of both sexes had lower levels of education and lower levels of occupational and income aspiration than had the less remote respondents. Since local off-farm occupational opportunities were generally of a lower status level and paid relatively low wages, the aspirations of the more remote respondents could be more easily satisfied locally. These off-farm opportunities were, however, concentrated in the centre, so that geographical factors could have counteracted the effects of their lower aspiration levels. This did not happen, however, as disproportionate numbers of such jobs at the centre were occupied by respondents from the more remote areas of the community. On the other hand, respondents from the centre, having aspirations for occupations and incomes of a much higher level than others, planned to migrate to other centres in Ireland or abroad, so that they could fulfill these aspirations. This unexpected support for one of Ravenstein's much earlier findings[1] may, however, only amount to a temporary postponement of migration, since population decline in the long run is most rapid in the more remote areas of the community. On the other hand, people from the more remote areas of the community may gradually be

[1] Ravenstein, E. G., "The laws of migration," *The Journal of the Royal Statistical Society*, 1889, Vol. 48, 2, 167, 235; and Vol. 52, 2, 241–305.

replacing the more migratory centre population, a trend earlier remarked upon by Arensberg.[2] The follow up study will be able to throw some light on those problems.

Migration Systems

Only a very small minority of respondents had no uncles or aunts living outside the community, but variation in these kinship contacts with "foreign" communities appeared to bear little relationship to the actual migration intentions of respondents. It appeared to play only a minor role in migration. An opposite conclusion was reached in the case of sibs, however. Those with a higher proportion of migrant sibs had higher levels of occupational and income frustration and showed greater tendencies to migrate than others. Such family influences appeared to play an independent role in migration. Some of the ways in which this influence is exerted will be explored in the follow up study.

This concludes the presentation of the results of the first study. In it, we have attempted to explain variations in the migration plans of a certain group of rural youth. We assumed that we would be able to explain and ultimately predict variations in actual migration behaviour if we could understand why some people planned to migrate and others to stay at home, as well as how these migration motives and plans were related to an individual's position in the social structure of his home community. By and large, we have succeeded in elucidating the major motivational and social structural variables involved in migration planning. We assumed that the same motives and the same differentials would be involved in actual migration behaviour. This was no more than an assumption, however. To see whether this assumption was in fact justified, a follow up study of a large sample of the original respondents was carried out in Spring 1968—just three years after the field work on the first study was completed. The following two chapters report the results of this restudy, while the subsequent and concluding chapter attempts to pull together all the results of both studies, and comes to some final conclusions about the migration behaviour of rural adolescents.

[2] Arensberg, C. M., *The Irish Countryman*, Peter Smith, 1959, 164–8.

Part Two—The Follow-up Study

8. Migration Intentions and Subsequent Behaviour

1. Introduction

There have been relatively few longitudinal studies of any kind in sociology or social psychology. This is so, even in areas where these studies are especially relevant; where attitudes, aspirations or intentions are taken as indicators of future overt behaviour. The validity of the assumption—that attitudes do predict subsequent behaviour—has only been tested in a few instances.[1] Even fewer studies have examined the relationship between occupational aspirations and subsequent attainments.[2] A yet smaller number of researchers studying migration planning have carried out follow up studies to see if their respondents subsequently behaved as they said they would.[3] In almost all cases, attitudes and aspirations appear to be only very moderate predictors of subsequent behaviour.

Intentions, particularly migration intentions, are likely to be

---

[1] See Newcomb, Turner and Converse, *Social Psychology*, Holt, Rinehart and Winston, 1965, 67ff.; Tittle and Hill, "Attitude measurement and prediction of behaviour", *Sociometry*, 1967, 30, 2, 199–213; and Fendrich, J., "Perceived reference group support; racial attitudes and overt behaviour", *American Sociological Review*, 1967, 32, 6, 960–9; for discussion and references.

[2] See Kuvlevsky and Bealer, "The relevance of adolescents occupational aspirations to subsequent job attainment", *Rural Sociology*, 1967, 32, 3, 290–301; and Haller, Sewell and Portes, "Education and Occupational Achievements of Wisconsin farm boys", paper delivered at the joint session of The Rural Sociological Society and American Sociological Association, San Francisco, August 1967; for discussion and references.

[3] Bohlen, J. M. and Wakely, R. B., "Intentions to migrate and actual migration of rural high school graduates", *Rural Sociology*, 1950, 15, 4, 328–34; Harp, J., Morton, M. and Ruff, G. E., *Expectations and Realities: A Study of Migration Behaviour of Youth*, Cornell University Agricultural Expt. Stn., Bulletin No. 69, March 1967.

even less predictive of subsequent behaviour than attitudes or aspirations. One's intended behaviour toward a social object need not be consistent with one's feelings toward it. As a result, persons who actually dislike taking a particular (intended) course of action would be very open to changing their plans if any opportunities to do so arose. In this study, for instance, many respondents who intended to migrate from Cavan would have much preferred to stay there. One third of the intending migrants were highly attached to the community. In contrast, only about half of those who were highly alienated from the community definitely intended to migrate. In these instances, changes in circumstances would most likely lead to major changes in plans. In this situation, a study of the extent to which actual behaviour conformed to previous intentions is especially useful, both from the point of view of testing the validity of the argument put forward in our original study, and from that of elucidating the major variables that intervened between what people intended to do and what they finally did. This was the major purpose of the follow up study.

Three general research questions are explored in the study. The first examines the extent to which respondents' intentions in 1965 predicted their behaviour in 1968. The second examines the extent to which the original personal motives involved in migration decision-making in 1965 were afterwards involved in actual migration behaviour, as well as the extent to which new variables intervened. The third question concerns the extent to which the differentials in migration decision-making—by education, sex, social class, remoteness etc.—observed in 1965 persisted into actual migration.

2. Methods

The field work was carried out from May to July 1968, slightly over three years after the original interviews in 1965. A 63 per cent random sample of respondents was prepared from the original list of 446 respondents who lived within the community boundaries in 1965[4] The respondents themselves were interviewed if they had not migrated. If they had already migrated, their mothers or guardians were interviewed about the occupations and migration

---

[4] The standard error of a proportion is roughly 2 per cent at p = .50. Therefore, the maximum confidence limits around a 50 per cent estimate for this data is approximately ± 4 per cent at 95 per cent confidence.

behaviour of the migrants. Table **XLI** summarises the details of the numbers interviewed and the extent of, and the reasons for, non-contact.

TABLE XLI: DETAILS OF SAMPLE AND THE NUMBERS INTERVIEWED OR NOT CONTACTED

	Number
Total number of respondents from the community interviewed in 1965	446
Total number selected for re-interviewing in 1968	281
Contacted	
Both respondents' and mothers' interviews completed	145
Number of mothers' interviews completed, respondents not contacted, but not migrated	3
Mothers' interviews completed, respondent migrated	121
TOTAL CONTACTED	269
Not contacted	
Number of complete families migrated from the area since 1965	8
Number of respondents who could not be contacted even on 6–7 callbacks	3
Number of mothers and respondents who refused to be interviewed	2
Number of respondents who had died since 1965	2
TOTAL NUMBER OF RESPONDENTS RESIDENT IN THE COMMUNITY BUT NOT CONTACTED	5

Out of a total of 279 eligible respondents, 129 had already migrated by 1968. Eight of these accompanied their families in migrating while 121 had migrated on their own, their parents and other family members remaining at home in the community. Of the eight families that had migrated out of the area, two were incomplete: the respondents leaving the area with other brothers and sisters on the death of both parents in one case, and on the remarriage of a widowed mother in the other. In the other six cases, the whole family had migrated together. Two families had sold the home business to move to work in Dublin. In another case, a local civil servant was transferred to Dublin, while in the three remaining cases the whole family moved to England to be with their father who had previously migrated there. Three respondents could not be contacted even after six calls, primarily because of their unusual work hours. In only two cases were interviews directly refused. Even in these cases, the interviewer was able to get some information before the interview was terminated.

Questions were asked about the respondent's occupational and educational history since the 1965 study; his actual residence movements, or his proposed ones if not yet migrated; characteristics of the sponsors or expected sponsors of his migration; main reasons for changing his mind about migration, if he had done so; his occupational and income aspirations and beliefs as to the feasibility of fulfilling them in the home community, if he was still there; his attitudes toward personal and institutional relationships and social provisions in the home community etc. Most of the variables dealt with were the same as those in the 1965 study, and were measured in exactly the same way. Information on the respondent's migration sponsors—those who helped him directly in his migration—was gathered for the first time, as were mothers' attitudes towards their children's migration. Any new variables introduced in the analysis will be explained in footnotes.

The following sections report the findings of this study, comparing them in each case to the 1965 results to see to what extent they conform with expectations. Each section has a short theoretical introduction setting out the major considerations that guided the research, and then goes on to report the relevant results. The first section will examine the actual migration behaviour of respondents in 1968, comparing it with their 1965 intentions. The major purpose here is to see to what extent intended migration behaviour in 1965 predicted subsequent behaviour. A second purpose is to see whether the personal motives involved in migration decisions—the frustration of occupational and income aspirations, Community Satisfaction and Family Obligations etc.—predict actual migration as efficiently as they predicted intended migration. The analysis will also attempt to assess whether any different motives that did not appear to be important influences on intended migration in 1965 became important in actual migration behaviour.

The major differentials in migration—by education and social class, sex, remoteness etc.—are each dealt with in the following chapter. The analysis is there concerned with the extent to which the conclusions about migration differentials, previously made on the basis of intended behaviour, also hold good in the case of subsequent actual behaviour.

MIGRATION INTENTIONS AND
MIGRATION BEHAVIOUR

It has been implicitly assumed up to this point that the respondents' 1965 migration plans resulted from an evaluation of the effects of all of the independent "motivating" variables taken together. Such plans, therefore, should have been more predictive of subsequent behaviour than any of the five independent variables taken in isolation. It is possible, however, that the joint effects of two or more of these independent variables might be more predictive of actual migration behaviour in 1968 than the 1965 plans taken alone. There are a number of reasons for this. Respondents' 1965 intentions were assumed to be the result of a number of attitudinal, belief, and role expectation variables acting together. The evidence available strongly supported this assumption. If these background variables continue to act in the same way, as the respondent comes to make the actual choice between staying or moving, they should predict his actual behaviour at least as well, if not better than his previous statement of intention.[5]

Some of these background motivating variables, however, should be more predictive of subsequent behaviour than others. Variables that are less subject to changes in magnitude or direction should remain more predictive of actual migration, while others that are more open to change become less predictive.

Respondents' obligations and attitudes (Family Obligations, Community Satisfaction, Community Evaluation) are less likely to alter than their beliefs (Occupational and Income Frustration). A relatively higher correlation would thus be expected between these obligations and attitudes and actual migration behaviour,

[5] See Campbell, A., et al., *The American Voter*, Wiley, NY, 1960; summarised in Newcomb, Turner and Converse, *Social Psychology*, Holt, Rinehart and Winston, 1965, 70–71; where a battery of relevant attitudinal variables predicted actual voting behaviour better than previous intentions.

than between them and intended migration. Rather than his attitudes, a subject's original beliefs about his ability to fulfill occupational and income aspirations locally will be far more likely to be open to change because of situational factors. Hence, one would also expect a lower degree of association between these variables and actual migration, than between them and intended migration. The following sections explore each of these areas in turn.

(i) Migration Intentions and Subsequent Behaviour

A simple comparison between respondents' intentions in 1965 and their migration position in 1968 shows an apparent close relationship between the two. Thirty-six per cent of the respondents in 1965 definitely intended to migrate, while just over 46 per cent had in fact already migrated by 1968. On the other hand, exactly the same proportion (26 per cent) of respondents had been definite in their intentions to stay locally in 1965 and 1968. This seems to indicate that most respondents were consistent in their migration plans over the whole period. However, as the results presented in Table XLII below clearly show, what has happened is that many of those who had intended to stay in 1965 had in fact migrated by 1968, this loss being compensated for by an approximately equal number who had, in 1965, intended to migrate but in 1968 intended to stay.

Although there is a relatively high correlation between intentions and subsequent behaviour, as the Gamma index indicates, many respondents have not acted as they had intended. Less than half of those who had definite intentions to remain in the home community in 1965 still had such definite intentions by 1968, while almost a third of them (31 per cent) either had already migrated or planned to do so shortly. Those who intended to migrate in 1965 seem more consistent: 70 per cent of them had already migrated by 1968, or still intended to do so. On the other hand, half of those who were unsure about their intentions in 1965 had migrated by 1968 or intended to do so, whereas only one fifth intended to stay. In general, therefore, although respondents did tend to act as they said they would, a considerable proportion changed their minds between 1965 and 1968. As a result, the overall correlation between intentions and actual behaviour is only moderate, as is indicated by Gamma. Indeed, this correlation is much smaller than that between either Occupational or Income Frustration 1965 and migration intentions. (Gamma = .64 and .55 respectively.) Therefore, from the individual's point of view, intentions appear to be only moderately predictive of subsequent behaviour.

TABLE XLII: PROPORTIONS OF RESPONDENTS HAVING MIGRATED OR REMAINING IN THE COMMUNITY IN 1968 RELATED TO INTENTIONS TO MIGRATE OR STAY IN 1965

Migration position in 1968	Migration intentions 1965			
	Definitely intend to stay	Not sur e whether to stay or migrate	Definitely intend to migrate	TOTAL
	%			
Definitely intend to stay at home	48	21	15	68
*Not sure but probably will stay there	14	16	7	33
*Not sure but probably will migrate	7	12	7	25
Definitely intend to migrate	3	8	7	17
Have already migrated	28	42	63	121
TOTAL %	100	100	100	
N	69	99	96	264

X^2 = 28.7; P < .001; Gamma = .418

* It was possible to divide the "not sure" category of the 1965 variable into two categories given for 1968. In one case, although respondent is not definite about migrating, he has made some contact with migrants and made some tentative plans.

The well known characteristic of prediction studies — that they work better for a whole group (prediction of rates) than for a single individual — had been borne out by this research.[6] Errors made in individual predictions are cancelled out to some extent so that in predicting, for instance, the proportion of respondents definitely intending to remain at home, the 1965 figures are almost identical to the 1968 ones. A comparison of the two sets of marginals in Table

[6] Lazarsfeld, P. F. and Rosenberg, M., *The Language of Social Research*, Free Press, 1955, 204.

XLII shows this very clearly. Since the immediate interest, however, is in individual decisions, this aspect of prediction will be left aside until dealing with migration differentials.

In dealing with individual predictions, however, the moderate predictive power of the 1965 intentions demands explanation. In dealing with the cause of these changes in plans, there appear to be two possible explanations. Entirely new variables may have intervened between 1965 and 1968, thus bringing about these changes, or the original motivating variables remain the only important ones but they themselves had changed in magnitude and direction in the intervening period. Before investigating these possibilities, however, it will be worthwhile to examine the performance of the original motives in predicting actual migration. The individual or joint effects of some of these variables may be more predictive of actual migration than intentions have been.

TABLE XLIII: CORRELATIONS BETWEEN RESPONDENTS' ACTUAL MIGRATION BEHAVIOUR IN 1968 AND SIX INDEPENDENT VARIABLES MEASURED IN 1965, COMPARED WITH THOSE BETWEEN SOME OF THESE VARIABLES AND RESPONDENTS' 1965 INTENTIONS. (GAMMA IS USED AS AN INDEX OF ASSOCIATION)

	Migration intentions 1965 X_1	Occupational frustration 1965 X_2	Income frustration 1965 X_3	Community Satisfaction 1965 X_4	Family Obligations 1965 X_5	Community Evaluation 1965 X_6
Y Migration behaviour 1968	.418 *(.453)	.400 *(.401)	.222 *(.237)	.161 *(.182)	−.386 *(.405)	.164 *(.108)
X_1 Migration intentions 1965	X	.640	.548	.355	−.302	.137

* The five values of the migration behaviour variable (see Table XLII) are here collapsed to three to make statistics comparable in the case of migration behaviour and migration intentions. The three new categories are: (1) "Definitely stay"; (2) "Not sure, but probably will stay," and "Not sure, but probably will migrate"; and (3) "Definitely intend to migrate" and "Have already migrated".

If, as we assumed, respondents' (1965) migration plans resulted, so to speak, from an evaluation of the effects of the five independent variables taken together, it may be that when the individual was faced with the real choice of migrating or staying at home (rather than being asked to forecast that choice) these independent variables would turn out to be more predictive of his final decision than his intended behaviour. Table XLIII presents the correlations[7] between these five independent variables and actual migration.

As hypothesised, no single variable is more highly correlated

[7] Correlation is used here and subsequently to refer to the strength of association between two variables.

with actual migratory behaviour than the respondents' previous intentions, although both Occupational Frustration and Family Obligations are almost as highly correlated. Two clear trends stand out when comparing the two sets of correlations in the table. Firstly, and in line with the hypothesis proposed, only one of the independent variables—Family Obligations—is more highly correlated with actual migration than with intentions to migrate. Contrary to this hypothesis, however, the two attitudinal variables have lower correlations with actual than with intended migration. They thus behave in a manner similar to Occupational and Income Frustration. It may be that, contrary to our hypothesis, these two attitudes arc as opcn to change as are beliefs about local economic opportunities. On the other hand, they may be so poorly predictive of actual migration, whether they change or not, that they can be safely ignored as causes of migration, despite their moderate association with migration intentions. This question of change in the values and consequent predictive power of these variables will be explored and, it is hoped, resolved in a later section.

One of the results of these changes in the relative predictive abilities of the five independent variables is that Family Obligations has become almost as predictive of actual migration as Occupational Frustration. By combining the effects of Occupational Frustration and Family Obligations, the results presented in Table XLIV clearly show that their joint effects are more highly predictive of actual migration in 1968 than are respondents' intentions.

Although Occupational Frustration and Family Obligations are highly—but negatively—correlated with each other (Gamma = −.505) they have major additional joint effects on migration. At all levels of Family Obligation, increasing levels of Occupational Frustration have consistent additional effects on migration. Among those with no Family Obligations, the proportion migrating increases from roughly half to almost 90 per cent. Among respondents with medium-high obligations, the proportion migrating increases from 10 per cent to 80 per cent as the level of Occupational Frustration rises. Although variation on the latter variable is at its maximum at low to slight levels of Family Obligations, its effect on migration is much less than at higher levels of obligation. When examining the conditional effects of Family Obligations, however, the picture is slightly different. When respondents are frustrated in their occupation aspirations, variation in levels of family obligation makes no consistent difference to migration; whereas it makes a great difference where respondents are not frustrated. This, in fact, reproduces the pattern present when these two variables were cross-classified against migration intentions.

TABLE XLIV: PROPORTIONS ALREADY MIGRATED OR STILL DEFINITELY INTENDING TO MIGRATE (1968) BY LEVEL OF OCCUPATIONAL FRUSTRATION AND FAMILY OBLIGATIONS (1965)

Occupational Frustration (1965)	Family Obligations (1965)					
	None		Very Slight		Med.–High	
	Percentages migrated or to definitely migrate (1968)					
	%		%		%	
Not frustrated	52	(25)	52	(70)	10	(30)
Not sure	58	(31)	48	(25)	67	(9)
Frustrated	89	(18)	72	(25)	80	(5)
TOTAL	74		120		44	

In general, then, the combined effects of these two variables predict migration behaviour in 1968 better than migration intentions themselves, as a comparison of the data in Tables XLII and XLIV clearly indicates. Between 80 and 90 per cent of those thwarted in their occupational aspirations have migrated, or intend to do so shortly, at all levels of Family Obligation. Only 70 per cent of those who definitely intended to migrate had done so or still intended to. On the other hand, of those with medium-high levels of Family Obligations who were satisfied they could fulfill their occupational aspirations locally, only one tenth had migrated by 1968 or still intended to do so, while this was so for over 30 per cent of those who definitely intended to stay in 1965. The combined effects of the two variables then predict actual migration more efficiently than the subjects' earlier intentions.[8]

[8] Pearsonian correlational methods were attempted on the data by assigning numbers from 1 to 5 to the corresponding ordinal categories of the dependent and six independent variables. Although this kind of data manipulation breaks many of the assumptions of the Pearsonian model when it is used only as a measure of linear relationship between two or more variables, it does allow one to test the significance of individual correlations and of the difference between correlation coefficients. This is not possible with Gamma, since it does not have a probability distribution. The results yielded coefficients somewhat lower than Gamma in each case, but the overall conclusions remained the same. Family Obligations

The reason why Family Obligations increased its predictive power is because a much higher proportion of those with high obligations are staying at home than intended to, while a much higher percentage of those with low obligations have actually migrated than intended to in 1965. Sixty two per cent of those with no obligations had already migrated or definitely intended to do so by 1968, although only 49 per cent of these intended to do so in 1965. On the other hand, although three of the 17 respondents with high levels of obligation definitely intended to migrate in 1965, only one had actually left by 1968,[9] while the other two intended to remain at home. It appears that many respondents, thinking they could ignore their obligations, intended to migrate in 1965 in pursuit of purely personal goals. They have apparently discovered that they could not, in fact, ignore these obligations when it came to the actual decision. On the other hand, the absence of family ties and obligations led to much greater rates of migration than the frustration of such personal aspirations would have suggested in 1965. As the figures presented in Table XLIV show, where respondents are not frustrated in their occupational aspirations and they have no or very slight obligations, less than half of them intend to stay locally. The presence or absence of such family ties and obligations, therefore, appears to be almost as important in migration as are beliefs about the availability of economic opportunities locally.

It appears, therefore, that both the respondents' 1965 intentions to migrate and the variables then assumed to be the major influences on these decisions, are only moderately predictive of actual migration. Only one of these "motivating" variables increased its predictive power. It is possible that the other variables are far less important in actual migration than in influencing previous statements of intention to migrate, and that other unconsidered factors intervene between such foregoing intentions and subsequent behaviour. On the other hand, these original motivating variables may have

---

become slightly more predictive of actual migration than Occupational Frustration, but the differences are not significant. The multiple correlation of Occupational Frustration and Family Obligations with migration yielded a coefficient ($R = .401$) which was higher than that between migration intentions and behaviour ($r = .335$). The addition of any of the other variables added very little to the size of the multiple R. See Cronholm, J. M., "Note on the Use of Correlation Coefficient", *Psychological Reports*, 1965, 16, 668, for a discussion of the use of the Pearsonian 'r' in a case like this.

[9] As later discussions will show, this individual's obligations to his family had in fact changed to very minimal levels by 1968.

changed in magnitude and direction between 1965 and 1968, as the individual moved closer to actual migration. If migration decision-making resembles occupational decision-making—from fantasy choices, to tentative more realistic choices, to the final choice which precedes movement into the first full time occupation[10] —then, as respondents move into the final stage of realistic choice and begin actively to seek occupational opportunities locally, and try to fit themselves into local adult occupational and community roles, their beliefs about local occupational and income opportunities and their attitudes toward local community institutions may change radically. The following section examines these changes in the original motivational variables* and relates them to changes in migration plans for those respondents who were still in the community in 1968. Equivalent data is, of course, not available for those who had already migrated. In these cases, respondents' mothers were interviewed and their responses will be examined.

(ii) Changing their Minds

There are essentially two ways of investigating the causes of these changes in plans: through cross-tabulation against changes in the causal factors proposed, and through relating plan changes to the reasons given by respondents for changing their minds.[11] Both approaches are employed. Unfortunately, since the analysis of changes in the causal factors will be limited to those living in the community in 1968, it deals with only a proportion of those who changed their minds in this way. However, the mothers of respondents who had migrated, despite their intention to stay in 1965, were interviewed on the reasons their children had changed their minds. By examining both types of data, it should be possible to get an overall assessment of the major factors which brought about these changes. Dividing those who changed their minds into two groups— those changing from "staying" to "migrating" (the inconsistent

---

[10] See Ginzberg, E., Ginsburg, S. W., et al., *Occupational Choice*, Columbia U.P., NY, 1951; and Burchinal, L. G., Haller, A. O. and Taves, M. et al., *Career Choices of Rural Youth*, University of Minnesota, A.E.S., Bulletin No. 458, 1962.

* For ease of presentation the adjective "causal" will be subsequently used to refer to the 5 motivational variables originally used. No claim is made that these represent the only necessary and sufficient conditions which cause migration.

[11] Zeisel, H., *Say it With Figures*, Routledge and Kegan Paul, London 1958, 226–43.

migrants), and those from "migrating" to "staying" (the inconsistent residents)—the next two sections examine changes in the five predictive variables, and the reasons given for changing plans for these two groups in turn.

Inconsistent Migrants

Nineteen of the 69 respondents who intended to remain at home in 1965 had already migrated by 1968 while a further seven, resident in the community, still intended to migrate. In addition, 42 respondents who were uncertain about migrating in 1965 had already migrated by 1968, while another twenty of them still intended to migrate. In total, therefore, 61 respondents who had already migrated, and 27 who still intended to migrate, had changed their minds about migrating over the three year period. Changes in the causal factors, however, can only be examined for these latter 27 respondents who were re-interviewed in the community in 1968.

(i) *Causal Factors:* Table XLV relates changes in migration plans to changes in the causal factors. Since those who had persisted in their original (1965) intention to stay locally could also have changed their beliefs about, and attitudes toward, the local community, they are included as a comparison group in the table. If changes in the motivating factors are important influences here, those who had changed their migration plans should have become significantly more pessimistic in their beliefs and attitudes than the comparison group. The results show that there are significant differences between these two groups in the extent of changes in only two causal variables —occupational and income frustration—while changes in the other two variables — Community Satisfaction and Evaluation — are roughly similar in both groups. Roughly half of those respondents who had changed their minds had become more pessimistic about local occupational and income opportunities, while this was true of only 10 to 20 per cent of those who persisted in their original intention to stay. And these small changes toward more pessimistic beliefs in this latter group were more than counterbalanced by the numbers who had become more optimistic about local opportunities.

Changes in migration plans are, therefore, closely related to changes in beliefs about local occupational and income opportunities, but do not appear to be related to changes in attitudes

TABLE XLV: Of those who definitely intended to remain at home in 1965 or who were not sure whether they would or not, the numbers showing changes in the Causal Factors as related to Migration Intentions in 1968

	Changes in Causal Factors		
	Change in Causal Factor which could lead to migration (i.e. have become more pessimistic)*	No change in Causal Factor*	Change in Causal Factors toward staying (i.e. have become more optimistic)*
1. Occupational Frustration			
To stay, 1968: (79)	8 (10% change)	60	11 (14%)
**To go, 1968: (26)	15 (60% change)	9	2 (8%)
		$X^2 = 25.8$; $p < .001$	
2. Income Frustration			
To stay, 1968: (73)	15 (21% change)	30	28 (38%)
**To go, 1968: (26)	12 (46% change)	9	5
		$X^2 = 6.9$; $p < .05$	

*Those who have become more pessimistic in their beliefs had changed from being "not frustrated" in their occupational and income aspirations in 1965 to being "not sure" or "frustrated" in 1968; or had changed from being "not sure" to "frustrated". Those who have become more optimistic had changed in these variables in the opposite direction. Since there were no significant differences between these two groups for Community Satisfaction and Community Evaluation, these tables were excluded.

**Those who changed their minds about migration.

toward the community. These changes are neatly summarised in the fact that only 5 of the 26 respondents changing their minds toward migrating were completely pessimistic about either occupational or income opportunities in 1965 while 18 of them were so pessimistic in 1968. And, although there were some unexpected changes in the pessimistic direction amongst these other respondents who had persisted in their intention to stay, the changes toward more optimistic beliefs were far more evident. Thirty seven (47 per cent) of these respondents were completely satisfied in 1965 with either local occupational or income opportunities, while this number had increased to 53 (67 per cent) in 1968.

A considerable proportion of these latter respondents, however, intend to stay, despite being frustrated in either their occupational or income aspirations (21 out of the 79 respondents). On the other hand, a small number of respondents who had changed their minds toward migrating are neither frustrated in their occupational or income aspirations (5 of the 26 respondents). Other non-economic factors, therefore, are intervening in these cases. These non-economic factors, however, are not apparently related to the two attitudinal variables examined—Community Satisfaction or Community Evaluation. The analysis of the reasons given for changing migration plans, which is to be examined in the next section, should provide some answers to this problem.

(ii) *Reasons:* Twenty one of the 69 respondents who had intended to remain at home in 1965 had changed their minds completely by 1968—the 19 who had already migrated and the two who still intended to. These latter two respondents and the mothers of the other 19 who had already migrated were interviewed on the reasons why they had so completely changed their minds.

Five of these migrants had not worked in the home community before migrating. These, together with one respondent who had worked locally, left the area because of required mobility in their chosen vocations. Two of these had unexpectedly gone to university in Dublin. Two had taken up posts as skilled apprentices with the Electricity Supply Board, and the remaining two had taken up positions as bank clerks. All four jobs had been secured through success in formal competitive examinations. Once accepted, these jobs require successful candidates to move to any of the branch offices designated by the firm. Migration was therefore an unforeseen educational or occupational requirement for these six respondents, and resulted from unforeseen offers of social mobility chances which were not attainable in the local community.

Seven more respondents left the area because of dissatisfaction with their previous jobs and incomes in the community — the dissatisfaction arising subsequent to the 1965 interview. Four other respondents left, not because they were dissatisfied with local economic opportunities, but primarily because of the influence of sibs and friends who had already migrated from the area. Two respondents had left to get married, and another to escape from a disagreeable personal problem, although he had a very satisfactory job locally. No information was available on the remaining migrant.

The majority of these respondents (13 of the 21) had therefore changed their minds for reasons connected with education, jobs and incomes. Excluding the five respondents who had not worked locally before migrating, the other 8 migrants had not left because of the lack of jobs of an acceptable status level locally—i.e. Occupational Frustration. They had, however, either become dissatisfied with the poor remuneration from their jobs or, in some cases, to the poor conditions of work. This dissatisfaction arose from unfavourable comparisons with the reported remuneration and conditions of work enjoyed by their migrant peers. This is an indirect influence of migrant contacts, through providing a comparative reference group against whose situation an individual's own progress is evaluated. The influence of migrant sibs and friends was more direct, however, in the case of four respondents. These were not frustrated in their personal aspirations by restricted local opportunities. They migrated in direct response to very enticing job offers, and to unsolicited offers of direct help in migrating made by migrant peers. These unsolicited offers of help appeared the exception rather than the rule, however. In general, although almost all respondents had direct contacts with sibs and friends who had migrated, these did not make a definite job offer or definite offers to help in the migration process without being requested. A rather general offer to help in migration is often made, however, even to relatively satisfied non-migrants. The influence of these rather general offers of help in migration, made by sibs and friends when writing home or when returning on holidays, was not unfortunately explored in this study. Migrant peers, however, always act as a normative and comparative reference group for the non-migrants, affecting their level of satisfaction with jobs and incomes and community roles and facilities.[12] Besides acting as points of comparison for self-assessment, the influence of migrant peers can be more direct in bringing about direct changes in aspirations and values. The changes in the level of income frustration, for instance, between 1965 and 1968 were not due to the frustration of the individual's 1965 aspirations but to the increase in the level of aspiration in the interim. Such adjustments in the level of aspiration and satisfaction of non-migrants, therefore, appear to be primarily due to the changing influences of migrant reference groups. Such influences would be at a minimum in 1965. A very small proportion of the age group concerned had migrated by that time. Also, only a small proportion were in their first full time occupation—the majority being in the final stages of occupational decision-making or in the first "trial" occupations.[13] As these enter the labour force and as occupational and income aspirations become directly relevant to the individual—instead of being only of vicarious interest as previously —and as more and more of the age group migrate, the influence of migrant reference groups can be expected to grow.

In conclusion, both analyses agree that roughly two thirds of the migrants had changed their minds for reasons connected with local occupational or income frustrations. Of the remainder, about one fifth had altered their plans because of the direct influence of migrant peers, although the indirect influences of migrants was more important than this proportion would suggest. In the remaining cases, migration resulted from girls marrying men resident outside the community (2 cases) or from unusual personal circumstances.

Inconsistent Residents.

Twenty one of the 96 respondents intending to migrate in 1965 had completely changed their minds by 1968. Fourteen now definitely intended to stay at home, while another seven had become unsure but probably would stay. Although proportionately fewer of this group changed their minds than did the former one, the number changing is still substantial.

[12] Kelley, H. H., "The two functions of reference groups", reprinted in G. E. Swanson, and E. L. Hartley, *Readings in Social Psychology*, Holt, NY, 1952, 410–4.

[13] Ginzberg, *op. cit.* and Burchinal, Haller and Taves, *op. cit.*

TABLE XLVI: OF THOSE WHO DEFINITELY INTENDED TO MIGRATE IN 1965, THE PROPORTIONS SHOWING CHANGES IN THE CAUSAL FACTORS AS RELATED TO MIGRATION INTENTIONS IN 1968

	Changes in Causal Factors		
	Change in Causal Factor which could lead to migration	No change in Causal Factor	Change in Causal Factor which could lead to staying
	1. Occupational Frustration		
Migration intentions 1968			
*To stay: (21)	3	8	10 (48%)
To go: (14)	4	4	6 (43%) X², n.s.**
	2. Income Frustration		
*To stay: (21)	3	5	13 (62%)
To go: (14)	4	2	8 (59%) X², n.s.**

* Those who had changed their minds.
** The two categories on the left were collapsed for the Chi Square test.

(i) *Changes in Causal Factors:* Table XLVI summarises changes in the causal factors and relates them to changes made in migration plans since 1965. The comparison group used in the table are those who still intended to migrate in 1968. Unfortunately, the numbers involved are very small. Of these 96 respondents who intended to migrate in 1965, only 35 were still at home and re-interviewed in 1968. Of these, 21 then intended to stay and 14 still intended to migrate. The latter group can be regarded as being consistent in their plans, although the date of departure had been postponed. If changes in the causal variables are important in bringing about changes in migration plans, these should show up in differences between the two groups.

Of the 21 respondents who had completely changed their minds, 10 had become more satisfied with local occupational opportunities and 13 with local income opportunities. In total, only two of these respondents had been satisfied with both occupational and income opportunities locally in 1965, whereas by 1968 this was true of twelve respondents. However, those who still intended to migrate in 1968 had also become more satisfied with local opportunities. In fact, the differences between the two groups in these respects, were not statistically significant. Similarly, the differences between the two groups in changes in Community Satisfaction, and Community Evaluation were not significant. As a result, except in the case of Family Obligations, those who still intended to migrate in 1968 were just as likely to have developed more positive attitudes toward the community as were those who intended to stay, the small differences between the two groups not being statistically significant. Such radical alterations in plans, therefore, cannot be explained by changes in the causal factors.

Although there are small consistent differences between the two groups on all the causal variables in changes toward a greater degree of satisfaction, these could have occurred by chance. If "true" differences exist between the two groups on these causal variables, these are very small and might have resulted after migration plans had been altered for other reasons, and the respondents might subsequently have shifted their beliefs and attitudes into conformity with their changed behaviour. Also, the fact that one third of the 21 respondents who had completely changed their minds about migrating, now intending to stay, still felt frustrated in either their occupational or income aspirations in 1968, suggests that non-economic factors are of major importance in these cases. Some light can be thrown on this question by considering the reasons given by these respondents for changing their minds.

(ii) *Reasons:* The fourteen respondents who had radically altered their plans—from definitely going to definitely staying—were questioned on the reasons why they had done so. Four of these had stayed at home because of changes in family circumstances (death of one of the parents) which imposed a firm obligation on them to remain at home. Another respondent who had earlier mentioned his family obligations, but thought he would evade them and migrate, had found he was constrained to stay. Family obligations were also important in the case of another respondent, an only son who had taken over management of the home farm; but these came into play only after he had failed his first year university examination. Failure in adjustment to migrant conditions was also important in the case of another respondent who had migrated to find an un-skilled manual job in England, but had quickly returned disillusion-ed after finding life there more difficult than he had expected. Six other respondents said they had unexpected luck in getting good jobs locally, and in only one of these cases was the job with a con-cern that had opened since 1965. One girl did not migrate because her mother would not allow her to do so, and she subsequently got a satisfactory job locally.

Less than half of the respondents, therefore, had changed their minds because of unexpected windfall opportunities locally. Equally important were family pressures, and newly emerging Family Obligations arising because of the death of one of the parents. In these latter cases, respondents appeared to have adjusted their aspirations to fit local opportunities. These changes in migration plans, therefore, are as much caused by family pressures as by unexpected windfall opportunities, i.e. by changes in the level of occupational and income frustration.

In conclusion, therefore, the study of these deviant cases shows that changes in migration plans arise almost as much from pressures exerted by family and friends as from changes in the causal variables. Roughly one third of those who had changed their minds from staying to migrating had done so because of the influences of migrant sibs and friends, and roughly half of those who had changed from a clear decision to migrate to a clear decision to stay had done so because of obligations to parents. Similarly, one fifth of the former who now intended to migrate were completely satisfied with both occupational and income opportunities locally; while one third of the latter, who now intended to stay locally, were frustrated in either their occupational or income aspirations. It is clear, therefore, that somewhat over one third of all respondents who had changed their minds about migrating had done so for reasons other than an attempt to maximise their individual satisfactions when these are considered in isolation.

These conclusions, however, refer only to those who had changed their minds and were still living in the community in 1968. They do not refer to those already migrated, nor to those who were consistent in their intentions to stay at home in 1965 and 1968. We need some equivalent information for these groups before coming to a conclusion on the question of migration motives. An overall examination of the schedules of these respondents who had already migrated was therefore attempted for this purpose.

(iii) Reasons Given for Migration

The following table summarises the reasons given for migration by the mothers of the 121 individuals concerned. Of the total of 121 migrants, almost half (57) had left because of the pursuit of higher level aspirations which could not be fulfilled locally. The maxim that "the pursuit of social mobility leads to migration"[14] certainly holds in their case. None of these migrants could have found comparable outlets locally. Some of them may return, however; particularly some of the nurses and teachers when they complete their training. None of them appeared to have any definite intention of doing so, however, at least as perceived by their mothers.

A further 11 migrants, all girls, had taken up lower level non-manual jobs—mostly as office clerks and typists. Only two of these had worked locally, although many jobs of this kind were available there. The preconceived beliefs of the other girls had biassed them against seeking local jobs. This was patently not the case, however, for ten other migrants who had worked locally in service (mostly shop assistants) and manual jobs before leaving. All of these had lost their jobs for various reasons. If shop assistants, they were let

[14] Kaufman, H. H., et al., "Social stratification in rural society", *Rural Sociology*, 1953, 18, 1.

TABLE XLVII: CLASSIFICATION OF MIGRANTS ON THE BASIS OF THEIR
                REPORTED REASONS FOR MIGRATION

Reasons given for migration	Total number migrating	Number working locally before migrating
1. Entering higher non-manual jobs unavailable locally	22	3 (temp.)
2. Entering University, Teacher or Nursing Training	35	4 (temp.)
3. Entering intermediate non-manual jobs of a kind available locally	11	2
4. Entering service or manual jobs (a) Lost local job and frustrated in attempt to find alternative	10	10
(b) Left local job because of dissatisfaction with present and prospective income opportunities	21	21
5. No reported local difficulties with occupations or incomes	22	15
TOTAL	121	55

go because they were deemed to have completed their "apprentice-ship" and were being replaced by younger people. All of these had searched around for local jobs before migrating.

In addition to these ten latter "occupational migrants", 21 other migrants had worked locally at service and manual occupations, but had left these jobs because of dissatisfaction with current and prospective income opportunities in the home community.

None of the remaining 22 respondents appeared to leave because of basic difficulties in establishing themselves in satisfactory jobs locally, or in achieving satisfactory incomes. Ten migrants left because they "wanted to travel", to "see the world", or just "wanted a change out of Cavan". All of these were girls. Six of them had given up satisfactory jobs locally, most of them in service occupations. The other four were secondary educated girls, two of whom had become au-pair girls on the Continent. Seven additional migrants left because of the direct influence of friends and sibs who had migrated, although all of these appeared to be satisfied with their jobs and income locally. All were in service or manual jobs locally, and only two of them were boys. Such peer group influences, therefore, appeared to have been far more important for the girls, especially the more poorly educated girls.

Out of a total of 121 migrants, therefore, 99 (83 per cent) had left because of the pursuit of economic and social mobility goals of a status higher than is available locally, or because of the frustration of similar but lower level aspirations. There are two different types of occupational frustration involved here, however: that resulting from aspiring to jobs of a higher level than are available locally, and that resulting from a scarcity of well paid lower level non-manual jobs or of manual jobs in general. Even if the community were to develop rapidly, the resultant expansion of local opportunities would be minimal at the upper non-manual levels. Those who aspired to manual, service and lower non-manual jobs, and who now migrate because of the scarcity of these jobs or of their poor remuneration, would be the ones most likely to benefit from such developments.[15] Of all migrants, they would also be the ones most likely to stay if such opportunities were to improve.

"Apprentices" in shops or apprentice tradesmen make up roughly half of the total number of these latter "economic"-type migrants. Very few of these apprentices actually take up full time work in shops once their apprenticeship is completed. Only ten of the 47 respondents who had first taken up service occupations locally were still in their jobs in 1968 and intended to remain in the community. All but three of the remainder had already migrated, or intended to shortly. Their vacated places, however, are quickly filled by younger replacements coming on to the labour market for the first time. These poorly paid service jobs serve only as temporary or trial occupations for new entrants to the labour force. They help to socialise neophytes into adult occupational life, but only a small minority of these will be able to take them up as permanent full time occupations locally. The local prospects for those qualified in a skilled trade are somewhat better. Here, most of those starting

---

[15] In the period 1961–6, for instance, although there was a decline of 6.6 per cent in the total number of people constructively occupied in County Cavan, this decline was restricted almost completely to agricultural and unskilled manual occupations. There were increases in the numbers of persons engaged in other occupations, but 77 per cent of the total increase in employment occurring in these expanding occupations occurred in skilled and semiskilled manual and service occupations. *Census of Population of Ireland*, 1966, Vol. IV, 1968.

their apprenticeship in a skilled trade are likely to complete the course. Of the 34 respondents who first entered apprenticeship to skilled trades locally, 24 were still in skilled trades by 1968. Only 13 of these are likely to stay permanently in the home community, however. In both cases, however, the proportion who had taken up lower status occupations on changing from their original jobs was much smaller than expected. Most of the service workers, in fact, and about half of the skilled workers increased their status as a result of migration and occupational changes.

These figures for migrants suggest that occupational and income aspirations appear to be more important than our discussions in previous sections might have suggested. Less than 20 per cent of the migrants appeared to have left without "adequate cause", and less than 5 per cent because of the direct influence of migrant peers. However, the information on these motives was not gathered from the respondents themselves, and there may be an element of rationalisation involved in mothers' responses. The fact that only half of the migrants' mothers supported them completely in their migration, and that a third thought that they should have stayed at home, suggests that such rationalisations might be important. These latter figures also suggest that the direct and indirect influence of migrant sibs and peers must have been of greater importance than appeared from the mothers' responses. This question of the influence of parents and peers on migration will be discussed in the concluding section on motives. Before considering these, however, we attempt in the following section to summarise the evidence on migration motives and to estimate the relative influence on the actual migration choice of the five different motivational variables proposed.

SUMMARY

Of the five variables originally proposed as influencing migration decisions, only three—Occupational Frustration, Family Obligations, and Income Frustration—have retained their importance. As an examination of Table XLIII clearly shows, these are the only variables which predicted actual migration with any degree of efficiency. The examination of the main influences involved in the decisions of the actual migrants came to much the same conclusion. The frustration of occupational status and consumption aspirations appeared to be the major factors involved. Over 80 cent of the migrants had left for these reasons and they were generally supported by their parents in these plans, although those migrating for consumption reasons were less strongly supported than those going for social mobility reasons. On the other hand, the majority of those intending to remain in the community are either those who could best fulfill their occupational and consumption aspirations there, or (a small minority) those who had been obliged to stay and adjust their aspirations to community opportunities because of family expectations and obligations.

Much the same conclusion emerged from the examination of the causes of changes in migration plans. Of the original causal factors proposed, only changes in levels of Occupational Frustration and Family Obligations appeared to be highly correlated with changes in plans. On the other hand, changes in the level of Community Satisfaction and Community Evaluation were unimportant. Changes in the level of Occupational Frustration arose because many previously optimistic respondents had unforeseen difficulties in obtaining local satisfactory employment, while others who were previously highly pessimistic had no difficulty at all in getting satisfactory jobs locally. The Family Obligations of many respondents had also changed in the meantime. Of the eleven migrants who had stated in 1965 that they had medium to high levels of family obligation, nine had experienced a complete removal of these obligations before 1968. In six cases a dependent parent had died, thus releasing them from their obligations. In the other three cases, younger siblings had taken over their older brother's obligations as they grew older. On the other hand, the obligations of five other respondents had changed in the opposite direction because of counteracting changes in family circumstances.

The following table summarises the relationship between these two independent variables, as measured in 1965 and 1968, and migration. The changes in the independent variables between 1965 and 1968 are estimated from parental responses for those who had migrated by 1968. The 1968 figures for the migrants are an estimate of their position on these variables at a time just prior to their movement.

The overall correlations between these two independent variables as measured in 1968 and migration, as estimated by Gamma or the Pearson Product Moment Correlation, are much greater than those between the same two variables and migration intentions in 1965.

TABLE XLVIII: THE RELATIONSHIP BETWEEN MIGRATION BEHAVIOUR IN 1968 AND OCCUPATIONAL FRUSTRATION AND FAMILY OBLIGATIONS IN 1965 AND 1968

Migration 1968	Occupational Frustration				Family Obligations			
	1965		1968		1965		1968	
	Not frustrated	Not sure or frustrated	Not frustrated	Not sure or frustrated	None or slight	Medium or high	None or slight	Medium or high
	%	%	%	%	%	%	%	%
Definitely stay	34	16	43	5	20	51	17	67
Not sure stay	16	8	16	8	12	16	11	18
Not sure go	10	9	10	10	11	6	10	7
Definitely go	7	6	6	8	7	4	7	4
Already gone	33	61	26	70	51	22	54	4
TOTAL (100%) N	144	119	144	118	216	49	220	45
	* P < .05 **γ = .400 **r_xy = .291		P < .05 γ = .724 r_xy* = .538		P < .05 γ = .386 r_xy1 = .333		P < .05 γ = .520 r_xy1* = .456	

* Estimated from Chi Square analysis.
** These correlations are estimated for five values of the migration variable, three values of the Occupational Frustration variable and four values of the Family Obligations variable.

This again emphasises their major importance in migration behaviour.

The joint effects of both variables were estimated through the uses of the Pearsonian multiple correlation coefficient. This co-efficient reaches .609 when the two independent variables are combined to predict migration. The joint effects of both variables then predict actual migration even better than they (R = .542) predicted migration intentions in 1965. There are many errors involved in estimating equivalent values of Income Frustration and Community Satisfaction for the respondents already migrated, but even using the most optimistic intercorrelation estimates, however, the multiple R is not increased much beyond that obtained when only Occupational Frustration and Family Obligations are used on their own.[16] The former two variables therefore appear to have had little independent relationship to migration.

CONCLUSIONS

In concluding this chapter on migration motives, it will be useful to discuss first of all some of the assumptions underlying our approach. We had assumed, rather naively it now appears, that with the exception of family obligations, the individual makes up his own mind about migration in isolation from his major role expectations, and other influences exerted by his family and friendship groups. The only role to which sufficient attention was paid was that of son or daughter within the family. Here it was shown that the expectations and associated sanctioning behaviour of parents and other family members was of major importance in migration behaviour. It appears now that the direct and indirect influence of migrant sibs and peers is almost as important. This influence of migrant peers corresponds rather closely to the two well known functions of reference groups: acting indirectly as points of comparison for self-assessment and

[16] For instance, the zero order correlation between Community Satisfaction (X_4) and Migration Behaviour '68 (X_1), and the two independent variables— Occupational Frustration (X_2) and Family Obligations (X_3)—are: $r_{14} = .365$; $r_{24} = .222$; $r_{34} = .151$ when the calculations are restricted to the sample re-inter-viewed in 1968—excluding the respondents already migrated $(N = 148)$. If the migrants' responses are estimated from their 1965 statements and included in the calculation $(N = 269)$ the following intercorrelations result: $r_{14} = .381$; $r_{24} = .311$; $r_{34} = .229$. Multiple $R_{1.234} = .650$ using the former set of intercorrelations, and .632 using the latter set: the additional influence of Income Frustration is minimal, R reaching .641 only when it is added in the latter case.

influencing the non-migrants level of satisfaction with their roles in the home community; and normatively as sources of change in their levels of aspiration and in norms and values generally.[17] Both of these influences are indirect and would be reflected in changes in the five independent variables measured. However, the expectations and complementary sanctioning behaviour of migrant peers also appears to have a more direct influence on migration. This influence appears to be somewhat similar to that exerted by the family in constraining some people to stay at home. Since less than 5 per cent of the age group had migrated in 1965, the relative lack of influence of migrant peers on migration plans was understandable at that stage. However, by 1968, 46 per cent of the group had migrated and migrant influences had greatly multiplied. Unfortunately, this was not foreseen at the research design stage and was not directly measured. This autonomous effect of the dominant expectations and attitudes within the primary groups—in influencing an individual's behaviour independently of his own attitudes—has been demonstrated in a number of studies. Blau called this the "structural effect" and demonstrated its individual influence on the behaviour of social workers.[18] Similarly, the expectations and influence of peers has been shown to be very important in educational achievement.[19] Besides these limitations of the individual decision-making model used, there is also another aspect in which it is inadequate—the degree to which parents expect their children to take responsibility for such major decisions and the degree to which they support them in these decisions once taken.

The model of extreme individualism implicitly assumed in the original study appears to hold good for the middle class and large farm class secondary educated respondents. Here, parents generally expected their children to take responsibility for their own occupational and migration decisions, and they usually supported them in the attainment of their goals, once chosen. This is much less true

[17] Kelley, H. H., *op. cit.*; See also R. H. Turner, "Migration to a medium sized city", *Journal of Social Psychology*, 1949, 30, 2, 229–50, where it was shown that the influence of migrant friends on the migration of girls was especially important.

[18] Blau, P. M., "Structural effects", *American Sociological Review*, April 1960, 25, 2, 178–93.

[19] Simpson, R. L., "Parental influence, anticipatory socialisation and social mobility," *American Sociological Review*, 1962, 27, 3, 517–22 Sewell, Haller & Portes, "Educational and occupational achievements of Wisconsin farm boys." Paper delivered at the Joint Session of the Rural Sociology and American Sociological Association Meeting, August 1967, San Francisco.

of working class or small farm class respondents who have only received a primary education.

Some data gathered in the course of the study clearly illustrates this phenomenon. The mothers of all migrants were asked whether they had supported their children's migration. Roughly sixty per cent of all mothers said they had expected their children to migrate, although about half of these said that they did not actively encourage them to do so. On the other hand, over a quarter of these mothers thought that their children should have stayed at home, and had not expected them to leave. This parental support for, or opposition to migration was very closely related to the status level of the family and the status of the occupation entered by sons or daughters. Nearly 90 per cent of the socially mobile respondents entering the higher non-manual occupations got strong material support for migration, and none of these were strongly opposed. This was, however, only true for 60 per cent of those entering lower non-manual occupations, and only 45 per cent of those entering skilled manual and service occupations. At the other extreme, less than a quarter of those entering semiskilled and unskilled manual occupations had strong maternal support for migration. In this last case, in fact, the majority of the higher non-manual workers come from middle class or large farm backgrounds, while those taking up manual jobs come almost exclusively from working class or small farm backgrounds. As one moves down the status scale, therefore, migrants get decreasing maternal support for migration, to the point where most migrants entering lower manual occupations had left home without the active support of their mothers. As already remarked, the counteracting influences of migrant reference groups is at its maximum for these groups of migrants. These latter migrants therefore were subject to many conflicting pressures, which they had resolved in favour of the migrant group. The direct and indirect influence of migrant peers is at a maximum, therefore, amongst those entering manual occupations.

Some evidence of this indirect and direct influence of migrant peers is provided by relating changes in migration plans between 1965 and 1968 to the number of other migrant sibs in the family. The results presented in Table XLIX show clearly that respondents with two or more migrant sibs were more likely to change their minds toward migrating between 1965 and 1968 than those with one sib migrated or none at all. Both amongst those who intended to stay in 1965, and amongst those who were then unsure about their plans, between two thirds and three quarters of those with two or more migrant sibs had already migrated by 1968 or intended to do so shortly. The equivalent figures amongst those with no sib migrated are one third and one half respectively. The percentage differences involved are between 20 and 30 percentage points. Curiously, the position is exactly the reverse in the case of those respondents who had intended to migrate in 1965; those with the smaller number of migrant sibs were more likely to persist with their original plans, whilst those with two or more migrant sibs were more likely to change their mind and stay locally. The percentage differences in this case are much smaller, however. Although these findings are not conclusive, they clearly indicate the important influence of migrant peers in migration behaviour. Any future research in this area should attempt to measure these influences directly.

TABLE XLIX: PROPORTION OF RESPONDENTS MIGRATED OR INTENDING TO MI-GRATE IN 1968 AS RELATED TO THE NUMBER OF SIBS MIGRATED AND MIGRATION PLANS IN 1965

MIGRATION INTENTIONS 1965	Number of sibs migrated					
	None		One		Two or more	
	Percentage migrated by 1968 or intending to migrate					
	%		%		%	
Definitely stay	36	(33)	20	(20)	67	(15)
Not sure	52	(31)	63	(27)	71	(41)
Definitely go	88	(26)	79	(19)	73	(51)

In conclusion, therefore, there appear to be two major classes of variables involved in migration decision making: those related to occupational and consumption aspirations and perceived oppor-tunities, and those related to the expectations and sanctions of one's family and peers. Variations in both sets of variables appear to explain most of the differences in migration decisions. The relation-ships between these variables could be diagrammed as follows: where the arrows represent hypothesised causal relationships

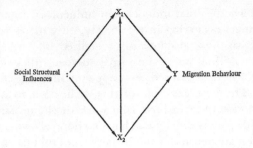

X_1 = Occupational status and consumption aspiration variables.

X_2 = Expectations and sanctions of parents and peers; i.e. Family Obligations and migrant peer influences.

both X_1 and X_2 are hypothesised to have a direct causal influence on Y. X_2 has also an additional indirect effect through its effects on X_1. This would occur through the reference group effects of migrant peers on non-migrant aspirations and satisfactions, etc.

It is noteworthy that Community Satisfaction has disappeared out of the model entirely. In this study at least, it appeared to have minimal independent effects on the final decisions. From a theoretical point of view, however, it is such an important variable that it would need to be investigated further before completely rejecting it. Major cultural and structural differences still exist in many countries between rural and urban communities. The family, religious and educational institutions differ widely between urban and rural areas, as do neighbourhood and community structures. The socialisation and social control processes also vary, as do beliefs and values. It seems highly likely that differences in levels of cultural alienation, or alternatively of high levels of attachment to the home community, should influence migration plans. However, in this study the attitude scale used had only a limited relationship to migration when the effects of Occupational Frustration were controlled. The variable is highly correlated with Occupational Frustration and to some extent appears to "lie behind" or to buttress the decision to stay of many respondents who are happily working away in traditional occupations which provide only a low level of living and appear to have very poor prospects for the future. At this level, however, the variable is so highly correlated with Family Obligations and Occupational Frustration that it appears to have minimal independent influence. Despite the major cultural changes occurring in the society, very many young people appear to have been so efficiently socialised into traditional roles that they are willing and even eager to spend their lives in roles which to their more urbanised peers appear stultifying or even highly frustrating. The best example of this dedication to a traditional system is the case of farm boys who work the home farm, who receive very little pocket money and have no hope of ownership or of an independent managerial role on the farm until middle age. Marriage has also to be postponed for the same period, if, indeed, they can hope to get married at all. Of course, these latter considerations do not become important to the person until his late twenties. Football playing, dancing, occasional courting, and all the other sporting and recreational activities of a young man employed on the home farm provide a very satisfying life for him even with the little pocket money available. However, considerations of ownership and of marriage, and the continuous irritations of a bossy father who leaves no initiative in one's own hands, may drive many of these people out of the home community in their late twenties. In the long run, therefore, this variable of structural alienation is likely to have an independent influence. However, at the present stage it appears to have little independent effect. The variable, however, has many unresolved problems of conceptualisation and measurement which still need to be ironed out before coming to a final conclusion on its place in the migration behaviour of young rural people.

In the original study, variation in the motivational variables was satisfactorily explained as being due to a corresponding variation in certain social structural factors. Differences in a person's position in the social structure—by social class or occupational background, educational level, sex, distance of one's home from the centre etc.—were shown to have a direct influence on levels of aspiration, beliefs about their local attainment, levels of family obligations etc., and consequently on migration plans. However, the intervening effects of migrant peers were at a minimum in 1965. These effects might have subsequently reduced or changed the magnitude of these differentials in actual migration. The following chapter examines the effects of these structural factors, to see to what extent the previously observed differentials are upheld in actual behaviour.

9. *Actual Migration Differentials*

In this chapter, all the major structural variables examined in chapters 5 and 6 are reconsidered to see to what extent the originally observed differentials and the reasons for them also hold good in actual migration. Firstly, occupational and educational differentials are examined. Secondly, sex differentials are examined, remoteness is considered, and in conclusion there is an investigation of social class differentials.

(i) LEVEL OF OCCUPATIONAL ACHIEVEMENT AND EDUCATION

The results presented in Chapter 5 showed a very close relationship between levels of aspiration or attainment and migration intentions. Less than one tenth of the non-manual aspirers definitely intended to remain locally, while more than one quarter of the manual aspirers intended to do so. This selectivity in migration was shown to be due to the decreasing extent that opportunities matched aspirations as the level of respondents' aspirations and qualifications increased. Does the same situation obtain in actual migration? The results presented in Table L clearly indicate that occupational status is certainly very highly related to the opportunity of getting one's first job locally.

Overall, just over three quarters of all respondents took up their first job locally. Almost all of those who first entered lower manual occupations or farming were able to do so locally. At the other extreme, less than one tenth of those entering professional-managerial, and only two thirds of those entering intermediate non-manual positions, were able to do so. Those entering service and skilled manual occupations appear to be almost as likely as the unskilled to take up the first job at home. These results seem to give very strong support to the original argument. However, very many of those who had first taken up a job locally had already migrated by

TABLE L: PROPORTION OF RESPONDENTS ENTERING THEIR FIRST JOB LOCALLY BY THE OCCUPATIONAL STATUS OF THE JOB CONCERNED

Location of first job		Level of occupational status of first job					
		Professional, semi-prof. and managerial	Farming	Intermediate non-manual	Skilled manual	Service	Semiskilled unskilled
Percentage in home community	%	7	100	66	88	87	93
TOTAL	N	14	44	74	34	47	41

TABLE LI: PERCENTAGES OF RESPONDENTS INTENDING TO MIGRATE OR STAY BY THE STATUS LEVEL OF OCCUPATION ACHIEVED BY 1968

Level of Occupational Achievement 1968

	*Professional Semi-professional and Managerial	Farming	Inter-mediate Non-manual	Skilled Manual	Service	Semiskilled and unskilled Manual
	%	%	%	%	%	%
(i) Migration Intentions 1965						
Percentage who def. intend to stay	12	65	13	39	33	20
	%	%	%	%	%	%
(ii) Migration Behaviour 1968						
Def. or prob. stay	5	88	38	53	29	38
Prob. or def. migrate	—	12	17	26	19	23
Already migrated	95		45	21	52	40
TOTAL %	100	100	100	100	100	100
N	41	26	71	38	48	40

$X^2 = 52$, $P < .05$; Gamma (excl. Farming) $= .280$ (5 values of migration), $= .230$ (3 values).

* Including 15 university and training college students in their second or third years at college.

1968, and many more still intended to migrate. Consequently, the location of the first job is not necessarily indicative of one's final location. Table LI relates the 1968 level of occupational achievement of respondents to their migration position in 1968, as well as their previous migration plans in 1965.

The results here show that the relationship is in fact greatly reduced from what appeared to be the position in 1965 (See Table LXXVIII, Appendix IV, also). Although a higher proportion of professional and semi-professional workers have migrated than intended to in 1965, a much higher proportion of intermediate non-manual and skilled manual workers have stayed and intend to stay in the home community than formerly intended to. Almost forty per cent of intermediate non-manual workers now intend to stay locally, in contrast to only slightly more than one tenth who intended to do so in 1965. The position is not so extreme for the skilled manual workers, but far more of them now plan to stay than intended to in 1965. On the other hand, service workers especially have been more migratory than one would have expected from their 1965 intentions, while the poorly skilled manual workers, although not as migratory as the service workers, are far more migratory than the skilled workers. The overall relationship between the two variables is, therefore, curvilinear rather than linear, with the highest proportions migrating from both the top and the bottom of the scale.

It appears, therefore, that many more of those in intermediate non-manual and skilled manual occupations, and far fewer of those in service occupations, were able to get satisfactory jobs locally than had expected to. This was in fact the case, since only slightly more than a quarter of the 47 skilled and intermediate non-manual workers who now intend to stay in the home community had definitely intended to stay in 1965, while just over one third had actually intended to migrate in 1965. On the other hand, only three of the 29 service and poorly skilled manual workers had so dramatically changed their minds from intending to migrate in 1965 to intending to stay locally in 1968. Of all the (21) respondents who had changed their minds toward staying in this way, 15 were in non-manual or skilled manual occupations. Very few of the poorly skilled met with such unexpected opportunities. Most of them, in fact, appear to have been far too optimistic about opportunities in 1965, while the non-manual appear to have been too pessimistic.

Census figures bear out this explanation.[1] In the period 1961-6 the decline in the number of unskilled manual workers in County Cavan was even greater than that occurring amongst farmers or farm workers—a decline of 17 per cent compared to a decline of 13 and 15 per cent respectively amongst farmers and farmers' relatives, and farm labourers. These three groups combined comprise over two thirds of the total labour force in the county. Although there has been considerable expansion in skilled manual and non-manual employment in the county—the number in skilled manual employment increased by 21 per cent and in all non-manual employment by 4 per cent in the period 1961–1966— the base is so small that it cannot possibly absorb all the off-farm migrants. Although the rate of decline in unskilled manual opportunities is greater in Cavan than in other counties, this decline is nevertheless general throughout rural Ireland. There are some exceptional counties, however, where local industries utilising relatively unskilled labour have been expanding. Even though in Ireland as a whole the number of unskilled manual jobs remained relatively stable in the period 1961–66, the high rate of unemployment in the country is almost completely restricted to the unskilled.[2] This decline in unskilled manual employment is widely prevalent in more industrialised countries. The British figures showed a decline of 3 per cent in unskilled manual employment in the period 1956–61,[3] while the United States figures showed a similar decline for the period 1960–1965.[4]

It appears, then, that persons seeking jobs at the service and lower manual levels are almost equally unable to get satisfactory openings locally as are those seeking higher non-manual jobs. It is highly significant in this respect that of the 88 respondents who first entered service, semiskilled and unskilled manual employment, exactly half had already migrated by 1968, and of these just over 70 per cent had left the country. On the other hand, of the 95 respondents first entering non-manual employment, 54 had already left the community, and of these only 20 (37 per cent) had left

[1] Census of Population of Ireland, Vol. IV, 1966, *Occupations*, and Vol. IV, 1961.

[2] *Investment in Education*, Department of Education, Stationery Office, Dublin, 1965, 178; and a forthcoming publication by Geary and Hughes in the ESRI Series.

[3] *Ministry of Labour Gazette*, "Occupational changes in Great Britain, 1951–1961", January 1968, 6–7.

[4] *Statistical Abstract of the United States*, 1965.

the country. This clear distinction in the destination of migrants cannot simply be explained on the basis of the relative distribution of opportunities. There is, in fact, a much faster expansion in non-manual jobs in Britain than in Ireland, and a proportionately greater contraction in unskilled and semiskilled employment opportunities there, as already noted.[5] However, the employment of unskilled manual workers is still increasing in the construction and manufacturing industries in Britain.[6] Since there are almost five times as many unskilled manual workers in the British construction industry as in all industries in Ireland, the attraction of these two British industries for Irish unskilled workers can easily be appreciated. Given these facts and the generally higher level of education of native British entrants to the labour force, plus the appreciably higher wage rates in Britain, this demand for Irish unskilled labour will probably continue for some time.

In general, therefore, these characteristics of migration and emigration from this community reflect national patterns pretty closely, and support Lynch *et alii* in their conclusions about the characteristics of emigration from Ireland.[7]

Migration from this community appears, therefore, to be selective of both the high and low achievers. This is due primarily to the relative number of satisfactorily renumerated opportunities becoming available at different occupational levels in the local community. The initial assumption that respondents aiming for higher non-manual employment would be more highly migratory than all others needs to be revised in the light of contracting opportunities at the lower manual level also. Of course, if an expansion in employment occurred at the lower manual level, as has occurred in some counties, migration selection would be somewhat closer to that originally hypothesised.[8] To determine the bases on which migrants

[5] All non-manual workers increased by 27 per cent in Britain in the period 1956–61, while the equivalent increase in Ireland in the period 1961–66, when expansion was faster, was only 9 per cent.

[6] *Ministry of Labour Gazette, op. cit.*

[7] *Investment in Education, op. cit.,* 178, 180, 201; See also The Economist Intelligence Unit, *Studies on Immigration from the Commonwealth,* London 1963. This data shows that there is a considerable over-supply of poorly educated unskilled workers in the Irish labour force, and that the majority of Irish emigrants to Britain are very poorly educated and are concentrated in manual worker categories.

[8] The County of Westmeath, for instance, showed a major expansion in unskilled employment in the same period, due primarily to the activities of Bord Na Mona. Census of Population of Ireland, 1966, Vol. IV, *op. cit.*

will be selected in any community, therefore, the structure of each new cohort's educational and occupational aspiration level has to be matched against the structure of new and permanent occupational opportunities that become available at the time that these people first enter the labour market. Both structures can vary widely among communities and, therefore, the bases on which migrants will be selected will also vary.

In this connection it is important that the jobs be permanent, since so many jobs available to poorly educated adolescent workers in rural communities are "dead-end" jobs—e.g. shop assistants, petrol pump attendants, lorry drivers' helpers, temporary farm and non-farm labourers, etc. These serve only as temporary jobs until the individual is old enough to migrate to better employment elsewhere. For this reason, the extent to which the individual is able to get his first job locally is a poor indication of subsequent migration, although the characteristics of first employment do strongly support the original hypothesis.

The highly unsatisfactory nature of these local jobs can be easily gauged from the fact that, before leaving home, the average wage earned by those migrants who had started off in service, semiskilled and unskilled jobs locally was only £3.10s. per week. On the other hand, the average wage of those currently in similar status jobs, and who intend to stay, was (in 1968) £7 per week. These latter jobs also were of a more permanent nature—in factories, creameries, etc. These particular "manual migrants" make up the bulk of those who leave for primarily economic reasons, and would be those most likely to stay if economic conditions were to improve in this area. They are also the most affected by migrant reference group factors, and are least likely to have the support of parents in their migration.

In conclusion, occupational selectivity in migration operates in a less clearcut manner than at first hypothesised. Nevertheless, it remains the major selective force in migration. The extent and characteristics of migration from each new cohort depends on the extent its skills can be utilised and aspirations fulfilled in the local community context. The kind of skills that can be utilised or the kind of aspirations that can be fulfilled depends primarily on the local labour market. Aspirations and skills can, of course, also vary. The major factor influencing both of these latter variables is education. Communities exist where the local educational system is so good that it raises the level of entry of its school leavers into the labour force above the level present in the locality, although there are plenty of well-paid manual jobs available locally.[9] As a result, most of the local highly educated cohort migrate, while local manual jobs are filled by less well educated in-migrants. On the other hand, where the educational system is poorly developed, many of the higher non-manual positions in the community may also be filled by in-migrants.[10]

This concludes consideration of occupational selectivity factors. The following section examines the relationship between level of education achieved and migration behaviour. Considering the results just examined, this relationship is unlikely to be as clearcut as appeared to be the case in Chapter Five. The improved prospects in skilled manual and intermediate non-manual employment should be to the advantage of the vocationally educated. The primary educated, on the other hand, may be more migratory than expected. The following section examines these possibilities.

Education

In the original survey, migration plans were found to be highly related to education. In the total population surveyed, roughly one tenth of the secondary educated, one quarter of the vocational and one third of the primary educated had definitely intended to remain at home. As can be seen below (Table LII), the sample figures are slightly different,[11] but a similar trend remains.

There are minimal differences between the primary and vocational group in either their 1965 or 1968 migration plans or behaviour. Roughly one third of these in 1965, and one half in 1968, intended to remain locally. Less than half that proportion of the secondary educated group intended to do so, however, while more than twice as many of the latter had already migrated. If we restrict consideration to the off-farm workers amongst the primary educated, however, it emerges that only slightly more than one

---

[9] Williams, J. L., "Some Social Consequences of Grammar School Education in a Rural Area in Wales", *Brit. Journal of Sociology* (1959) 10, 2, 125 ff.

[10] Geschwind, R. D. and Ruttan, V. W., *Job Mobility and Migration in a Low Income Rural Community*, Purdue University A.E.S., September 1961, Bulletin 730.

[11] The main reason for these differences, amongst the vocationally educated particularly, is the restriction of this sample to respondents within the community boundaries who are therefore more likely to get a satisfactory job locally.

TABLE LII: MIGRATION INTENTIONS AND BEHAVIOUR OF RESPONDENTS IN 1965
AND 1968, BY LEVEL OF EDUCATION RECEIVED

	Level of education received		
(i) *Migration intentions, 1965:*	Primary	Vocational	Secondary
Percentage who definitely intend to stay %	31	33	15
(ii) *Migration behaviour, 1968:*	%	%	%
Definitely or probably stay	49	49	20
Definitely or probably migrate	20	17	12
Already migrated	31	34	68
TOTAL %	100	100	100
N	85	89	95

$X^2 = 17.3$; $P < .05$;   Gamma $= .415$.

third of these will stay locally—somewhat more than the secondary
educated group, but far less than the vocationally educated group.

It was hypothesised that any educational differences in migration could be explained on the basis of occupational selection alone.
The more highly educated are more migratory, not because of
their education *per se*, but because they enter non-manual occupations to a far greater extent than others, and these occupations are
concentrated in urban areas to a far greater extent than others.[12]
If this is the case, therefore, and we control for the effects of occupational status achieved, education should have minimal additional
effects on migration behaviour. The following table (LIII) was set
up to see if this is, in fact, the case.

The results presented in this table show minimal differences
between the primary and vocational group in their migration
plans. Any small differences present in the percentages staying
locally between these two groups could easily be accounted for by
errors due to aggregation in the case of the manual group, or to
random error due to the small numbers involved in other cases.
For instance, for those entering all manual occupations, the vocational group are less migratory than the primary because over half
of the former but only one seventh of the latter had taken up skilled

[12] Hofstee, E. W., *Some Remarks on Selective Migration*, Martinus Nijhoff, The
Hague, 1952.

TABLE LIII: THE RELATIONSHIP BETWEEN EDUCATIONAL LEVEL ACHIEVED AND
MIGRATION, CONTROLLING FOR THE EFFECTS OF OCCUPATIONAL STATUS ACHIEVED

EDUCATIONAL LEVEL ACHIEVED	Occupational status of current job (1968)			
	Farming	All non-manual	All manual	Total number
	Percentages quoted are of the numbers in each cell who definitely or probably intend to remain at home			
	%	%	%	
Primary	88 (16)	50 (6)*	34 (62)	84
Vocational	100 (5)	47 (30)	46 (54)	89
Secondary	80 (5)	16 (77)	25 (12)*	94
TOTAL N	(26)	(113)	(148)	267

*A number of exceptional cases reduced the correlation between education received and occupation achieved. Six primary educated respondents entered non-manual occupations. One of these had taken up a partnership in a local small furniture manufacturing firm, two were employed as book-keepers in local shops; and one, an exceptionally intelligent girl, had emigrated to New York to take up a job as a waitress. She had made such a favourable impression on one of her customers, however, that she was taken into a stockbroking firm to train as a receptionist. A somewhat similar situation held in the case of some of the secondary educated who had taken up manual jobs. Some of these had to remain at home because of family obligations and had taken up manual employment to supplement a low income from the home farm.

manual occupations. Far more of the vocational group also entered the lower level non-manual occupations which provided a better opportunity to remain locally than the lower manual occupations entered by the primary group. By and large, therefore, occupational selection explains the differences in migration behaviour between the primary and vocational group.

This conclusion, however, does not hold good in the case of the secondary group. A far lower proportion of the secondary group entering non-manual occupations plan to stay locally than is true in the vocational group. Part of this difference is again explained by the far greater tendency of the secondary group to enter the higher professional occupations. Almost none of these higher non-manual achievers intend to remain locally, compared to nearly half of the intermediate non-manual group who do intend to do so. The major part of the difference is explained on this basis alone. However, when we restrict consideration to the intermediate non-manual group itself, it transpires that the secondary group is still far more migratory than the vocational. Roughly half of the vocational, but only one quarter of the secondary group, intend to stay locally. This is the only group, in fact, in which the two percentages are significantly different.

The differences between the vocational and secondary group respondents entering intermediate non-manual occupations appear to be of two kinds. First, there were some intrinsic differences in the kinds of jobs entered. The majority of the vocational group took up jobs as office clerks and typists etc., and almost all of them were girls. The secondary group, on the other hand, entered a far wider range of jobs—as bank clerks, policemen, laboratory technicians, reporters etc., and almost a third of them were boys. Even given these sex and occupational differences, however, many secondary girls who had migrated had taken up the same kind of occupation as non-migrant vocational girls. The differences here were not concerned with the type of job taken up, but with the status of the firm worked with. Working as a clerk typist in a local firm, shop, solicitor's office or the County Council, etc., does not appear as prestigious or attractive to the secondary educated girl as working in the same kind of job for a bank, the civil service etc., or with a national prestige firm such as Aer Lingus. Many of these girls, in fact, when asked for their occupational aspirations, had specified the firm they wanted to work for, rather than the particular occupation desired. Besides this factor of firm prestige, however, almost two thirds of the secondary educated girls, as compared to less than one quarter of all others, had said that they would not remain at home permanently, even if they could fulfill all their occupational and consumption aspirations there. There appears to be a complex of aspirations and attitudes involved in the migration of the secondary educated girls, of which occupational prestige is only a part. They appear to be a deviant group in this respect, however. In the case of all others, if their occupational and consumption aspirations can be fulfilled locally they are nearly all likely to stay there. With this one exception, therefore, occupational selection explains the educational differences observed in migration.

In conclusion, therefore, it is the close association between education and occupational status achieved that explains educational differentials in migration. Occupational achievement is very closely related to education received. Over four fifths of the secondary educated entered non-manual occupations, compared to one third of the vocational and only slightly more than one twentieth of the primary educated. At the other extreme, the primary educated are almost as equally concentrated in service and poorly skilled manual occupations as the secondary are in the non-manual. Both extremes are almost equally oversubscribed in terms of the numbers seeking opportunities locally. With some minor exceptions, therefore, differences in migration among educational groups are due to corresponding differences in occupational opportunities. Occupational selection is the main selective force at work.

It was initially hypothesised that occupational selection would also account for sex differences in migration. The evidence considered in relation to migration intentions strongly supported this hypothesis. However, subsequent migration has not always conformed to original plans. The following section examines the extent to which sex differences in actual migration conform to previous differences in migration intentions.

(ii) SEX SELECTIVITY IN MIGRATION

Sex differences in migration intentions (1965) were very clearcut, and were explained as being due to three local selection processes, all related to occupational selectivity. The first of these referred to the male domination of farming as an occupation. In a community with a large proportion of farm families, at least one male in every family can remain on the farm, while a very small number of farm girls can or would like to do so. As a result, unless local off-farm opportunities are heavily biassed toward female employment, far more girls will migrate. A second factor had also intervened, however: the higher level of education received by those girls who were not employed on their home farms. A third factor related to the tendency of vocational educated girls to aspire to occupations of a higher level and a lesser availability than vocational educated boys. However, we have already seen that far more intermediate non-manual jobs—mostly open to girls—and far fewer manual jobs—almost completely dominated by boys—were available locally than had been expected. In this situation, actual sex selectivity in migration may not be as clearcut as respondents' intentions had suggested.

The results presented in the following table demonstrate that something like this must have occurred, since far more girls have stayed at home than would have been expected from their 1965 intentions.

TABLE LIV: MIGRATION INTENTIONS (1965) AND MIGRATION BEHAVIOUR (1968) OF MALES AND FEMALES

Migration, 1965 *and* 1968		Migration intentions 1965		Migration behaviour 1968	
		Male	Female	Male	Female
Definitely intend to stay		35%	17%	28%	23%
Not sure but probably will stay		32%	44%	14%	11%
Not sure but probably will migrate				12%	7%
Definitely migrate		33%	39%	6%	6%
Already migrated				40%	52%
TOTAL	%	100	100	100	100
	N	142	126	139	126

$$X^2 = 10.16; \ P < .05 \qquad X^2 = 5.9; \ P > .75 \\ < .90$$

The proportion of males intending to stay at home in 1965 was more than twice that of females. However, by 1968 only five per cent more males than females definitely intended to stay, although a further three per cent more males than females said they probably would stay. In total, therefore, the proportion of males actually remaining permanently in the home community is only slightly greater than the proportion of females. In fact the 1968 sex differences in migration behaviour are not statistically significant by conventional standards.

It appears from this that more of the girls were able to find satisfactory roles locally than had expected to, while the reverse seems to be true of the boys. An analysis of the sex characteristics of respondents who actually changed their minds about migration in the interim appears to bear this out. Of the 58 males who now plan to remain in the home community, 31 had definitely intended to stay in 1965 (53 per cent), whereas this was true of only 12 of the 43 females (28 per cent). The girls, therefore, appear to have been too pessimistic in 1965, whereas the boys were, if anything, over-

TABLE LV:

SEX OF RESPONDENTS	Professional managerial and proprietorial	Farming	Intermediate non-manual	Skilled manual	Service	Semiskilled and unskilled manual
	%	%	%	%	%	%
Male (N = 143)	13	15	13	26	18	16
Female (N = 125)	18	4	42	2	13	20

optimistic. These unexpected changes in plans by the girls are probably due to the greater number of opportunities at the intermediate non-manual level that are available locally. Since girls enter these occupations to a much greater extent than boys, many more of them than had previously expected to were able to get satisfactory jobs locally. Table LV shows the distribution of jobs amongst the two sexes.

This also means that such migration plan changes would be far more likely to occur amongst the vocationally educated girls, since these girls enter such non-manual jobs to a much greater extent than the primary educated, and are also far more likely to stay than the secondary educated girls if these aspirations are satisfied locally. The results below appear to bear this reasoning out.

TABLE LVI: THE PROPORTION OF RESPONDENTS INTENDING TO STAY AT HOME IN 1965 AND 1968 AS RELATED TO EDUCATIONAL LEVEL AND SEX

	Level of Education received by respondents					
	Primary		Vocational		Secondary	
	Male	Female	Male	Female	Male	Female
	%	%	%	%	%	%
(a) *Migration intentions* 1965 Definitely intend to stay	33 (55)	27 (30)	55 (44)	18 (45)	18 (44)	12 (51)
(b) *Migration behaviour* 1968 Definitely and probably stay	49 (55)	50 (30)	59 (44)	40 (45)	20 (44)	20 (51)
	X^2 n.s.		$X^2 = 3.2$; $p > .90 < .95$		X^2 n.s.	

These figures show that the major sex differences in migration planning in 1965 occurred amongst the vocationally educated. Three times as many vocational males as females had intended to stay at home in 1965. There were minimal sex differences amongst the other educational groups, although slightly fewer females intended to stay in each case. In 1968 there are no sex differences within the other educational groups, and the only sex difference occurring in the vocational group is much smaller than in 1965, and in fact is not statistically significant. The sex difference observed in this group is due to the major difference between the sexes in their aspirations and school training. Over 60 per cent of the vocational girls entered non-manual positions, most of them into intermediate positions. On the other hand, only two of the boys entered non-manual positions, but over 60 per cent entered skilled manual occupations—i.e. the boys entered more available occupations than the girls.

More of the primary educated girls have been able to stay locally than one might have expected, given their very low level of occupational achievement. In general, they are the least migratory of all educational groups, while the vocational group is the least migratory amongst the boys. However, these differences between the primary and vocational educated are not statistically significant.

A third factor influencing sex selectivity in migration was the high level of education received by the girls. Seventy six per cent of the girls received a postprimary education, compared to only 62 per cent of the boys. The fact that there were so few primary educated girls (see Table LVI) probably accounts for their relatively greater success in finding satisfactory roles locally.

Actual sex selectivity in migration, therefore, is greatly reduced. What still remains is due firstly to the greater migration tendency of the vocationally educated girls than boys, and secondly to the larger proportion of girls receiving a postprimary education. As previous analyses have shown, this educational selectivity is restricted to those from a farm background, although girls from a skilled manual and service background also tended to receive a better education. An examination of sex differences in migration by occupational background reveals that only in the farm group do consistent sex differences exist. (Table LVII).

The only place where consistent and significant sex differences appear is amongst the farm origin group. Here, nearly 50 per cent more boys than girls intend to remain locally, while the proportion of girls already migrated is almost twice that of boys. The greater proneness to migration of the farm girls is accounted for by the greater tendency of the farm males to stay at home on the farm, and by the greater tendency of the farm girls to go on for further education.

These results do not consistently support the original hypotheses and rationale, except in this latter case where sex selectivity is

TABLE LVII: MIGRATION BEHAVIOUR (1968) BY SEX AND OCCUPATIONAL BACK-
GROUND

Migration 1968	Father's occupation					
	All non-manual		Farmer		All manual	
	Male	Female	Male	Female	Male	Female
	%	%	%	%	%	%
Definitely and probably intend to stay	14	13	57	42	34	40
Probably and definitely migrate	38	16	16	8	23	19
Already migrated	48	71	27	51	43	40
TOTAL %	100	100	100	100	100	100
N	21	31	75	53	47	42
	X^2 n.s.		$X^2 = 9.5; p < .05$		X^2 n.s.	

indeed restricted to those from farm backgrounds. Although the
sex differences are not statistically significant for the vocationally
educated group, they remain the only place where migration differences are consistently reproduced. The lack of significance appears
to be due to two factors: sex differences in general are much smaller
than expected, and the numbers involved are too small to show
significant differences where this is the case. It seems very likely,
in fact, given the results of the significance tests in the case of
occupational groups, that real sex differences are present amongst
the vocational group, and that they are accounted for by the factors
proposed.

The arguments put forward to account for the greater migratory
tendency of girls assumed that boys and girls migrated for more or
less the same set of motives. The reason why girls tend to migrate
more than boys is due primarily to the fact that a larger proportion
of them aspire to higher status and generally less available jobs
than boys, and not to any unique set of factors which do not affect
boys. Marriage chances, unique recreational needs, etc., might be
some of these other unconsidered factors, and could be important.
If this assumption were valid, the strength of the relationship
between the original set of motives proposed and migration behaviour in 1968 should be approximately equal for both boys and

girls. Is this, in fact, the case? The following table summarises these relationships, using Gamma as an index of association.

TABLE LVIII: The association (Gamma) between the five motivational variables as measured in 1965, and migration behaviour in 1968, controlling for sex

Migration behaviour 1968	Occupational frustration 1965	Income frustration 1965	Family obligation 1965	Community Sat. 1965	Community Evaluation 1965
Males	.488	.248	.454	.128	.068
Females	.348	.111	.327	.197	.289

There are in fact no significant differences between boys and girls in any of these correlations.[13] In general, although the socio-economic variables appear to predict better for males than for females while the reverse is the case for the attitudinal variables, these differences could be due to chance. Occupational Frustration and Family Obligations still remain the two most predictive variables for both sexes. Income Frustration appears to be the third most predictive for males, but it is the least important for females. Community Evaluation, in fact, becomes almost as predictive as Family Obligations for females. The additional effect of Community Evaluation for females is, however, considerably reduced by the much higher correlation it has with Occupational Frustration. As a result, even if these differences are statistically significant, the joint effects of Occupational Frustration and C.E. are somewhat less for females than for males. In general, therefore, although the assumption of similar migration motives for both sexes is not strongly supported by the evidence, there is, on the other hand, no strong evidence to reject it.

Sex differences can, therefore, be explained on the basis of occupational selection alone. There is no need to propose a unique set of motives which are operative for females but not for males. The only case where unique motives seem to be important is in the case

[13] The significance tests were carried out by initially calculating the Pearsonian correlations for each of the relationships, and testing for the significance of the differences between the two correlations for each relationship. See Walker and Lev, *Statistical Inference*, Holt, Rinehart and Winston, NY, 1953, 255–6.

of secondary educated girls. Here, however, they are so highly correlated with other considered factors that they do not add very much to the explanation given. Since, in any case, these secondary educated girls would not be able to get the kind of jobs and opportunities they want in the local community, even if it were to industrialise rapidly, the additional motives concerned in their migration would not come into play. In the case of other girls, although the evidence suggests that socio-economic factors are somewhat less important for girls than boys, the main factors operating in selecting for migration are educational and occupational factors.

One cannot, however, apply generalisations based on these results to an older age group. The respondents were aged between 20 and 21 in 1968. As far as the girls were concerned, marriage opportunities, although much more important to them at this time than in 1965, were still not a vital concern. The great majority did not expect to get married until 23 or 24. Although they were all highly involved in dancing and courtship, marriage was still in the future for them. By 1971 or so, however, it may seem to many of these girls that marriage has passed them by. If not engaged, or at least "going steady" by that time, very many of them are likely to reconsider their migration decisions on this basis alone. Much the same situation would hold in the case of farmers' sons working at home on the farm. The frustrations involved in the deferment of full adult status due to this role are not likely to reach "boiling point" until their late 20s or early 30s. The relevance of different migration motives, therefore, are likely to change over time as the person enters a different stage in the life cycle. Occupational, consumption and recreational factors are likely to be very important for the adolescent. Marriage is still viewed as being in the distant future. By the late 20s or early 30s, however, such considerations would become vital and the motives that would be significant at an earlier age may drop out of the reckoning. If one cannot generalise from one particular community context to another, it is even more dangerous to generalise from one age group to another.

At this particular point in time, however, the original hypotheses which were put forward to explain sex differences in migration have been generally supported. The following section examines the extent to which this is also true for the effects of remoteness, or of distance of respondents' homes from the centre.

(iii) REMOTENESS AND MIGRATION DIFFERENTIALS

The original study had shown a clear relationship between the remoteness of respondents' homes and migration, the more remote being the least migratory and the most likely to take up full time jobs in the community. The data from the follow up study shows rather similar trends, as is evident from the following table.

TABLE LIX: Migration Intentions and behaviour of Respondents in 1965 and 1968 as related to the level of remoteness of their homes

	Remoteness		
Migration Intentions 1965	Centre and up to 2 miles from centre	All other towns and areas within 4 miles	More than 4 miles from centre
Percentage who definitely intend to stay	18	26	31
Gamma = .225			
Migration behaviour 1968	%	%	%
Definitely and probably stay	30	37	44
Definitely and probably migrate	18	18	14
Already migrated	52	45	42
TOTAL %	100	100	100
N	61	62	146

X² = 3.9;   P < .75;   Gamma = .157.

The results show a clear trend of decreasing migration with remoteness from the centre. However, as the Chi Square test has shown, these differences could be due to sampling errors. Nevertheless, the differences are so consistent and so similar to the original 1965 results that this seems very unlikely. Even if it is significant, however, the relationship is reduced, as the respective Gamma indexes indicate. This reduction in the relationship appears to be due to the fact that almost twice as many of those from the centre had stayed than intended to, while far fewer of the most remote respondents had changed their minds in this way. The proportions who had actually changed their minds toward staying at home support these conclusions. Exactly one third of those from the centre who now intend to stay permanently at home had actually intended to migrate in 1965, whereas this was true for only one sixth of those from the most remote areas. Local opportunities, therefore, appear to have been more favourably distributed to those from the centre than they had expected, whereas those from the most remote areas had been less successful in this respect.

A breakdown by education of respondents revealed that migration declined with remoteness for both the primary and secondary educated respondents, but the reverse was the case for the vocational educated. In this latter case, from half to two thirds of those from the centre and contiguous areas intended to remain permanently at home in 1968, while only 40 per cent of those from the most remote areas intended to do so. More than half of the latter had in fact migrated by 1968, compared to less than one fifth of the former. It appears from this that the vocationally-dominated skilled and non-manual jobs, almost three quarters of which are situated in the centre, are also disproportionately filled by respondents from the centre or neighbouring areas. On the other hand local semiskilled and unskilled manual jobs, dominated by the primary educated and only one quarter of which are situated in the centre, are correspondingly filled by respondents from the most remote areas. In both cases, therefore, the location of the job itself discriminates in favour of the least remote of the vocationally educated and the most remote of the primary educated; and since over three quarters of those currently in farming and intending to remain permanently in the community come from the most remote areas of the community, the occupational discrimination in favour of the most remote for the primary educated is further emphasised. In the case of service occupations, almost all of which are situated in the two least remote areas, however, nearly two thirds of the jobs are filled by respondents from the most remote areas.

In conclusion, therefore, the relationship of remoteness to migration has been reduced. Although the great majority of the non-migrants in local manual and service jobs who intend to remain at home do come from the most remote areas of the community, this is counterbalanced by an opposite selection of the least remote who are in skilled and non-manual jobs locally. The more remote in these latter cases have not only a poorer chance of getting any of these jobs locally but are also somewhat less likely to remain in the community full-time, even if they do take up a first job at this level locally. Unfortunately, the samples in each of these cases are so small that these conclusions are tentative rather than conclusive. In general, however, this data on remoteness supports the original findings, with the exception of the vocational group.

(iv) SOCIAL CLASS AND MIGRATION

The social class origins of respondents was shown to be closely related to educational achievement, level of aspiration and migration planning. More than 90 per cent of respondents from non-manual backgrounds had received a postprimary education, while this was true of less than half of those from lower manual backgrounds. Those whose fathers were skilled manual or service workers, or farmers, held intermediate positions. Much the same situation held within farming. While roughly four fifths of those from farms of over £30 valuation received some postprimary education, this was true for less than two thirds of those from poorer farm backgrounds.

TABLE LX: The migration intentions and migration behaviour of Respondents by occupational background

	Fathers' occupations			
(i) *Migration Intentions* 1965	All non-manual occupations	Farmers	Skilled manual and service occupations	Semiskilled and un-skilled manual occupations
Percentages who definitely intend to stay %	17	37	18	18
(ii) *Migration behaviour* 1968	%	%	%	%
Definitely and probably stay	13	51	39	35
Definitely and probably migrate	15	13	21	22
Already migrated	71	37	39	43
TOTAL %	100	100	100	100
N	52	128	38	51

$$X^2 = 39.8; \quad P < .05$$

These educational differences are naturally reflected in migration planning and behaviour, as the results presented in Table LX clearly show. Although there were, in fact, minimal differences between those from non-manual and manual backgrounds in their 1965 migration plans, there are considerable differences between these groups in their subsequent migration behaviour. Only slightly more than one tenth of the non-manual group definitely intended to stay at home in 1968, whereas this was true for well over one third of the manual and over half of the farm group. Those from farms are the least migratory, while those from non-manual backgrounds are the most migratory. The farm group showed this greater non-mobile tendency both in 1965 and 1968. On the other hand, a comparison of the 1965 and 1968 results shows that the non-manual and manual groups behave in exactly opposite ways to one another. The non-manual group have been even more migratory than they had intended to be in 1965, while the manual group have been far less inclined to migrate than one would expect from their 1965 intentions. Over twice as many of the manual group intended to remain locally in 1968 than had intended to in 1965, while the reverse was the case for the non-manual group, fewer of whom intended to stay in 1968 than in 1965. The farm group, on the other hand, had been only slightly more stationary than intended, the proportions staying increasing only from 37 to 51 per cent.

When we classify intentions ('65) against subsequent migration behaviour, these differences in plan changes become clearer. None of the seven respondents from non-manual backgrounds who now intend to stay locally had intended to migrate in 1965. On the other hand, over a third of the 33 manual respondents now staying had changed their minds in this way. The farm group was intermediate, with only one seventh changing their minds. These figures clearly reflect the educational and occupational differences between the different groups, with the manual-vocational group being the most likely to find unexpected opportunities locally.

There is, therefore, a very clear relationship between social class background and migration, much of it explainable on the basis of the relationship of both variables to educational mobility. But what is the relationship of social class and migration to social mobility? Not all of the middle class respondents who receive a secondary education are upwardly mobile, and not all of those who received only a primary education are downwardly mobile. Educational advancement and social mobility are not synonomous processes. Within classes or educational levels, therefore, the chance to achieve social mobility at home or in foreign countries is likely to be indirectly related to migration. Those who come from non-manual backgrounds obviously have much smaller chances of increasing or even maintaining their status by remaining in the home community than those from the bottom of the local class pyramid. A boy or a girl from a lower manual background who becomes a motor mechanic or a clerk typist in the home community experiences social mobility to the same extent as does any boy or girl from a non-manual background who becomes a doctor and has to migrate to become one. The unexpected increase in the proportion of the working class respondents who stayed locally may be partly due to the extent to which manual respondents were able to get these kinds of opportunities locally.

One major difficulty arises, however, in determining whether a respondent has achieved a higher status than that of his father. Farm respondents, as has already been noted, are not easily assigned to status categories comparable to the non-farm respondents. The solution adopted was to assign farmers to those non-farm occupational prestige categories which they most resembled in terms of average income. A farmer with an income equivalent to the average income enjoyed by skilled manual workers was assigned to that category. By using this approach, and by controlling for occupational

TABLE LXI: THE PROPORTION OF RESPONDENTS HAVING MIGRATED OR DEFINITELY PLANNING TO MIGRATE BY SOCIAL MOBILITY EXPERIENCE—COMPARING FATHERS' OCCUPATIONS TO THE CURRENT OCCUPATION OF RESPONDENTS—AND BY FATHERS' OCCUPATIONAL GROUP

Respondent's current occupation status relative to that of his father	Fathers' occupational status					
	All non-manual		Farmers		All manual	
	Percentage of respondents having migrated or definitely planning to migrate					
	%		%		%	
Higher	91	(11)	53	(40)	47	(49)
Same	78	(18)	30	(37)	54	(28)
Lower	73	(22)	26	(38)	88	(8)

background, Table LXI was set up to see whether social mobility is related to migration in the same way for each occupational class.

Although the numbers on which these percentages are based are generally too small to be confident of their statistical significance, a number of trends are so consistent that some clear implications are obvious.

Firstly, the higher the social status of one's father, the greater the need to migrate in order to increase or even maintain one's status. Conversely, the lower one's status background, the better one's chances of achieving upward mobility within one's home community. Non-manual respondents who occupy higher or even the same occupational status as their fathers have migrated to a far greater extent than have equally mobile farm or manual respondents.

Secondly, with the exception of the manual category, the higher the level of social mobility achieved the greater the rate of migration. The downwardly mobile amongst those from farms and non-manual backgrounds are less likely to migrate than the upwardly mobile. In fact, those from farm backgrounds who are downwardly mobile—mostly remote farm boys in manual occupations—are the least migratory of all occupational groups.

This is a very unusual pattern of mobility and migration. One would have expected that farm youth would not be any more likely to stay locally than working class youth in the same occupations. In fact, given their greater loss of prestige, one would have expected them to have been far more migratory, yet they are almost twice as likely to stay at home as are working class youth who achieved upward mobility. Prestige factors are apparently far less important for these youth than had been previously thought to be the case.[14] The reason why working class youth are not content with these jobs is because of the very poor wages offered. The remote farm youth have far lower levels of consumption aspiration, and prestige factors appear to be far less important than originally thought.

What is equally as interesting as this pattern of local recruitment is that the working class youth who are upwardly mobile — mostly girls in clerical work and boys in skilled manual work — are far more content than others to stay locally. New opportunities

---

[14] See Vercruijsse, E. V. W., *The Shannon Hinterland Survey*, Leyden University, Dept. of Sociology, Mimeo, 1961; and McNabb, P. "Social Structure" in Rev. J. Newman (Ed.), *The Limerick Rural Survey*, 1958–1964, 215 ff.

in the centre allow them to move up the social scale in a setting where such upward mobility is most relevant to them. Those who are able to move up statuswise into new opportunities seem to be the most likely to stay locally, with the single exception of the more traditional farm males who seem to be willing to stay locally under almost any circumstances.

An overall view of these results suggests that the local community is being denuded of its middle class elements and being replenished by people from farms and, to a lesser extent, from manual background. This can be illustrated by considering the origins of the total sample studied and of the respondents who intend to remain in the community permanently. Slightly less than one fifth of all respondents in the sample came from non-manual backgrounds, one third from manual, and slightly less than half from farms. However, of those respondents now intending to remain permanently in the home community, only slightly more than one twentieth came from non-manual backgrounds, slightly less than one third from manual, and two thirds from farm backgrounds. This fits in neatly with previous conclusions about the extent to which non-manual families from the centre were being replaced by remoter farm families, but also apparently by upwardly mobile manual families from the centre. A few reservations are in order, however. First, many of the higher non-manual positions in the community are being filled by outsiders, while this internal migration pattern is primarily limited to manual, service, and some intermediate non-manual and proprietorial positions. Secondly, some of those from the community who were at university in 1968 might later return to the community. However, this is very unlikely to be true of any more than four or five respondents in all. Thirdly, a rather high proportion of the fathers of respondents currently in local manual and non-manual positions were only one or two generations removed from farming themselves. There appears to be only a small proportion of current manual or no-manual parents who are more than two generations removed from the land. In other words, there is a limited traditional middle class or working class pool in the community, and these, when present, would tend to be restricted to the centre. Unfortunately, no directly relevant data was gathered on this, so that these conclusions are necessarily imprecise. The results, however, generally bear out Arensberg's argument of the gradual replenishment of the local middle class by those from a farm background and the gradual migration of the original middle class from the local community, as their sons and daughters move up into professional and semi-professional positions in more urbanised places in Ireland or abroad.[15]

(v) EDUCATION, CLASS AND MIGRATION

The main reason why more of those from a farm background were able to find satisfactory niches locally is due to two factors: firstly, their chances of being ascribed occupations on the home farm, and secondly, that they have a greater tendency than the non-manual group to move into vocational schools. Indeed, if respondents currently engaged in farming are excluded, there remain no differences in the migration behaviour of farm and manual origin respondents receiving a primary or vocational education. And, as previously noted, over twice as many vocational educated as secondary educated respondents are likely to remain locally. As a result, since over four fifths of the non-manual group achieving postprimary education went to secondary school and less than half of the farm group did so, their greater migration tendency was assured. On the other hand, there were some differences within the secondary educated group. Respondents from manual backgrounds were least likely to migrate. The farm group were intermediate, while the non-manual group were by far the most migratory. Since those who had left secondary schools before completing the course were concentrated amongst the manual and small farm group, and most of these had taken up intermediate non-manual jobs locally, this is, again, easily explainable. In each case here, however, the numbers involved become so small that these conclusions are disputable. Nevertheless they neatly fit in with previous discussions.

CONCLUSIONS

This completes the presentation of the results of the restudy. In general, the findings bear out the conclusions based on the 1965 results. There is one major exception in regard to occupational and educational selection: the primary educated or the low achievers generally have been far more migratory than was expected or indeed than they expected themselves. They were too optimistic about

[15] Arensberg, C. M., *The Irish Countryman*, Peter Smith, 1959, 146–80.

opportunities in 1965. On the other hand, the vocationally educated or those entering intermediate occupational statuses generally were too pessimistic in 1965. Their initial beliefs about local opportunities seem to have been biassed by other intervening factors. This may have been simply due to their increasing maturation since 1965. At that time, the young primary educated respondents were far more content with low paid dead-end type jobs, while their future perspectives were very limited. At the same time, the beliefs of the vocationally educated may have been biassed by their somewhat more negative attitude toward general community relationships. Their low levels of Community Satisfaction may have biassed their perceptions of the local opportunity structures at a time before they actually sought openings in it. It came as a very pleasant surprise to many of them that the picture was not quite as black as they had imagined it. The reverse seems to have been the case for the primary educated.

With these exceptions, the other findings on actual migration differentials—sex, remoteness and social class, etc.—confirmed previous findings.

The final chapter attempts to rationalise all the various trends of the study, and endeavours to reach some final conclusions about the motives involved in migration and the differentials observed. The monograph is then concluded with a final section on some of the practical implications of the study for the community concerned, and for the country generally.

10.   Conclusions and Implications

THIS monograph deals with two studies. The approach taken to these studies and the results presented have, it is hoped, elucidated many aspects of migration behaviour which have hitherto been unexplained. At the same time, the results from the two studies have appeared to contradict one another at many points. Some readers will no doubt wonder why both sets of results should have been presented in this way. However, since both studies dealt with the same people at different stages in their life cycle, it was necessary to discuss them separately. The purpose of this chapter is to attempt to correlate both sets of results, to resolve as far as possible any of the apparent contradictions present, as well as to indicate the utility of such longitudinal studies.

(1) Migration Motives and Decisions

Overall, the utility of the theoretical orientations which guided the research has generally been validated. The approach taken has emphasised that migration is due primarily to the frustration of certain aspirations in the community of origin. The hypotheses emphasised the predominant importance of occupational and consumption aspirations in explaining migration decisions and migration differentials. The main explanatory variable employed related to the facility or difficulty experienced by people in finding jobs locally which, in terms of their status and remuneration, satisfy the individual's aspirations. This process of local occupational selection has, in fact, proved a crucial variable in explaining individual decisions and in explaining why certain groups of individuals tend to be more migratory than others. This was true for both studies. It even helped to explain why many respondents had changed their minds between 1965 and 1968.

Family obligations were of equal importance, although they predicted actual behaviour better than they predicted intended behaviour. The degree of satisfaction with recreational and other social provisions in the home community proved to be relatively

237

unimportant in explaining the initial migration intentions or subsequent behaviour. If people are satisfied with their jobs and incomes, dissatisfaction with social provisions in the home community does not appear to influence migration behaviour to any great extent. This appears to be somewhat less true of girls than of boys, but the evidence here is not conclusive.

Much the same conclusion holds in regard to Community Satisfaction. Although it was highly related to intended migration it was a very poor predictor of actual migration. The reason for the decline in its predictive power appeared to be due to the fact that the highly attached respondents had overestimated their chances in 1965, while the highly detached had underestimated them. Such strong feelings of attachment to or detachment from the local community appeared to bias perceptions of the local community's opportunities in the initial stages of occupational decision-making. However, when the individual actually becomes involved in looking for a job instead of merely projecting what it is going to be like, or when he is actually working for a few years in his first trial occupations, such biasses appear to become relatively unimportant. Besides this apparent initial influence on biassing perceptions, such orientations toward the local community were also important for some particular types of non-migrants. Many respondents who intend to stay permanently in the home community are working in traditional occupations which appear to their more sophisticated peers to be highly unsatisfactory or even highly frustrating. This is especially true of boys and girls remaining on the home farm and working under the supervision of parents, who have no hope of an independent managerial role until their late thirties or so, and who have no hope of marriage until at least that age. Most of these have been so effectively socialised into this traditional system that they do not appear to find this frustrating. In this case, and in many others besides, the degree of dedication to the traditional system appears to be very important in their decision. For instance, many of those who migrated did not spend much time looking for local opportunities although many suitable ones were available. In this case also, one's dedication to or alienation from the traditional system would be an important differentiating variable. The fact that it did not appear to be so for this study may be due to the deficiencies of the scale used to measure this variable. This needs to be corrected in future research.

There may also be another reason why both attitudinal variables were more highly correlated with intended behaviour than with actual behaviour. This reason seems to revolve around the meaning of "intended migration" in 1965. The question had asked respondents to project themselves forward in time in order to tell us what they intended to do at some unspecified date in the future. In most cases, the responses expressed a previously existing state of mind which had been present for some time before the interview. Even in this situation, however, such an intention is necessarily based only on poorly-validated beliefs, and in this conjectural situation a statement of one's intentions may be partly an expression of what one would like to do at that particular time. Similarly, current feelings may easily bias one's perceptions of local opportunities. The final decision to stay or go is so contingent upon other future outcomes, many of which cannot be foreseen, that subsequent changes in plans appear inevitable. The important intervening conditions seem to be closely related to the success of one's job-hunting experiences and with the influences exerted by one's family and friends. For those who change their minds, the influences of family and friends seem to be as important as the outcome of one's search for local opportunities.

For these reasons, it appears that one cannot readily generalise about migration from data collected in two different periods of the life cycle. Migration decision-making amongst a particular cohort of adolescents growing up in any community proceeds in a series of stages which appear to duplicate each stage in the occupational decision-making process. When interviewed in 1965, the great majority of respondents were aged between 15 and 17, and were in the tentative or early trial stages of occupational decision-making. Less than five per cent of their peers had already migrated. By 1968, when the majority of respondents were aged between 19 and 21, almost all of them were in the final trial of stable stage of occupational decision-making, and almost half of them had already migrated. If we consider the occupational decision as preceding the migration decisions in the majority of cases,[1] then, as the person moves

[1] A very reasonable assumption, as some previous research and the general results of this study strongly indicate. See Harp, J., Morton, M. and Ruff, G. E. *Expectations and Realities: A Study of Migration Behaviour of Youth*, Cornell University Agric. Expt. Station, Bulletin No. 69, March 1967; and Payne, R., "Development of occupational and migration expectations among urban, small town and rural adolescent boys," *Rural Sociology*, 21, 2, June 1956, 117–26.

from the tentative to early trial stage of occupational choice, many previously unconsidered factors connected with job-seeking become important. And, as more and more of one's peers migrate, changes in occupational and consumption aspirations and beliefs about the desirability of different locations to fulfill these aspirations become more likely. The circumstances in which migration decisions are being taken have been radically altered. In 1965, the decisions were somewhat tentative and hypothetical. This would be especially true for respondents who had not made up their minds about the kind of jobs they wanted. By 1968, however, they had all been working for some years, and their familial, recreational, peer group and courtship roles had altered considerably. The group contexts in which decisions were being taken had changed. And, since the expectations and sanctions of others in these groups are of crucial importance in such a decision, the constraints that these introduce are apparently sufficient to overcome purely personal feelings.

If this is true of the period between 15 to 21, it is probably also true of later life. The migration intentions of respondents in 1968 are likely to be subject to change in the future, although these changes are very unlikely to be as great as they were during the period when respondents were first becoming involved in occupational life. Nevertheless, the roles an individual plays (as well as the relative importance of these roles) change as time passes. What was highly relevant, for instance, to an adolescent girl becoming involved in the world of work for the first time is likely to be very different to the major concerns of a girl of 25 or 26 who has been working

TABLE LXII: RANK ORDER OF ROLES IN TERMS OF THEIR RELATIVE IMPORTANCE
TO THE INDIVIDUAL AS SHE GROWS OLDER

	Age		
	13–16	17–20	22–25
RANK OF IMPORTANCE OF ROLES	1. Familial roles 2. Educational 3. Recreational and courtship 4. Occupational	1. Occupational 2. Courtship and recreational 3. Familial	1. Courtship and marriage 2. Occupational

locally for some time, and who has no steady boyfriend and no prospect of one. The table opposite attempts to set out the likely changes in the type and relevance of different roles for girls as they grow older.

The individual assumes new roles as he or she grows older, and their importance varies at different times. A girl in her late twenties, for instance, is likely to get very worried about local marriage chances if she is not dating regularly. Such considerations are likely to have over-riding importance at this stage of a girl's life, although they were relatively unimportant at an earlier stage. Such marriage considerations, however, are unlikely to become important for boys until somewhat later. Similarly, boys who work on the home farm but who have not yet been given an independent managerial role and who have no hope of being left the farm for some time are very likely to get worried about this in their late twenties or early thirties. Either of these considerations are, therefore, likely to lead to migration out of the community at a later stage, even where people are perfectly satisfied with occupational and consumption roles. The purposes that would be served by migration, therefore, are very likely to change over the life cycle.

Given these likely changes in the aspirations and concerns of these respondents in the next five or ten years, it is likely that many respondents will change their minds about migration in the future. It is likely that some of the original cohort who have already migrated will return to the community. In each case, however, migration can best be understood as an attempt to attain some goals or purposes that the individual believes cannot be attained in the home community.

The prevalence of these continuing comparisons of the relative attractiveness of one's own community and alternative communities can easily be appreciated from the following. Over the whole period from 1965 to 1968, less than one sixth of all respondents had not seriously considered migration at one time or another, and almost a third of all respondents had completely changed their minds about moving in the three year period. Except for a small minority, therefore, almost all respondents at some time or another in the three year period made seriously considered comparisons of their own with other communities as a place to live in, to the disadvantage of their own home community. Only a very small proportion—mostly of the remoter farm boys—are so locality-

bound by their membership and reference group contacts that they
did not appear to engage in such invidious comparisons. Almost
all respondents are very highly involved in migrant networks,
whether familial or friendship, etc. Through these contacts, as well
as via mass media and other sources, they are very conscious of
conditions in outside communities. They live in anything but an
isolated cultural system. Not only do these migrant influences affect
their residence plans by influencing their aspirations and satisfaction with local opportunities etc., but these networks also make
it easy for migrants to move to new communities.

The direct and indirect influence of these migrant reference
groups became very obvious in the restudy. They were especially
important amongst respondents entering manual occupations. The
direct role they play in migration can be easily gauged from the following figures. Of 162 migrants or intending migrants who had made
definite plans for migration, over half had been helped by family
members and friends who had previously migrated, and the arrangements for helping in this movement had been made before leaving
the home community. This help given by previous migrants usually
took the form of arranging jobs and accommodation for the migrant,
of financial help where necessary, and of meeting the new migrant
and smoothing the way for him in his new environment.

Except for a very small proportion (7 per cent) who had migrated
on their own without having made any prior arrangements, all of
the other migrants had arranged jobs, and in most cases accommodation also, through formal channels before leaving the home
community. These formal channels included examinations, newspaper advertisements, writing directly to employers, etc. Even in
these cases, however, informal contacts were important, both in
informing potential migrants about opportunities, and in providing
accommodation for them.

Formal channels were rarely used by those entering manual
occupations. Only one sixth of those taking up manual or service
work used such formal channels, and even in most of these cases
they had also used informal channels. On the other hand, over half
of those who entered non-manual occupations utilised only formal
channels.

Besides giving help in the migration movement, once the individual had decided to go, previous migrants occasionally made a
direct offer of a highly enticing job and of help in transport and

accommodation to a non-migrant who was relatively satisfied at home. This was, however, rather unusual. Their usual influence operated through influencing non-migrants' aspirations, attitudes and levels of satisfaction with local opportunities. Once these changes in aspirations brought about changes in residence plans, then help was requested. In regard to these indirect effects, the main variables influenced appeared to be occupational and consumption aspirations. These appear to be the only variables where changes can be directly linked to migrant contacts. They are also the only variables involved in changes in migration plans.

In view of the considerable changes in migration plans between 1965 and 1968, it is remarkable when one considers them in aggregate that the 1965 responses are such good predictors of the proportions actually migrating or planning to stay permanently at home. Almost exactly the same proportion of respondents definitely planned to stay in 1965 and 1968. The proportion who had already migrated by 1968 was only slightly greater than the proportion who had definitely planned to migrate in 1965. If the intention to stay at home or to migrate is taken as a decision contingent on the respondents' assessments of the local community's opportunities, it appears that respondents' assessments in 1965 had been relatively realistic. Many of the respondents were overoptimistic, but this was approximately balanced by the proportion who were too pessimistic, so that in aggregate the 1965 assessment was not very different from the subsequent one. If these changes in plans were roughly the same within each group of migrants—males and females, primary and secondary educated, etc.,—this conclusion would be supported. However, the optimists and the pessimists were not balanced within each group, but were actually from different groups. The pessimists were concentrated amongst the vocationally educated, while the optimists were equally concentrated amongst the primary educated. It was not merely that one overpessimistic primary educated respondent was balanced by an equally overoptimistic primary educated one. Rather, it was that the primary ˈeducated in general were too optimistic in 1965, while the vocational were too pessimistic. The assessment of opportunities in the community had changed considerably between 1965 and 1968. The fact that the proportions planning to stay in 1965 and 1968 are very similar does not mean that the 1965 views of the community are, in aggregate, efficient predictors of subsequent views. The similarity

R.E.—I

appears more fortuitous than causal. It appears that in their early adolescence, the poorly educated—largely those from small farm and manual backgrounds—are strongly biassed in favour of the home community. Their views of its opportunities are more optimistic than reality will afterwards force them to accept. Their parents also are strongly opposed to their going away. The vocationally educated, on the other hand, were too pessimistic in 1965. Their pessimism probably stems from the fact that they are inclined to use the secondary educated as a reference group in their assessment of the local community. When they actually start looking for a job, many of them find that these views are unjustified. In general, therefore, the original assessments cannot be taken as realistic, despite their predictive value. The previous discussion about the role of Community Satisfaction in migration decision-making supports these conclusions. The primary educated were the most satisfied in 1965 and tended to overestimate local opportunities. The vocationally educated were the most dissatisfied and tended to underestimate them.

(2) Migration Differentials

The main causal factor proposed to account for variations in rates of migration from different groups in the home community—social class, education, sex, remoteness, etc.—was occupational selectivity. It is the extent to which a group's occupational aspirations can be met in the home community that determines differences in rates of migration. The initial hypothesis stated that the higher the level of aspirations the lower the probability of fulfilling them locally. This hypothesis is strongly confirmed at the upper end of the status scale, since only one twentieth of those entering higher non-manual occupations remained in the home community. Any background factor that increases the probability of having such higher levels of aspirations will therefore be equally related to migration. The higher rates of migration of the secondary educated can be explained on this basis alone. The greater rates of those from non-manual backgrounds, farm girls, and of the less remote can also be explained on this basis because of their greater tendency to receive a secondary education.

The converse of this pattern does not hold good, however. The primary educated are not the least migratory, as was expected.[2] In fact, the primary educated who were working off the farm were far more migratory than the vocationally educated. Although almost all of these got their first job locally, these were either dead-end jobs which only kept the respondents employed for two or three years, or, if of a more permanent nature, paid very poor wages. The only place where jobs are expanding in this community — and indeed this appears to be the case in most rural communities in Ireland—is at a level that favours the vocationally educated rather than the primary. As a result, the vocational group is the one least subject to migration.

One of the main reasons why there has been such little progress with research on migration differentials is that community differences in the type of education given each new cohort of job entrants, and in the level of occupational opportunities available locally, have not been controlled for in intercommunity comparisons. In any other community, migrants would probably be selected on a different basis, especially if there were plenty of well paid unskilled and semiskilled manual jobs available locally, or if the educational system were so efficient that very few new entrants to the labour force had received only a primary education. A comparative study of a number of rural communities varying along the dimensions of job opportunity structure, and of the educational structure of the local adolescent entrants to the labour force, would lead to very fruitful findings about the dimension along which migrants are selected.

Because of the fact that many of the primary educated had over-estimated their chances in 1965, and many of the vocational educated had underestimated theirs, many of the differentials in migration behaviour were less pronounced in 1968 than in 1965. This is true of sex differences and of remoteness differences especially. Far more girls have stayed at home than were expected to, given their intentions in 1965. This is only true, however, of the vocational educated girls. Approximately twice as many of the vocational girls intended to stay at home in 1968 than in 1965. This was due to the fact that there were far more jobs available at home at the intermediate non-manual level than they had

---

[2] There are many US studies which show a similar selection of emigrants from both extremes of educational or occupational achievement. See OECD Report, No. 75, *Geographic and Occupational Mobility of Rural Manpower, op. cit.,* 43.

expected. It was in fact the vocational girls that were overpessimistic in 1965, not the boys.

Remoteness differentials were reduced in exactly the same way and due to the same reasons. In 1965, the proportion of the most remote respondents who intended to stay locally was roughly twice that of the least remote. However, almost twice as many of those from the centre had stayed than intended to. This reduction was again due to the change in the position of the vocational educated. More of these had stayed than intended to, especially those from the centre. As a result, the migration rate actually increased with remoteness for the vocational educated, but decreased for the primary and secondary educated. It appears from these results that the vocational-dominated skilled and intermediate non-manual jobs, most of which are situated in the centre, are also disproportionately filled by respondents from the centre and surrounding areas. The reverse is the case for the secondary and primary educated.

These 1968 results differ from some of the 1965 findings. This is especially true as regards the position of the more remote respondents who were working in service and manual jobs in the centre. When employing shop assistants especially, employers from the centre appeared to discriminate in favour of farm over working class applicants from the centre. On the other hand, it may have been that the remoter farm adolescents were the only ones with sufficiently low levels of aspiration to be satisfied with many of the low paid service or manual jobs available at that time. In any case, this initial discrimination in favour of the local employment of the more remote respondents quickly disappeared. Most of the service workers, especially the shop assistants, migrated within a very short time after first taking up the job. Disillusionment with the limited opportunities available locally and with the very low wages available there quickly dampened their initial enthusiasm—especially as their level of aspiration increased. Despite this, however, and despite the fact that the vocational educated from the centre have an advantage over the more remote in finding satisfactory long term opportunities locally, actual overall migration remains greater among those from the centre. This occurs despite the fact that population decline actually increased with distance from the centre. This latter fact, however, illustrates the dangers in inferring total gross migration rates from such derived factors as net population changes which lump together the various sources of population change—births and deaths, in-migration and out-migration. What may be true of net migration, therefore, may not be at all true of total rates of out-migration, with which we are dealing here.[3]

As a result of these local educational and occupational selection processes, social class differentials in migration were especially clearcut. Only slightly more than one tenth of those from non-manual backgrounds intended to remain at home in 1968, compared with more than half of those from farm backgrounds. The proportion of manual origin remaining is slightly greater than one third. As a result of these differences, although a little more than one fifth of all respondents in the sample came from non-manual backgrounds, only one twentieth of those respondents now intending to remain in the community are from non-manual backgrounds. Most of the others come from farm backgrounds where, although they make up less than half of the total number of respondents, they comprise more than two thirds of those remaining at home. The proportion of manual origin respondents amongst those intending to remain at home stays roughly the same as their proportion in the total population overall. Farm people, therefore, appear to be replacing the non-manual stock in the community. This is a process that has apparently been characteristic of many Irish rural communities for some time, as Arensberg has pointed out.[4]

These emphases on occupational considerations may tend to over-estimate the importance of a purely economic interpretation of migration behaviour. We have explained migration differentials especially by stressing the varying extent to which local job opportunities can satisfy the aspirations of the different social groups in the community. In this discussion, the aspirations themselves were taken as given. When we examine these aspirations, however, it becomes clear that major cultural changes are occurring in this community—especially in the farm sector. These adolescents' aspirations show a massive departure from identification with the traditional occupational roles of their own family, or even of their

---

[3] See Hathaway, D. and Perkins, B., "Farm labour mobility and income distribution", *American Journal of Agric. Econ.*, 50, 2, May 1968, 342–53, where the use of gross out-migration and in-migration figures contradicts many of the normally accepted generalisations on migration behaviour—generalisations which have been based on net figures. They also found that out-migration rates did not increase with distance from urban centres.

[4] Arensberg, C. A., *The Irish Countryman*, reprinted Peter Smith, Boston, 1961, 146–80.

home community. By and large, they appear to show many of the same occupational values as their urban counterparts. There is a massive downgrading of farming as an occupation. Less than one twentieth of farm girls and one fifth of farm boys remained on the home farms.[5] There was evidence also that this depreciation of farming was widely shared by the respondents' parents, especially by the mothers. A similar movement away from unskilled manual occupations also occurred, although far too many of the farm-reared were still seeking jobs at this level.

This very pronounced depreciation of farming was not unfortunately translated into effective educational strategies by the respondents concerned or their families. Far too many farm and working class youth were still receiving the minimum of education.[6] This limited their possible occupational achievements to poorly remunerated and poorly skilled manual and service occupations. Since well paid opportunities at this level are usually contracting in rural areas, the very poorly educated have to migrate to almost the same extent as the very highly educated. However, the poorly educated are in a far more unfortunate position, in that they have to emigrate to British cities to find these opportunities, while the better educated can find them within Ireland. Since they are least likely of all migrants to make a successful adjustment to any highly urban community, due to their poor educational level and their greater extent of internalisation of traditional cultural patterns, they are doubly disadvantaged from the point of view of satisfactory assimilation into their new communities.

In general, however, despite these exceptions, the level of aspira-

[5] The proportion of farmers' sons remaining on the home farm is remarkably similar to those observed in Britain and the United States. See R. Gasson "Occupations chosen by the sons of farmers", *Journal of Agric. Economics*, 19, 3, 17–23 & 26, 1968; and for OECD Documentation in Agriculture and Food, see Report No. 75, *Geographical and Occupational Mobility of Rural Manpower*, 1965.

[6] See, A. O. Haller, "The occupational achievement process of farm-reared youth in urban industrial society", *Rural Sociology*, 1960, 25, 3, 321–33; and R. Gasson, *op. cit.* In both Britain and the United States, farmers' sons seem to be equally disadvantaged. In both cases it is explained as due to the early development of occupational self-conceptions by farmers' sons who tended to identify very strongly with farming as an occupation. These self-conceptions precluded consideration of other alternatives and greatly limited their educational aspirations, since they did not consider it necessary to acquire a prolonged postprimary education to become a farmer. This educational restriction greatly limited occupational achievement when they were finally forced to move out of farming. See *Geographical & Occupational Mobility of Rural Manpower*, 45, where studies are quoted and show that this situation also holds good in some European countries.

tions and expectations of the majority of the cohort has more in keeping with a modern industrial city than one might have expected. Occupational identifications are highly urbanised and often have no local equivalent for comparison. Similarly, the level of consumption aspiration has risen (in most cases) far above that enjoyed by respondents' family of origin. Since there has been considerable migration out of this community for at least a century or more, such processes of urbanisation have been going on for a long time through contact with migrant family members and peers. The influence of migrant reference groups, however, is likely to have greatly expanded in recent times. Since migration has switched from the United States to Britain in recent decades, communication with migrants has greatly improved. Also, the great improvements in the means of transport and communication have meant that even in the case of American migrants communication is much easier. Birmingham is not much further than Cork city in terms of cost or time spent in travelling. Inexpensive charter flights across the Atlantic make it very much easier for recent migrants to keep in touch than was true of their uncles and aunts. Similarly, the intrusion of radio and television has made a major impact in involving rural families in national and international affairs. Unfortunately, this research did not specifically examine the causes of these generational changes in aspirations and expectations. From the point of view of developing industries locally, however, such a study appears vital—especially where one of the inducements offered to prospective industrialists is the lower wages required by local workers.

IMPLICATIONS

There are some clear policy implications of this study for Cavan itself, and indeed for the Irish industralisation and population conservation policy in general.

Firstly, the community which these people form is a very "open" one. The great majority of adolescents growing up there have very extensive personal contacts with relatives and friends living and working in extremely urban communities outside their own community. Their aspirations and attitudes are highly influenced by these extra-community reference groups. No doubt, with some exceptions, the majority of the migrants or prospective migrants would have been satisfied to stay at home if they were able to get a job that satisfied them there, even for rather smaller wages than they knew they could get if they went away. (Unfortunately, this study did not gather information on this.) The size of this differential will obviously vary with the kind of group involved. Most respondents, however, are so tightly integrated into migrant networks that the reference group effects of these contacts will ensure somewhat comparable levels of aspiration. Any industrialisation or community development policy would need to keep this clearly in mind, at least in the initial stages of development. If, however, industrialisation were to gather such rapid momentum that it was possible to employ almost all members of each new cohort locally, the effects of the migrant reference groups would be greatly attenuated.

Secondly, almost all of the respondents interviewed in this study had in their adolescence seriously considered migrating at one time or another. Although only 40 per cent had left the community by 1968, roughly five sixths of all respondents had seriously considered migration at one time or another, and only one sixth throughout all the period continued to maintain that they intended to stay locally. The decision to migrate or stay at home was, by and large, contingent on their success in finding a local job which satisfied both their occupational and income aspirations. It is a matter of whether the individual can find the desired level of job and income in the locality or, in the case of the secondary educated, believes he can. The great majority of the primary and vocational educated respondents had taken up their first job locally and, if they had migrated, had searched around locally for suitable opportunities before migrating. The majority of them had also said that they would much prefer to stay than migrate. Very few had migrated on impulse or without "serious cause". Some do, but they are a very small minority. Contrary to popular opinion in Ireland, very few migrate without having made some prior arrangements about transportation, accommodation, jobs, or being met at the point of destination. The great majority make these arrangements either through family members or friends and neighbours who have previously migrated. Furthermore, they usually stay with these migrant contacts, either in the household or in accommodation arranged beforehand, for some time after migration. Isolated individuals rarely migrate. The use of these informal migration networks is especially marked amongst the poorly educated and the manual and service workers.

Non-manual migrants usually use formal liaison channels for job seeking and arranging accommodation, etc. Even in these latter cases, however, informal migration contacts are very important as sources of information about jobs, and for providing accommodation and help in adjustment to the new community. The great majority of migrants moving into manual or service jobs, therefore, had made serious efforts to find good jobs locally before going, and had taken considerable pains about looking for alternative opportunities outside the community before migrating. Even in this case, the majority of their mothers had expected them to stay at home.

Although a previous conclusion clearly indicated that any new industries in this area would have to pay competitive rates to hold their workers, these latter results hold out considerable hope for the success of any industrial development in this community. The great majority of manual and service workers who had migrated would have preferred to stay if they could find suitable opportunities at home. This is, perhaps, most clearly illustrated by the position of the skilled manual and intermediate non-manual workers who stayed in even greater numbers than the less skilled manual and service workers. Since non-economic considerations were more important in the migration of the skilled and non-manual workers (see Table XXVII, chapter 5) than they were for the unskilled, even more of the latter would have stayed locally if they had the chance.

If we assume that it is the absence of local occupational opportunities of a satisfactory status and remuneration level which is the main factor involved in the migration of these lower achievers, would the local development of industrial opportunities stem this migration? Would those migrants at present working in manual or service occupations in Britain, or in Dublin, have stayed at home if plenty of well remunerated factory jobs were available? Although this question was not asked the respondents concerned, we can attempt some clear answers. To begin with, the male respondents interviewed in the study assigned unskilled factory work to a prestige level higher than almost all other unskilled manual work available in the community, and even of many service occupations such as shop assistants, etc.* Skilled factory work was also assigned a prestige position higher than most other skilled manual occupations in the home community. In fact, somewhat less than half of the male respondents interviewed said that they felt they "would be

* See Appendix II.

letting down their family" if they were to take up unskilled factory
work, and less than one fifth of all male respondents said they felt
the same about skilled factory work.[7] In the case of girls, the situation was somewhat different. Roughly three quarters of the girls
outrightly rejected unskilled factory work as below the status acceptable to them. Unfortunately, the girls were not asked to assess the
social acceptability of skilled factory work, but if we assume that the
relationship between unskilled and skilled work would be the same
for them as for boys, nearly half of them would have rejected skilled
factory work for prestige reasons. The rejection of factory work was
also closely related to education. Almost all the boys and girls who
had received only a primary education said that they would accept
unskilled factory work. However, almost all the girls who had
received a vocational education rejected this work, whereas only
slightly more than half of the boys had done so. In the case of the
secondary educated, both skilled and unskilled factory work is
unacceptable to both boys and girls. There are therefore two main
reasons why factory work is less acceptable to girls in this community
than it is to boys. The first is the higher level of education received
by the girls (See Table IX, Chapter 3, and Table LVI, Chapter 9)
and the second is the greater reluctance of the vocational educated
girls to take these jobs. Given the extent to which these vocational
girls aspire to, are trained for, and enter non-manual jobs, their
greater reluctance is understandable. (See Table XC, Appendix IV).

If, therefore, enough factory jobs with a sufficient range of skills
and paying satisfactory wages had been available in the home
community, it is very likely that the great majority of boys and girls
who had received only a primary education or a vocational education would not have migrated. The predominance of occupational
and consumption motives in their migration has already been
commented upon. In 1965, almost 90 per cent of the primary
educated and 80 per cent of the vocational educated had said that
they would stay if they could fulfill their occupational and income
aspirations locally. Much the same conclusion, with regard to the
predominance of economic considerations in their migration
decisions, emerges from an examination of the motives involved in
actual migration. Of the 121 migrants who had left the community
by 1968, nearly half had worked locally in service and manual

[7] See Hannan, D. F. and Beegle, J. A., "Evaluations of occupations on the
basis of their prestige and difficulty of achievement", *Rural Sociology* (1969) 34, 3.

occupations. Poor job and income opportunities were the major factors influencing migration for over three quarters of these migrants. Overall, therefore, the rapid local development of factory employment would greatly reduce migration from these groups.

Providing suitable factory jobs is likely to be more successful in stemming the migration of the boys than the girls, however. Although almost all the girls who had received only a primary education said they would accept factory work if available, this is much less true of the vocational educated. It will be seen, then, that the growth of industries demanding female labour—especially labour that is perceived to demand few skills—is not, on its own, very likely to stem female migration; moreover, these industries may be starved of labour in a short time as educational levels increase.[8] There appear to be very negative connotations attached to "factory work" for girls—service work of many kinds has much higher prestige. The perceived skill that the job requires appears, however, to be very important in the case of boys in altering their evaluation of factory work, and the same may also be the case for girls. However, from other more casual observations made in the course of the survey, the main prestige objections to factory work for girls appeared to be based on many factors extrinsic to the particular skill demanded by the job concerned. The term "factory girls" has definite social class connotations which becomes particularly relevant for the recruitment of girls from farm or upwardly mobile manual backgrounds. It may be perceived to have deleterious influences on girls' recreational, courtship and marriage chances. In a comparable study of a small town in the west of Ireland, for instance, many of the girls employed in similarly unprestigious work found that the local boys would not even dance with them.[9] The consequences of these negative community evaluations of factory work for girls cannot be explored any further in this research. Nevertheless, any industrialisation programme would need to take many of these class connotations into consideration when planning for the kinds of factories that would attract female labour, when recruiting girls for factory work, or even when planning the siting or layout of

[8] See Ward, C., *The Drogheda Manpower Survey*, Dept. of Labour, Dublin, 1966 where an acute shortage of such female labour has been shown to exist for more, or less the same reasons.

[9] See Mulligan, M., *Youth in a Country Town*, unpublished M. Soc. Sc. thesis. Dept. of Social Science, University College, Dublin, 1967.

factories. With factories that demand a wide range of skills, with careful recruitment procedures which ensure that work in the factory is not exclusively associated with one social class in the town, and with success in creating a pleasant and clean environment for the work, many of the problems involved in the employment of girls may be eliminated. On the other hand, as each succeeding cohort of young people receive increasingly better education—especially secondary education—it may become more and more difficult to recruit female staff.

The position of the secondary educated is somewhat different to that of the vocational or primary educated group. Almost all of the secondary educated enter non-manual occupations, more than half of those being higher non-manual positions. A very small proportion take up permanent positions in the home community. Although it is likely that industrial expansion would lead to a considerable expansion in intermediate non-manual positions, the vocational educated are more likely than the secondary to make use of this development. (See Table LIV, Chapter 9, and the ensuing discussion). At the present time, however, the majority of the secondary educated stay within Ireland when migrating. The home community also gains from the in-migration of higher non-manual personnel into the community—a situation which is also likely to continue if it were to develop rapidly. From a national point of view, and even from the point of view of the community itself, this migration is not therefore necessarily dysfunctional. Concern about the migration of the "best brains" out of Cavan is rather unrealistic, given the inefficiency of the selection process for higher education and the in-migration of many non-manual workers. The migration of the secondary educated may, however, become dysfunctional if the current improvement in educational levels leads only to ever-increasing proportions of each new cohort entering the academically orientated secondary schools, while the vocational stream remains relatively fixed in size. Seen from the point of view of the local community, therefore, and even from that of the nation as a whole, vocational education rather than secondary education should be emphasised. This conclusion merely repeats the conclusions of the national survey on educational needs, and of a series of regional studies on labour requirements.[10]

Primary education is not *per se* a major drawback to the individual

[10] See *Investment in Education, op. cit.*, and *Drogheda Manpower Survey, op. cit.*

himself in finding satisfactory opportunities locally, but it must damage the migrants' chances of successfully adapting to life in British cities, where the majority of the primary educated migrants go. From a short term point of view, the high proportion of each cohort who receive only a primary education might increase the probability of retaining a bigger population at home by enticing manufacturers who employ only unskilled labour to move into the area. At present, the primary educated are mainly the people who will take this kind of job. In the long run, however, the proportion of any cohort remaining content with only a primary level of education is likely to become smaller and smaller. And, although the proportion of the vocational educated willing to take up relatively unskilled factory work is likely to gradually increase as the community becomes accustomed to industrial ways, it is unlikely ever to reach the proportions of the current primary group, no matter what the economic incentives may be. From these points of view, therefore, the satisfaction of local and national labour requirements requires emphasis on vocational rather than secondary education, but it equally requires attention to the kind of industries to be established.

Some of the problems met with by the primary educated can be illustrated by examining the kinds of jobs they first enter and their subsequent job movements. Viewed from the perspective of the home community, about two times too many are entering farming and service occupations for their first jobs. Much the same situation also holds good for those entering semiskilled and unskilled manual occupations, but the consequences are not as drastic in these cases. The work habits developed, the manual and social skills learned, the attitudes developed toward work itself and toward the person's place in the community, make it all the more difficult for both farm and service workers to adjust to industrial life. They bias both classes of workers against factory work. Those who have identified with farming will find it much easier to adapt to outdoor heavy manual work, where one can set one's own work pace—hence the popularity of working "on the buildings" for those from farm backgrounds. In regard to the service workers—mostly shop assistants— their close contact with the public, the light and "clean" nature of the work, the variation in the working tasks, etc., all make it very difficult for them to adapt to factory work. If both kinds of workers could be induced into vocational schools after completing their primary education, instead of taking up their first employment in such temporary and "dead-end" jobs, some of these problems could be avoided.

At the present time in Cavan, because jobs are not available for even half of the vocationally educated—the most highly adapted to local industrialisation—much of the foregoing discussion is irrelevant to its present population problems. If more people went into vocational schools at the present time, more would migrate, since the poorly paid lower manual jobs would be far less acceptable to them than to the primary educated who fill these positions at present. However, if Cavan were to develop, such considerations would be vital.

The "Buchanan Report" on regional development issued in early 1969 had tentatively proposed Cavan as a development centre for the region, but had not definitely come down in favour of Cavan as against the claims of other neighbouring centres.[11] Cavan town has obvious geographical advantages, not only in terms of its centrality for the surrounding hinterland areas of County Cavan itself, but also for counties Monaghan and Leitrim and parts of Meath, Longford and Louth; it also has many competitors for the required government funds. What if Cavan were not selected for development, however, and the main development of the region were concentrated in Dundalk or Drogheda—the latter just 40 miles away? Would the excess labour move freely from Cavan to these centres, either through commuting or through actual residence transfers? The evidence available from this study and corroborative evidence from many similar studies suggest that they would not.[12]

The migration of the poorly educated, and of those moving into manual and service jobs, generally takes place within the context of informal networks of friends and family who have previously migrated. Knowledge of job opportunities flows through these informal contacts. Direct aid in arranging accommodation and job finding, and in smoothing the way generally for the new migrant is given by his family and friends who have previously migrated. Such migration takes place "from home to home" as it were; from the home community to an enclave or colony established in a particular destination community. Such "migration systems" have a

[11] Buchanan and Partners, *Regional Studies in Ireland:*—a study summarised by the United Nations on behalf of the Government of Ireland, published by an Foras Forbartha, Dublin 1969, 153.

[12] See Mulligan, M., *op. cit.*, for corroborative evidence of another town in Co. Galway situated rather near the development centre of Galway city.

built-in inertia which is difficult to upset. How could young people become aware of opportunities in Drogheda or Dundalk if they had no friends there? How could they find a job there if they had no friends to help them with information, advice and influence? How could they adjust to life there if these towns are as "foreign" to them as Cork or Galway—the other side of the country—and far less familiar to them than Birmingham or London, where they have so many friends? As one moves outside the natural orp re-existing service areas—shopping, professional, educational and other services, and employment provision—of any new centre, such natural resistances to labour mobility will occur. It should be possible to overcome these natural resistances, but not through any formal mechanisms. It is likely, for instance, that wage differentials between the home and destination communities would have to be much greater to attract labour from a traditional out-migration area such as Cavan to a new employment centre than it would have to be to retain them at home, or even to attract them to British cities to which there had been considerable previous migration. Through personal recruitment of labour, through the arrangement and subsidisation of transport or accommodation, through employing a number of friends or acquaintances in the same factory, through the conscious use of local community, clique or friendship group networks to recruit labour, and through other such personal recruitment and adjustment methods, it should be possible to establish an initial pool of labour. Once such a pool or colony of local labour is established in a new centre, it is likely to be self-recruiting afterwards if the labour force is satisfied with the employment offered.

These appear to the author to be the major practical implications of the study. There are many others that could be remarked upon, but in most cases they are rather obvious from the previous discussion. The final section of this chapter deals with the limitations of the study.

LIMITATIONS OF THE STUDY AND PROPOSALS FOR FUTURE RESEARCH

The research design has generally proved to be satisfactory. The particular approach taken has provided clearcut answers to most of the research questions posed, as well as providing some very interesting data on other aspects of the life of young people in a particular community. There are three particular aspects of the design however, that need some further discussion: the restriction of the study to a particular community; the use of a small number of variables to explain the whole range of migratory behaviour; and some conceptual and measurement problems. There are some obvious merits in these aspects of the design, but there are also some obvious weaknesses that require comment.

The advantages of viewing migration from a community perspective were clearly demonstrated. Examining the mobility of a total cohort growing up within particular community boundaries gives more comprehensive and more precise information about migration planning and behaviour than any alternative approach. This is particularly apparent in the examination of the geographical or ecological factor in migration behaviour. There are clear physical and cultural factors that distinguish between respondents from or near the centre and those from the most remote areas of the community. At a time when cultural differences between the city and the countryside are being played down or regarded as being entirely eroded, the findings of this study—that there are major cultural differences between a small trade centre and its more remote hinterland—demonstrate that, in Ireland at least, these cultural differences are very much alive.[13] Besides this demonstration of the existence of such a cultural hiatus, there is a more general sense in which the advantage of studying migration within a particular community context is clearly demonstrated: that the structure of opportunities remains constant, although the respondents' views of it varied widely. It was possible, therefore, to examine the reasons for this variation without the need to control for corresponding variations in actual opportunities, which would have been required if a national sample had been used.

However, this community approach has its corresponding weaknesses. A considerable proportion of rural people are not so tightly integrated into service areas surrounding market centres as was the case for this study. Many of the outlying farm communities of Co. Cavan, for instance, are well out of the effective service range of Cavan town. These people seek their everyday consumption requirements in small local settlements, while their educational services, off-farm occupational outlets and secondary and tertiary

[13] Dewey, Richard, "The rural-urban continuum: real but relatively unimportant", *American Journal of Sociology*, 1960, 66, 60–6.

services are sought in centres which are less centralised and which are more distant from the home community. Had some of these more remote farm areas been included in the survey area, the effects of remoteness on educational mobility, level of aspiration, ability or inability to achieve aspirations locally, and rates of migration could have been investigated in a more comprehensive way. It is highly probable, for instance, that non-farm occupational outlets fall off very rapidly in these more remote areas, and that relatively fewer people find occupational outlets in Cavan or in similar local employment centres. Consequently, the hypothesis of migration rates increasing with distances from the centre might have held good, had these more remote areas been included.

The fact that the study was limited to one centre and its surroundings also places a considerable restriction on the generalisability of the study's findings. A comparative study of a number of rural communities which varied widely in the structure of their opportunities as well as in the characteristics of the local educational system would more effectively have tested the basic assumption of the study. This stated that such a variation would lead to corresponding differences in the rates of out-migration and in the type of migrants leaving the community. An investigation of these facets of migration would greatly add to the knowledge about the factors which give rise to variation in migration differentials and in rates of in- and out-migration.

With regard to the restriction of the number of variables considered as affecting migration decisions, the approach has some obvious advantages and disadvantages. The approach did allow us to explore all of the important interrelationships amongst these variables. A larger number of independent variables would have made this very difficult. An alternative approach that could have been used would have been to ask respondents for their *reasons* for behaving or intending to behave in particular ways. This approach may appear to give a more meaningful explanation than the one taken here, in that this is the usual everyday interpretation technique we use with each other when we are trying to understand behaviour that is not "traditional or routinised".[14] It would appear, therefore, to be a more satisfying approach from an explanatory point of view. However, there are so many dangers involved in this

14 See Gerth, H. and Mills, C. W., *Character and Social Structure,* where such a "social justification" view of motives is explored.

kind of approach that it is highly unreliable. There is a great danger, for instance, of conscious or unconscious rationalisation, especially where the individual is migrating for reasons which are not justified by the culture: i.e. to get away from highly unsatisfying personal relationships—low Community Satisfaction—where the individual is quite satisfied with the job.[15] There is a second danger of getting reasons which refer only to the most proximate irritation, rather than to any deep underlying reasons, whether the individual is aware of this or not.[16] However, the more important justification for the particular approach taken is related to the fact that in 1965 we were dealing only with projected or intended migration behaviour. Many of the respondents were also genuinely unsure about what they would do, or were not certain that they would actually do what they said they intended to, and in this situation, one could not ask them the reasons for their intended behaviour. The "general why" question has so many limitations that it could not be used in this case. The choice of independent variables to be considered as important influences on the behaviour to be explained, therefore, becomes very important. Information from previous research findings and the pilot studies had shown that the particular variables chosen were probably the most important ones. The results of the initial study showed that this was indeed the case. In the follow up study, however, we failed to get direct information on migrant peer influences. These were relatively unimportant in the 1965 study but became increasingly important as more and more of the cohort migrated. This oversight should have been corrected in the pilot phase of the study, but unfortunately it was not found to be significant in the pilot phase and was not fully appreciated until too late in the final survey. Future research, however, should pay very close attention to these migrant reference group effects.

Another limitation in the variables considered relates to the Community Satisfaction scale used. The conceptualisation of the variable includes two distinct ideas—the cultural orientation of

[15] See Forman, R. and Francis, R., *Some Ideological Aspects of Migration*, Paper No. 5220, Scientific Journal Series, A.E.S., University of Minn. St. Paul 1963; where there is evidence that certain "motives" for migration, such as seeking to avoid unpleasant duties or dissatisfaction with local relationships, are not approved of by people in general.

[16] The disadvantages of unsophisticated "reason analysis" have been so well documented elsewhere that there is no reason to labour the point here. See Rossi, P. H., *Why Families Move*, Free Press, 1955; and Zeisel, Hans, *Say It With Figures*.

respondents, and feelings of relative deprivation. The effects of both of these on attitudes toward personal and institutional relationships in the home community were assumed to be adequately indexed by the scale used. It is strongly recommended that these two dimensions be separated out in future research. There is no doubt that both dimensions are involved in these feelings of Community Satisfaction. The high degree of attachment of farm boys and the contrary alienation of farm girls could only be explainable on cultural differences alone. On the other hand, the lower rates of satisfaction of the vocational educated seemed to be explainable only on the basis of reference group factors. Both dimensions need to be separated, however, to get a clear picture of what is occurring. In general, cultural alienation did not appear to be so strong as to compel the migration of people with urbanised values out of a community where traditional cultural ideals are enshrined in many structures. Nevertheless, there was evidence that many respondents —expecially farm boys—had internalised these traditional models and intended to stay locally in situations which would frustrate most of their peers.

Attempts to refine the C.S. scale used were made in the follow up study. Responses to the ten items included in the scale were analysed using the scalogram method.[17] Five of the items yielded a quasi-unidimensional scale with a reproductibility of .86.[18] However, even this scale was no more efficient than the older Likert-type scale in predicting variations in migration behaviour. Only those with highly negative attitudes intended to any considerable extent to migrate in 1968, and there were minimal differences amongst the other respondents. Although this greater migratory tendency of the very highly alienated was also true in 1965, their intention was not carried into action. It is not clear why this should be the case. It may be that the cultural and reference group effects are operating independently of each other, and that the composite scale does not adequately represent these effects. Future research should try to separate out these two dimensions.

Attitudes toward recreational or other social provisions in the home community appeared to be relatively unimportant in migra-

[17] See Waisenan, F. B., "A notation scale for scalogram analysis", *Sociological Quarterly*, 1, 4, 1960; and Edwards, A. N., *Techniques of Attitude Scale Construction*, Appleton-Century-Crofts, NY, 1957, 172–200.

[18] The five items were: (e), (c), (d), (g) and (j), Appendix I, Question No. 70.

tion. In the original study, the scale used to measure this attitude had some major limitations. It was assumed that community provisions were viewed as a single dimension by respondents, although the items varied very widely in reference. Five items referred to recreational facilities, two to schools, one to roads, one to shopping facilities and one to the remoteness of the community itself. Although these limitations were to some extent removed in the restudy, even a revised unidimensional scale measuring attitudes toward recreational provisions in the home community had an even smaller association with migration than the original cruder Likert scale.[19] In general, such attitudes appear to be unimportant in migration— at least in the age group interviewed. Since, however, this age group is likely to be the one for whom these facilities are most relevant, they appear to be relatively unimportant in general. But in themselves, the great variation in these attitudes is very important, and their clear relationship to cultural and structural factors is very impressive. In future studies dealing with migration, however, this research suggests that the variable could very well be dropped in place of some other more relevant considerations.

Problems of measurement also arose in the case of the social status of the respondents' families. It is possible that some modification of the reputational technique[20] could have been used, although the community seemed far too large to get any overall reliable assessments of the relative prestige position of the different families in the sample. Had such an overall measure been available, the relation of class and status factors to educational, aspirational, occupational recruitment and migration behaviour could have been studied in depth. The fact that even the use of crude occupational indicators showed such very clear class differences in educational and occupational chances and in migration behaviour emphasises the importance of such social class considerations. Had it been possible, for instance, to compare farm and non-farm respondents on the social class variable, such class factors would have been explored in far greater depth. This aspect of migration planning should be studied more intensively in later studies.

[19] The seven items were: (e), (f), (b), (i), (h), (g), (h). As it contained two distinct ideas, item (h) was split into two in the restudy: (i) people showing interest in games, and (ii) spending time organising clubs and teams, etc. Appendix I, Question No. 66.

[20] See Warner, W. L., *Social Class in America*, Harper Torchbooks, NY, 1960, first published in 1949, for a description of the method.

Finally, what may appear to be the major limitation of the study is its one-sidedness. It dealt only with the new recruits to the occupational system and did not concern itself with the employers or potential employers of this youth, or with the actual opportunities in Cavan. From another point of view, its one-sidedness is an advantage. It examines the problems of employment and migration in Cavan completely from the adolescents' point of view. Since they are the ones making the decisions about migration, their views of local opportunities are the important ones and not the actual situation—even if it is somewhat different from the way these young people see it. By and large, they have a very pessimistic view of their home community. Those entering manual occupations often have a very hostile and recriminatory attitude toward the community that denies them the opportunity to remain at home. They are highly dissatisfied with the opportunities available locally, but at the same time they go marching off with many a backward glance. Their dissatisfaction with the home community seems, on the whole, to be restricted to the economic sphere. The migrant—from working class or farm backgrounds especially—who has received only a primary level of education, remains attached to his original culture in various ways. and this attachment to traditional norms will make it all the more difficult for him to adjust to urban industrial life in Britain—the destination of the majority of this kind of migrant. The situation of the more highly educated is rather different, especially for girls. A considerable minority of these would not stay in the home community, even if they could achieve all their aspirations there. The majority of these, in any case, will be able to find opportunities within Ireland. Given their more urbanised attitudes and values, and the greater cultural similarities between their home and destination communities, their adjustment should be all the easier. The analysis of these problems of adjustment will, however, have to await future research.

This final section has argued the need for future research in many areas of migration behaviour. The study has left many lacunae, even within its limited field of concern. Despite this, we think that it has added considerably to the knowledge of migration behaviour. It is limited in many ways—in particular, to a specific age group and to a specific community in a specific country. Nevertheless, most of the study's first assumptions and hypotheses—based on research done in the United States, Israel and the Netherlands—have been strongly confirmed. It appears that the same basic set of factors is involved in rural–urban migration in most Western countries. In many areas these propositions about such migration behaviour have been altered or expanded. They constitute a set of rough propositions about migration behaviour which can help to guide future research and planning in migration. Therefore, besides providing a narrative of the migratory characteristics of a unique group of rural adolescents, we hope that the study also contributes something toward the achievement of an overall theory of migration behaviour.

Appendix I—The Questionnaire*

THE OCCUPATIONAL AND RESIDENCE
PLANS OF IRISH YOUTH

Every year, thousands of young people like yourself face the problem of choosing a life occupation and making their own way in the world. Although each individual has to make his own decisions and face his own problems, the experience of others can provide valuable information which can help you to solve your problems. Similarly, your experience with the problems you are meeting can help others, if it is brought to their attention. The information that we are gathering in this survey will be of great value in developing ways to help people like you in the problems that they are meeting, when setting out to find a suitable job for the first time. It is for these reasons that we ask you to answer the questions that follow, as seriously, and as sincerely as possible. We are interviewing about 600 people in Cavan on this survey.

The information that you give will be treated in the *strictest confidence*, and will be used *only* for research purposes. Your name and address is required only for sampling purposes, and will *never* be *published* in *any* connection.

1. Name: ....

2. Home Address: ....

3. Name of Primary School that you attended:.....................

    ....

---

* Note: Some questions have been omitted from the questionnaire because they are not relevant to the purpose of this book and have not been discussed in it.

4. What year did you leave primary school? $\frac{1960}{(0)}$ $\frac{1961}{(1)}$ $\frac{1962}{(2)}$

$\frac{1963}{(3)}$

5. What was your age on last birthday? $\frac{14}{(0)}$ $\frac{15}{(1)}$ $\frac{16}{(2)}$ $\frac{17}{(3)}$ $\frac{18}{(4)}$

$\frac{19}{(5)}$ $\frac{20}{(6)}$ $\frac{21}{(7)}$

6. What did you do when you finished up in primary school?
   (Please check off (√) that statement which is most true in
   your case.)

   ( ) I did not go on for any more education   (0)

   ( ) I went to the vocational school for one year   (1)

   ( ) I went to the vocational school for two years   (2)

   ( ) I went to the vocational school for three years   (3)

   ( ) I went to the secondary school for one year   (4)

   ( ) I went to the secondary school for two years   (5)

   ( ) I went to the secondary school for three years   (6)

   ( ) I went to the secondary school for four years   (7)

   ( ) I went to the secondary school for five years   (8)

   ( ) I went to the secondary school for six years   (9)

7. How many older, living brothers have you?   ....

   How many older, living sisters have you?   ....

   How many younger, living brothers have you?   ....

   How many younger, living sisters have you?   ....

8. Please write in below the names, sex, age, educational level achieved, occupation, and current place of residence of each of your brothers and sisters. Start off with the oldest member of the family and include *ALL* living brothers and sisters, leaving a blank space for your own place in the family

Christian name	Sex	Present age	What is the highest educational level reached by each person so far				Occupation of each person. State job, and type of employment, trade, or profession	Present place of residence
			Primary school only	Vocational school	Secondary school	University		
1								
2								
3								

9. How many uncles have you?
        (a) on your father's side?   ....
        (b) on your mother's side?   ....
    How many aunts have you?
        (a) on your father's side?   ....
        (b) on your mother's side?   ....

10. As far as you know, did any of these have a secondary school education?
        Yes ( )   No ( )   Not sure ( )
        If yes, how many?   Uncles—father's side ....
                             Uncles—mother's side...............
                             Aunts—father's side ....
                             Aunts—mother's side...............

11. What are, or were, the occupations and residences of your uncles and aunts? If your aunts are married, what are the occupations of their husbands?

Names of all your uncles and aunts	State whether each one is your father's or mother's blood relation	What is each one's occupation or that of their husbands?	Where does each one live? Name of place
1			
2			
3			

12. (a) How many people live in your house at home?...............
     (b) How many separate rooms in the house?   ....
     (Do not include hallways, porches, bathrooms, or toilets, etc.)
     (c) What kind of lighting do you have in the house?...............
     (Please check off the statement that is most true in your case.)

            ( )   electricity
            ( )   gas
            ( )   oil lamps
            ( )   other. If this, what kind? ....

		Yes	No
(d)	Do you have a piped water tap in the house?	( )	( )
(e)	Do you have hot water on tap in the house?	( )	( )
(f)	Do you have an indoor flush toilet in the house?	( )	( )
(g)	Do you have a bathroom in the house?	( )	( )
(h)	Do you have a telephone in the house?	( )	( )
(i)	Do you have a radio in the house?	( )	( )
(j)	Do you have a TV set in the house?	( )	( )
(k)	Do you have a washing machine in the house?	( )	( )
(l)	Do you have a kitchen range in the house?	( )	( )
(m)	Do you have an electric or gas cooker in the house?	( )	( )
(n)	Do you usually eat your meals in the kitchen at home?	( )	( )
(o)	Does your family have a car?	( )	( )
(p)	Do you have a carpet in the sitting room?	( )	( )
(q)	Do you have linoleum on the floors of some of the rooms in your house?	( )	( )

(q) If yes, which rooms? ....

(r)	Have any new tiled fireplaces been put in your home in the past few years?	( )	( )
(s)	Is there an electric doorbell on the front door of your home?	( )	( )

13.	Do you get the daily newspaper at home every day?	( )	( )
(b)	Do you get the local newspaper at home every week?	( )	( )
(c)	Does your father read books regularly?	( )	( )

If yes, what kind of books does he read?

....

....

(d)	Does your mother read books regularly?	( )	( )

If yes, what kind of books does she read?

....

....

(e)	Do you get any weekly magazines at home? (incl. the "Farmers' Journal")	( )	( )

                                                                       Yes   No

(f) Does your family listen to the news on the radio every day? ( ) ( )

(g) Would they 'miss' the news if they didn't hear it? ( ) ( )

14. (a) Is your father a member of any organization? ( ) ( )
(e.g. N.F.A., Muintir na Tire, Red Cross, etc.)
If yes, what organizations is he a member of?
....
....

(b) Is your mother a member of any organization? ( ) ( )
If yes, what organizations is she a member of?
....
....

15. (a) Have you ever gone on holidays outside your home county? ( ) ( )
If yes, where did you go to? ....

(b) About how many times have you gone on holidays outside the county? ....

(c) Do your parents ever go on holidays away from home, even for a day or two? ( ) ( )
If yes, about how many times have they done so in the past ten years?........................
If yes, where do they usually go to?............
....

(d) About how often do you have visitors at home?
         ( ) Less than once a year
         ( ) A few times a year
         ( ) About once a month or so, or less
         ( ) A few times a month
         ( ) Weekly, or more frequently

(e) What proportion of these visitors come from outside the county?
         ( ) Most of them
         ( ) More than half
         ( ) About half or maybe less
         ( ) Very few
         ( ) None

                                                        Yes   No

(f) Have you ever been to Dublin or Belfast?   ( )   ( )
     If yes, about how many times were you in
     these towns altogether? .... times

16. (a) What is the principal occupation of your father?............
     (b) Does he have another occupation? If yes, what is it?

          ....

     (c) If he is employed: (i.e. paid a wage or salary while work-
          ing for somebody) state:
          (1) Type of work done?.....................................
          (2) Where he is employed? ....
          (3) Approximately how much is he paid per week?
          (Please check off the response that is most true in your
          case)
                    ( )   £ 2–4 per week   (1)
                    ( )   £ 4–6 per week   (2)
                    ( )   £ 7–8 per week   (3)
                    ( )   £ 9–10 per week   (4)
                    ( )   £11–12 per week   (5)
                    ( )   £13–14 per week   (6)
                    ( )   £15 –20 per week   (7)
                    ( )   Over £20 per week   (8)
                    ( )   Paid a salary on a monthly
                          basis   (9)
                    ( )   I don't know   (0)

     (d) If he is self employed (owns a farm, some kind of business,
          or has a profession), state exactly the kind of business or
          profession?

          ....

     (e) If he is a farmer, please state:
          (1) Size of farm in acres ...... [Are these Statute ( )
              or Irish ( ).]
          (2) If land is rented as well, about how many acres are
              rented?......
          (3) How many milking cows are kept on the farm?......
          (4) What is done with the milk if cows are kept?......

          ....

(5) How many other cattle are kept on the farm?
    Store Cattle ....
    Fat Cattle   ......
    Calves or yearlings ......
    Dry cows   ......
(6) How many pigs are kept?
    Sows   ......
    Weaners   ......
    Bacon pigs   ......
    Bonhams   ......
(7) How many sheep are kept? ......
(8) About how many acres of tillage are cultivated on
    the total farm, including rented land, this year?....
(9) How many acres of each crop?

    ....
    ....

Are they Irish ( ) or Statute ( ) acres?

17. What did your father's education consist of? Answer to the
    best of your knowledge. (Please check off (√) that statement
    that is most true in your case.)
        ( ) A National School education only   (0)
        ( ) 1–2 years of secondary school education (1)
        ( ) 3–4 years of secondary school education (2)
        ( ) Finished secondary school education   (3)
        ( ) Some vocational school education   (4)
        ( ) Completed vocational school education (5)
        ( ) Some University education   (6)
        ( ) Completed University education   (7)

18. What did your mother's education consist of? Answer to the
    best of your knowledge. (Please check off (√) the response
    that is most true in your case.)
        ( ) A National School education only   (0)
        ( ) 1–2 years of secondary school education (1)
        ( ) 3–4 years of secondary school education (2)
        ( ) Completed Secondary school education (3)
        ( ) Some Vocational School education   (4)
        ( ) Completed Vocational school education (5)

( ) Some University education   (6)
( ) Completed University education   (7)

....

25. When you finished up in primary school did any of your
    parents want you to go on for further education?
    ( ) Yes
    ( ) No   (0)
If yes, which of them?
    ( ) Father   (1)
    ( ) Mother   (2)
    ( ) Both   (3)
If yes, how strongly do you think they/he/she felt about this?
    ( ) Very strongly   (3)
    ( ) Strongly   (2)
    ( ) Didn't seem to care that much   (1)

If yes, what kind of school did they/he/she want you to go to?
    ( ) Secondary
    ( ) Vocational
    ( ) Other. If this, what kind?

26. Did your Primary school-teacher ever encourage you to go on
    for further education beyond primary school?
    ( ) Yes
    ( ) No   (0)
If yes, how strongly did he encourage you?
    ( ) Very strongly   (3)
    ( ) Strongly   (2)
    ( ) Didn't seem to care that much   (1)
If yes, what kind of school did he want you to go to?
    ( ) Secondary
    ( ) Vocational
    ( ) Other. If this, what kind?

27. Are you now, or have you been, working full time on a job,
    or on your home farm or business? Yes ( ) No ( )
    If no, go on to question no. 29.   0

If yes, and you have been working on your home farm, or in the family business go on to question no. 28.

If at other type of work, please answer the following questions.

(a) What kind of work have you been doing? ....

(b) Where or what organization have you been working with?
     ....

(c) Do you live at home? Yes ( ) No ( )

(d) About how much do you earn per week? ....

(e) Is this a whole time job? Yes ( ) No ( )

(f) Do you like this type of work? Yes ( ) No ( )
     Undecided ( )

(g) Do you think that you will stay permanently at this
     particular job? Yes ( ) No ( ) Not sure ( )
                        0   2   1

(h) If yes skip to questions no. 51 or 53.

(i) If no, skip to question 29.

28. If you have been working on the home farm or in the family
     business, please answer the following questions. (If you haven't,
     skip to the next question.)

     (a) Have you been paid a regular weekly or monthly wage
          for your work? Yes ( ) No ( )

     (b) If yes, how much have you been paid, about?
          £...s....d.... per week

     (c) If no, about how much pocket money do you get?
          ...... per week

     (d) Is this a whole time job? Yes ( ) No ( )

     (e) Do you like this work? Yes ( ) No ( )
          Undecided ( )

     (f) Do you think that you will get to own the home farm or
          business eventually? Yes ( ) No ( ) Not sure ( )
                                        0   1

          If yes, how sure are you of this?
                    ( ) Very sure   (5)
                    ( ) Somewhat sure   (4)
                    ( ) No opinion   (3)
                    ( ) Somewhat unsure   (2)

     (g) If yes, (you think that you will get to own the home farm
          or business) how old do you think you will be when you
          get to own it? ......years old.

(h) How sure are you of this?
     ( )   very sure
     ( )   somewhat sure
     ( )   no opinion
     ( )   somewhat unsure
     ( )   very unsure

(i) Has your father ever discussed this question with you?
Yes ( ) No ( )

(j) Has you mother ever discussed this question with you?
Yes ( ) No ( )

(k) Do you think that you will stay on working at this job permanently? Yes ( ) No ( ) Not sure ( )
If yes, please skip to Question No. 51 or 53.

(l) If no, at what age do you think you will start looking for another job? .... years old.

(m) If no, what plans have you of what you might do when you finish up? (If you have answered this question, skip to q. 29 next)
....
....
....

29. If you think that you will stay working at what you are doing now, please skip to q. 51 or 53. If not, and you are thinking of getting another job or you have still to start working, please answer the following questions. (All students in secondary and vocational schools should answer these questions as well.)

(a) What jobs (occupations) have you thought of going into?
1............................ 3............................
2............................ 4............................

(b) What job(s) would you really like to get?
1............................ 3............................
2............................ 4............................

(c) What is the first job(s) that you think you will get?
1............................ 3............................
2............................ 4............................

(d) What job(s) would you like to have when you are 30 years old?
1............................ 3............................
2............................ 4............................

(e) What is (are) the best job(s) you think you can get by the
     time you are 30 years old?
     1.......................................   3...................................
     2.......................................   4...................................

30. Now, in regard to choosing a job, how deeply have you thought
     about it? (Please check off that statement that is most true in
     your case.)
     ( ) I have thought a great deal about it.
     ( ) I have thought somewhat about it.
     ( ) I have not thought very much about it.

31. Now, in regard to choosing a job, how sure are you of your
     choice? (Please check off that statement that is most true in
     your case.)
     ( ) I am sure that my mind is made up.
     ( ) I am not sure that my mind is made up but I think so.
     ( ) I am not sure that my mind is made up.
     ( ) My mind is not made up.

32. In regard to choosing and getting a job, how anxious do you
     feel about it?
     ( ) I feel very anxious.
     ( ) I feel somewhat anxious.
     ( ) I feel just a little anxious.
     ( ) I don't feel anxious at all.

33. Of the jobs that you have just considered, do you think that
     you will be able to get any of them in or near your home
     community?
     ( ) Yes   (0)
     ( ) No   (2)
     ( ) Not sure   (1)
     If yes, which one(s)?...

33a. What kind of jobs could you get around here if you wanted
     them?
     ....

34. Now, supposing that you could get the sort of job(s) that you have just considered, in or near your home community, would you take it/them and permanently stay there?
( ) Yes   (0)
( ) No   (2)
( ) Not sure   (1)

35. Do you intend to leave this part of the country to get a job and live your life elsewhere?
( ) Yes   (2)
( ) No   (0)
( ) Not sure   (1)

36. If you intend to leave, do you know of any place, either in Ireland or abroad, where you could go to get a suitable job?
( ) Yes
( ) No
( ) Not sure
If yes, where is this place?...
How, or from whom, did you hear about this place?............
....

37. Has anybody offered to help you find a good job? Yes ( )
No ( )   If yes, who is this person? ....

38. Do you have a definite job waiting for you?
( ) Yes
( ) No
If yes, is it one of the jobs that you have just considered?
Yes ( ) No ( )
If it is not, what kind of job is it?.....................................
Do you intend to take it? Yes ( )   No ( )
Where is it located? ....

39. Which of the jobs that you have just considered do you know most about?

40. From whom, or how, did you get your information about that (these) job(s)?
....

40a. Who could give you the most help in getting a job?............

....

41. Now, about choosing a job, and getting a job: how fully, if ever, have you discussed this with your father?
    ( )   very fully
    ( )   rather fully
    ( )   vaguely discussed it
    ( )   never discussed it

42. How fully have you discussed this matter with your mother, if ever?
    ( )   very fully
    ( )   rather fully
    ( )   vaguely discussed it
    ( )   never discussed it

....

48. (a) What jobs do your parents think that you should go into?
    1............................. 3................................
    2............................. 4................................
    (b) Would you like to take up the kind of jobs that they want you to take up? Yes ( ) No ( )
    (c) If not, what is there about their selection of jobs that you don't like? ....

    ....

    (d) Could they help you to get a job that you wanted?
         Yes ( ) No ( )
    If yes, in what way could they help you?....................

    ....

49. Do you think that your parents expect you to take up a job locally? Yes ( ) No ( )
    Would they be disappointed if you went away to get a job?
    Yes ( ) No ( )
    Do they expect you to leave to get a good job?
    Yes ( ) No ( )

....

51. (FOR *BOYS ONLY*, GIRLS GO ON TO Q. No. 53)
For the following list of occupations, please check off (√)
all those occupations that you *feel you would be "letting down"*
your family with if you were to take them up!

( )   Co. Council road worker
( )   Farm labourer
( )   General unskilled labour
( )   Street sweeper
( )   Caretaker
( )   Manual worker on the buildings
( )   Factory worker—unskilled
( )   Messenger boy
( )   Doorman or Porter
( )   Creamery worker — unskilled
( )   Laundry worker
( )   Petrol pump attendant
( )   Lorry driver's helper
( )   Milk delivery man
( )   Bread roundsman
( )   Bus conductor
( )   Lorry driver
( )   Factory worker — semiskilled
( )   Bus driver
( )   Ticket collector on train
( )   Shoemaker or cobbler
( )   Barber
( )   Corporal in the army
( )   Assistant in a grocery shop
( )   Assistant in a drapery shop
( )   Postman
( )   Foreman over labourers
( )   Foreman on a building site
( )   Skilled factory worker
( )   Garage mechanic
( )   Painter
( )   Carpenter
( )   Plasterer or bricklayer
( )   Butcher
( )   Plumber
( )   Tailor

( )   Book keeper in shop, etc.
( )   Clerk in insurance or other office
( )   Clerk in the county council
( )   Bank clerk
( )   Inspector on the buses, etc.
( )   Garda
( )   Rate collector
( )   Reporter on a local newspaper
( )   Insurance agent
( )   Farmer, owning own farm
( )   Commercial traveller
( )   Primary school teacher
( )   Inspector for farm buildings or drainage, etc.
( )   Cashier in the bank, or equivalent
( )   Agricultural Advisor
( )   Secondary school teacher
( )   Engineer
( )   Accountant
( )   Solicitor
( )   Bank Manager
( )   Dentist
( )   Chemist
( )   Architect
( )   Doctor
( )   Judge

52. (FOR *BOYS ONLY*, GIRLS GO ON TO THE NEXT
     QUESTION)
     For the following list of occupations, please check off (√) *all
     those occupations you feel sure you would not be able to get,* even if you
     tried; and if plenty of these jobs were available!

          ( )   Co. Council road worker
          ( )   Farm labourer
          ( )   General unskilled labourer
          ( )   Street sweeper
          ( )   Caretaker
          ( )   Manual worker on the buildings
          ( )   Factory worker — unskilled
          ( )   Messenger boy

( ) Doorman or Porter
( ) Creamery worker—unskilled
( ) Laundry worker
( ) Petrol pump attendant
( ) Lorry driver's helper
( ) Milk delivery man
( ) Bread roundsman
( ) Bus conductor
( ) Lorry driver
( ) Factory worker — semiskilled
( ) Bus driver
( ) Ticket collector on train
( ) Shoemaker or cobbler
( ) Barber
( ) Corporal in the army
( ) Assistant in a grocery shop
( ) Assistant in a drapery shop
( ) Postman
( ) Foreman over labourers
( ) Foreman on a building site
( ) Skilled factory worker
( ) Garage mechanic
( ) Painter
( ) Carpenter
( ) Plasterer or bricklayer
( ) Butcher
( ) Plumber
( ) Tailor
( ) Book keeper in shop, etc.
( ) Clerk in insurance or other office
( ) Clerk in the county council
( ) Bank clerk
( ) Inspector on the buses, etc.
( ) Garda
( ) Rate collector
( ) Reporter on a local newspaper
( ) Insurance agent
( ) Farmer, owning own farm
( ) Commercial traveller
( ) Primary school teacher

( ) Inspector for farm buildings or drainage, etc.
( ) Cashier in the bank, or equivalent
( ) Agricultural Advisor
( ) Secondary school teacher
( ) Engineer
( ) Accountant
( ) Solicitor
( ) Bank Manager
( ) Dentist
( ) Chemist
( ) Architect
( ) Doctor
( ) Judge

53. (FOR *GIRLS ONLY:* BOYS GO ON TO Q. No. 56)
     For the following list of occupations, please check off (√) all
     those occupations that you feel *you would be "letting down" your
     family with if you were to take them up!*

( ) Domestic servant
( ) Wardsmaid in a hospital
( ) Unskilled factory worker
( ) Clothes presser in a laundry
( ) Housework at home
( ) Housekeeper for a Priest or doctor, etc.
( ) Cinema usherette
( ) Barmaid
( ) Waitress in hotel or restaurant
( ) Cook in an hotel
( ) Assistant in a grocery shop
( ) Assistant in a drapery shop
( ) Chemist's assistant
( ) Book keeper in a shop or office
( ) Telephone operator
( ) Post Office clerk
( ) Dressmaker
( ) Hairdresser
( ) Clerk in solicitor's office
( ) Clerks in other offices
( ) Clerk typist

( ) Civil servant clerk
( ) Bank clerk
( ) Nurse
( ) Executive officer in the civil service
( ) Teacher in a primary school
( ) Librarian
( ) Poultry Instructress
( ) Domestic Science teacher
( ) Teacher in a secondary school
( ) Manageress of an hotel
( ) Fashion Model
( ) Chemist
( ) Air Hostess
( ) Architect
( ) Dentist
( ) Doctor

54. (FOR *GIRLS ONLY:* BOYS GO ON TO Q. No. 56)
For the following list of occupations, please check off (√) *all those occupations that you feel you would not be able to get,* even if you tried; and if plenty of these jobs were available.

( ) Domestic servant
( ) Wardsmaid in a hospital
( ) Unskilled factory worker
( ) Clothes presser in a laundry
( ) Housework at home
( ) Housekeeper for a Priest or doctor, etc.
( ) Cinema usherette
( ) Barmaid
( ) Waitress in hotel or restaurant
( ) Cook in an hotel
( ) Assistant in a grocery shop
( ) Assistant in a drapery shop
( ) Chemist's assistant
( ) Book keeper in a shop or office
( ) Telephone operator
( ) Post Office clerk
( ) Dressmaker
( ) Hairdresser

( ) Clerk in solicitor's office
( ) Clerks in other offices
( ) Clerk typist
( ) Civil servant clerk
( ) Bank clerk
( ) Nurse
( ) Executive officer in the civil service
( ) Teacher in a primary school
( ) Librarian
( ) Poultry Instructress
( ) Domestic Science teacher
( ) Teacher in a secondary school
( ) Manageress of an hotel
( ) Fashion Model
( ) Chemist
( ) Air Hostess
( ) Architect
( ) Dentist
( ) Doctor

55. (FOR *GIRLS ONLY:* BOYS GO ON TO THE NEXT
     QUESTION)

   (a) Do you feel that when you are to get married, that you
        would like to be a farmer's wife? (Please check off that
        response that is most true in your case.)
        ( ) Definitely yes
        ( ) Yes
        ( ) Undecided
        ( ) No
        ( ) Definitely no
   (b) What is there about being a farmer's wife that you would
        particularly dislike?
        ....
   (c) Is there anything about being a farmer's wife, that you
        would particularly like? Yes ( ) No ( )
        If yes, what is it?...
   (d) Some people have said that even if good jobs were avail-
        able in this part of the country for girls, they would not

stay here anyway, beause there is so little chance of getting married in this part of the country.

Do you agree with this?   Yes ( )   No ( )

(e) For most girls of your age, at what age do you think they should be married? ...... years old.

(f) If they stayed around home, do you think that they would get married at that age?   Yes ( )   No ( )

....

61. Now, if you could get a permanent and otherwise suitable job, in a place of your own choosing, how much would the job need to pay per week before you would be satisfied with it? (Please check only that response that you agree most with.)

( )   £ 2–4   per week   (1)
( )   £ 4–6   per week   (2)
( )   £ 7–8   per week   (3)
( )   £ 9–10 per week   (4)
( )   £11–12 per week   (5)
( )   £13–14 per week   (6)
( )   £15–20 per week   (7)
( )   Over £20 per week   (8)
( )   I don't know   (0)

62. Now, for the type of income that you want to earn, do you think that if you stay in or near your home community, that you will be able to earn this income?
( )   Yes   (0)
( )   No   (2)
( )   Not sure   (1)

63. Now, supposing that you could get the sort of income that you want in or near your home community, would you stay there permanently?
( )   Yes   (0)
( )   No   (2)
( )   Not sure   (1)

64. Do you intend to leave this part of the country so that you can get a better income elsewhere?

    ( ) Yes   (2)
    ( ) No   (0)
    ( ) Not sure   (1)

65. If you are thinking of going, as a reason for leaving, is the fact that you cannot get a suitable income here (i.e. *if* you cannot get it) an important reason for leaving?

    Yes ( ) No ( )

    If yes, is it: ( ) more important than the lack of jobs as a reason for leaving?

    ( ) about as important as the lack of jobs as a reason for leaving?

    ( ) less important than the absence of jobs, as such, as a reason for leaving?

66. Some young people from your community have said that they would not live there always, but only in a community which had the following characteristics. How much do you agree with them?

    (a) Which was nearer to a big town than the one you live in? Strongly Agree ( ). Agree ( ). Undecided ( ). Disagree ( ). Strongly Disagree ( ).

    (b) Which had better roads than the one you now live in? Strongly Agree ( ). Agree ( ). Undecided ( ). Disagree ( ). Strongly Disagree ( ).

    (c) Which had better primary schools than the one you now live in? Strongly Agree ( ). Agree ( ). Undecided ( ). Disagree ( ). Strongly Disagree ( ).

    (d) Which was nearer to secondary and vocational schools than the one you now live in? Strongly Agree ( ). Agree ( ). Undecided ( ). Disagree ( ). Strongly Disagree ( ).

    (e) Which allowed you to enjoy your time off much better than in your home community? Strongly Agree ( ). Agree ( ). Undecided. ( ) Disagree ( ). Strongly Disagree ( ).

(f) Where a person would not have to go so far to enjoy a good dance or a good film?
Strongly Agree ( ).   Agree ( ).   Undecided ( ).
Disagree ( ).   Strongly Disagree ( ).

(g) Where the community has better facilities for games than this one has?
Strongly Agree ( ).   Agree ( ).   Undecided ( ).
Disagree ( ).   Strongly Disagree ( ).

(h) Where people showed more interest in games, and organized clubs and teams for young people to play and enjoy themselves?
Strongly Agree ( ).   Agree ( ).   Undecided ( ).
Disagree ( ).   Strongly Disagree ( ).

(i) Where there would be more young people to go to films and dances with, and to organize games with?
Strongly Agree ( ).   Agree ( ).   Undecided ( ).
Disagree ( ).   Strongly Disagree ( ).

(j) Which is nearer to shops and good shopping facilities than the one you live in?
Strongly Agree ( ).   Agree ( ).   Undecided ( ).
Disagree ( ).   Strongly Disagree ( ).

67. Now, suppose that you could enjoy all these things and similar amenities in your home community, would you stay there permanently?
( ) Yes   (0)
( ) No   (2)
( ) Undecided   (1)

68. If you have some idea of leaving your home community for elsewhere, is the fact that your home community lacks the amenities that you would like it to have an important reason for this decision?
( ) Yes ( ) No
If yes, is it: ( ) more important than the lack of jobs?
( ) more important than the fact that you wouldn't be able to earn enough money locally?
( ) less important than jobs, as a reason?

( ) less important than the fact of being unable
to earn enough money locally, as a reason?
(Please check off (√) only those statements that are true in
your case.)

69. Do you know of any place in which you could make more
money than at home, and which has all the amenities and
advantages that you think are satisfactory?

( ) Yes
( ) No
( ) Don't know.

If yes, where is this place?...

70. For the following set of statements, please check off (√) only
the one response that you most agree with in each case.

(a) I am looking forward to leaving this community.
Strongly Agree ( ). Agree ( ). Undecided ( ).
Disagree ( ). Strongly Disagree ( ).

(b) Any young people worth their salt should leave this
community.
Strongly Agree ( ). Agree ( ). Undecided ( ).
Disagree ( ). Strongly Disagree ( ).

(c) Not much can be said in favour of this community.
Strongly Agree ( ). Agree ( ). Undecided ( ).
Disagree ( ). Strongly Disagree ( ).

(d) No one seems to care how young people get on in this
community.
Strongly Agree ( ). Agree ( ). Undecided ( ).
Disagree ( ). Strongly Disagree ( ).

(e) There is too much bickering among people in this
community.
Strongly Agree ( ). Agree ( ). Undecided ( ).
Disagree ( ). Strongly Disagree ( ).

(f) This community is not too bad really.
Strongly Agree ( ). Agree ( ). Undecided ( ).
Disagree ( ). Strongly Disagree ( ).

(g) The future of this community looks bright.
Strongly Agree ( ). Agree ( ). Undecided ( ).
Disagree ( ). Strongly Disagree ( ).

(h) The people of this community are very friendly and help-
ful to one another.
Strongly Agree ( ).   Agree ( ).   Undecided ( ).
Disagree ( ).   Strongly Disagree ( ).

(i) This community is a good place to live in.
Strongly Agree ( ).   Agree ( ).   Undecided ( ).
Disagree ( ).   Strongly Disagree ( ).

(j) I am very eager to spend my life in this community, if I
can at all.
Strongly Agree ( ).   Agree ( ).   Undecided ( ).
Disagree ( ).   Strongly Disagree ( ).

71. Do you help out your family or some other relation in any way?
Yes ( )   No ( )
If yes, please give details of what you do............................
....

72. Do you think that your family, or any relations depend on
your help to any extent?
Yes ( )   No ( )
If yes, how much: ( )   A great deal
( )   Somewhat
( )   Undecided
( )   Not very much

73. Now, if you were to leave your community and home, could
somebody else do the work that you are doing for them?
( )   Yes, very easily
( )   Yes, somewhat easily
( )   I don't know
( )   No, not very easily
( )   Not except with difficulty

74. Now, if your family depend on you helping them out at home
to some extent, (or some relation does), would you feel guilty
leaving your family, in order to get work and live away from
home?
( ) Yes   ( ) No

If yes, how guilty would you feel?
 ( ) Yes, very guilty
 ( ) Yes, somewhat guilty
 ( ) I am undecided
 ( ) Not very guilty

75. If you are helping out your family by working at home, for how long will you be expected to do this?........................

76. What do you intend to do when you think your obligations to your family are finished?...

77. Now, if you are earning, or when you do start earning money, will you be expected to contribute some to the family?
     Yes ( ) No ( )
If yes, do you think that your family might depend on you for this support? (Please check that response that is most true in your case.)
 ( ) Yes, a great deal
 ( ) Yes, somewhat
 ( ) I am undecided
 ( ) No, not at all

78. Have you any younger brothers or sisters that have to be educated yet?
     Yes ( ) No ( )
If yes, will you be expected to help them out in any way?
     Yes ( ) No ( )
If yes, please give us some particulars of what kind of help you would be expected to give?...
....

....

(Question No. 79 omitted).

Appendix II:
Prestige Scaling of Occupational Titles by Male Adolescents

QUESTION 61 in the schedule (Appendix I) placed a list of 61 occupations before male respondents and asked them: "For the following list of occupations, please check off (√) all those occupations that *you feel* you would be letting down your family with if you were to take them up". The occupations were widely known in the area and were roughly presented in an ascending order of status according to the author's opinion from County Council road worker to Judge. As it happened, the respondents did not agree with the author's ranking at all, as a comparison of the original rank order and the respondents' ordering clearly indicates.

It was possible to rearrange and rank-order the items in terms of their degree of "difficulty" of rejection—i.e. the relative number of respondents who checked the occupation as being of lower status than that of their own family. The Waisenan technique of Guttman Scalogram analysis was used for this purpose.[1] A description of the method used and a fuller discussion of it is given in a paper in *Rural Sociology*, Vol. 34, 3, Sept. 1969. From the list of 61 occupations, 31 were successfully scaled, with a Coefficient of Reproducibility of .893 — a quasi-unidimensional scale by Guttman's standards. The final scale is presented below, with the original rank order presented in brackets after the occupational title.

[1] Waisenan, F. B., "A notation Technique of Scalogram Analysis", *Sociological Quarterly*, 4, 1, 1960.

Perceived Prestige of Occupations — Ascending Order of Rank	Original Rank Order
* 1. Street sweeper	(4)
2. Messenger boy	(8)
3. General unskilled labourer	(3)
4. County Council road worker	(1)
* 5. Petrol pump attendant	(12)
6. Caretaker	(5)
7. Doorman or Porter	(9)
* 8. Laundry worker	(11)
* 9. Farm labourer	(2)
10. Lorry driver's helper	(13)
11. Unskilled creamery worker	(10)
*12. Postman	(26)
13. Assistant in grocery	(24)
*14. Milk delivery man	(14)
15. Unskilled factory worker	(7)
16. Bread roundsman	(15)
17. Ticket collector on train	(20)
*18. Assistant in drapery	(25)
*19. Semiskilled factory worker	(18)
*20. Barber	(22)
21. Shoemaker	(21)
22. Painter	(31)
*23. Lorry driver	(17)
*24. Bus conductor	(16)
25. Manual worker on construction	(6)
*26. Corporal in the Army	(23)
27. Butcher	(34)
28. Foreman over labourers	(27)
29. Tailor	(36)
*30. Plumber	(35)
31. Plasterer or Bricklayer	(33)
32. Book keeper in shop	(37)
33. Bus driver	(19)
*34. Garage mechanic	(30)
35. Skilled factory worker	(29)
*36. Carpenter	(32)
37. Foreman on buildings	(28)

A comparison of the relative rankings of 15 occupations common to this and the North-Hatt scale (marked with an asterisk above) yielded a Spearman Rank Order correlation of .720. If the occupation "postman" is excluded, the correlation reaches .87.[2]

THE OCCUPATIONAL STATUS SCALE

This classification scheme is based on the Census classification "Social Groups", *Census of Population of Ireland*, 1961, Vol. III, 171–172, but as it is primarily a classification based on the relative prestige of the occupation, many occupations have been changed around and the relative positions of categories have been changed too. These changes have been made on the basis of prestige rankings of occupations delineated in the United States[3] and generally validated in Britain and Europe.[4] The author used his own opinions of how some occupations would be evaluated here for some occupations which were not mentioned in any of these reports.

1. *Higher Professional Workers*

As in Vol. III, *Census of Population of Ireland*, 1961, 171–172, *op. cit.*
Chemists are included here, however, from "the Lower Professional" category.

Doctor, Surgeon, etc.
Priest or Minister of
    Religion
Architect
Dentist
Solicitor
Engineer

Accountant
Veterinary Surgeon
Secondary School Teacher
Chemist
Agricultural Instructors
Other Professional Workers
    who require a University
    degree or equivalent in order
    to practise.

[2] See Hannan, D. F. and Beegle, J. A., "Evaluation of Occupations by Irish Rural Adolescents on the Basis of Prestige and Difficulty of Achievement", *Rural Sociology*, 34, 3, 1969.
[3] National Opinion Research Centre, "Jobs and Occupations: A Popular Evaluation", Opinion News, 9:3:13:1947. Reprinted in Bendix and Lipset, *Class, Status and Power*, Free Press, 1956.
[4] Inkeles, A. and Rossi, P. H., "National Comparisons of Occupational Prestige", *American Journal of Sociology*, 61:329–339; and Hannan and Beegle, *op. cit.*

2. *Lower Professional Workers*

Classified as in the above Census volume. But it also includes: Army officers, from the "Salaried Employees" class; Managers of large concerns—Creameries, factories, etc. from the "Employers and Managers" category and senior civil servants and local county officials etc.

Primary and Vocational School teachers who do not require a University degree.

Higher Bank officials and officials of large concerns, Managers, Secretaries, Cashiers in banks, etc.
Higher civil service and local county officials, Social Welfare officers, Customs and Excise officials, tax officers,
Army officers,
Nurses, Radiologists, Physiotherapists, etc.
Medical technicians.
Librarians
Editors and higher officers in newspapers.

3. *Employers and Proprietors of Wholesale and Retail Shops*

As in the census classification, *op. cit.*, but excluding all managers of large concerns to the "Lower Professional" category, and Managers of small concerns to the "Intermediate Non-Manual" category. It also includes all proprietors of wholesale and retail establishments whether employers or not, from the "Intermediate Non-Manual" category.

Owners or Proprietors of all manufacturing concerns. Shopkeepers, Merchants, etc., whether employers or not. Publicans, proprietors only, whether employers or not. Garage proprietors, whether employers or not, Hotel and Guest Home proprietors, and proprietors of restaurants.
Building Contractors
Hauliers and Agricultural Contractors, Livestock and Egg Dealers, etc.

4. *Farmers*

5. *Intermediate Non-Manual Workers*

This includes the remainder of the "Salaried Employees" and the "Intermediate Non-Manual Workers" from the above classification. But it excludes Shop Assistants, and Bartenders, to the following "Services" category. It also includes Managers of small concerns, retail and otherwise, from the "Employers and Managers" category.

Commercial Travellers
Insurance Agents
Press Agents or Reporters
Bank Clerks, etc.
Other office clerks, typists, etc. in other offices
Policemen, all ranks
Auctioneers, salesmen in garages, etc.
Rate collectors
Bus and other transport inspectors
Draughtsmen, etc.

6. *Skilled Manual Workers and Foremen*

As in the census report quoted.
Electrician
Machinist
Carpenter
Motor mechanic, fitter, etc.
Plumber
Butcher
Bricklayer, mason, plasterer
Tailor, dressmaker
Foreman, land steward, etc.

7. *Service and Sales Workers and "Other Non-Manual Workers"*

Includes the category "Other Non-Manual Workers" and the cited occupations from "Intermediate Non-Manual Workers". But it excludes all private domestic workers to the next occupational category below.

Shop assistants, Bartenders, and service assistants in garages, etc.,
other than petrol attendants
General salesmen
Bus, lorry, taxi, and van drivers
Postmen and post office sorters
Warehousemen and storemen
Barbers and hairdressers
Wardsmaids and ward orderlies
Housekeepers, roundsmen, soldiers, etc.

8. *Semiskilled Manual Workers and Lower Order Service Workers*
Includes all the occupations in the "Semi-Skilled Manual
Workers" category in the quoted Census volume. But it also includes maids and other lower order domestic service workers from
the "Other Non-Manual Workers".

Labourers with builders, electricity supply board, post office, etc.,
and land project
Semiskilled factory workers, in meat and shoe factories, other
machine operators
Labourers in creameries and other semiskilled labourers
Porters and doormen in banks, hotels, hospitals, etc.
Messengers
Caretakers, watchmen, and related workers
Lorry drivers' helpers, and other transport workers
Petrol attendants

9. *Unskilled Manual Workers*
Includes all those in the "Unskilled Manual Workers" category,
in the census classification, *op. cit.*, and those from "Other Agricultural Occupations".

Co. council labourers and navvies
General labourers and unskilled workers
Farm labourers
Gardeners and forestry labourers

10. *Unemployed and otherwise not classified*

Appendix III:
Tables for Chapter 4

TABLE LXIII: The Relationship between Occupational and Income Frustration

Income Frustration	Occupational Frustration			
	Not Frustrated	Partly Frustrated	Frustrated	Total
	%	%	%	
Not frustrated	52.8	13.7	8.2	152
Partly frustrated	22.1	48.4	18.2	145
Frustrated	25.1	37.9	73.6	197
Total N	231	153	110	494

Gamma = .595

TABLE LXIV: THE RELATIONSHIP BETWEEN INCOME FRUSTRATION AND MIGRATION INTENTIONS, CONTROLLING FOR LEVELS OF OCCUPATIONAL FRUSTRATION

	Occupational Frustration								
	Not Frustrated			Partly Frustrated			Frustrated		
	Income Frustration			Income Frustration			Income Frustration		
Migration Intentions	Not Frustrated	Partly Frustrated	Frustrated	Not Frustrated	Partly Frustrated	Frustrated	Not Frustrated	Partly Frustrated	Frustrated
	%	%	%	%	%	%	%	%	%
Definite intention to stay	53.3	25.5	29.8	38.1	4.1	3.4	22.2	0.0	6.2
Indefinite whether will stay or leave	33.6	54.9	42.1	38.1	75.7	39.7	11.1	35.0	13.6
Definite intention to migrate	13.1	19.6	28.1	23.8	20.3	56.9	66.7	65.0	80.2
TOTAL N	122	51	57	21	74	58	9	20	81
	Gamma = .346			Gamma = .566			Gamma = .305		

TABLE LXV: THE RELATIONSHIP BETWEEN LEVELS OF COMMUNITY SATISFACTION AND PLANS TO MIGRATE

Levels of Community Satisfaction

Plans to Migrate	Lowest Score				Highest Score		Total
	0 and 1	2 and 3	4 and 5	6 and 7	8 and 9		
Definite plans to stay	% 4.1	% 8.4	% 18.6	% 35.4	% 42.6		128
Indefinite whether will stay or leave	46.9	41.1	41.4	35.4	34.3		203
Definite plans to leave	49.0	50.5	40.0	29.2	23.1		191
TOTAL % N	100.0 49	100.0 95	100.0 140	100.0 130	100.0 108		522

Gamma = − 0.355

TABLE LXVI: THE RELATIONSHIP BETWEEN OCCUPATIONAL FRUSTRATION AND COMMUNITY SATISFACTION

Community Satisfaction		Occupational Frustration			Total
		Not Frustrated	Partly Frustrated	Frustrated	
		%	%	%	
Scores 1–3		19.4	32.2	39.6	137
Scores 4–5		24.6	25.5	34.2	133
Scores 6–7		29.3	25.5	13.5	121
Scores 8–9		26.7	16.8	12.6	101
TOTAL	%	100	100	99.9	492
	N	232	149	111	

Gamma = − .298

TABLE LXVII: THE RELATIONSHIP BETWEEN INCOME FRUSTRATION AND COMMUNITY SATISFACTION

Community Satisfaction		Income Frustration			Total
		Not Frustrated	Partly Frustrated	Frustrated	
		%	%	%	
Scores 1–3		13.8	27.8	39.4	142
Scores 4–5		21.9	25.0	30.5	133
Scores 6–7		30.0	26.4	20.2	127
Scores 8–9		34.4	20.8	9.9	105
TOTAL	%	100.1	100	100	507
	N	160	144	203	

Gamma = − .387

TABLE LXVIII: THE RELATIONSHIP BETWEEN INCOME FRUSTRATION AND COMMUNITY SATISFACTION, CONTROLLING FOR LEVELS OF OCCUPATIONAL FRUSTRATION

Community Satisfaction	Occupational Frustration								
	Not Frustrated			Partly Frustrated			Frustrated		
	Income Frustration			Income Frustration			Income Frustration		
	Not Frustrated	Partly Frustrated	Frustrated	Not Frustrated	Partly Frustrated	Frustrated	Not Frustrated	Partly Frustrated	Frustrated
	%	%	%	%	%	%	%	%	%
Scores less than 5	28.6	53.5	58.7	52.6	53	63.5	44.4	72.2	80.5
Scores more than 5	71.4	46.5	41.3	47.4	47	36.5	55.6	27.8	19.5
TOTAL %	100	100	100	100	100	100	100	100	100
N	98	43	47	19	66	52	9	18	77
	Gamma = − .451			Gamma = − .168			Gamma = − .427		

TABLE LXIX: THE RELATIONSHIP BETWEEN COMMUNITY SATISFACTION AND INTENTIONS TO MIGRATE, CONTROLLING FOR LEVELS OF OCCUPATIONAL AND INCOME FRUSTRATION

	Occupational Frustration											
	Not Frustrated				Partly Frustrated				Frustrated			
	Income Frustration				Income Frustration				Income Frustration			
	Not or Partly Frustrated		Frustrated		Not or Partly Frustrated		Frustrated		Not or Partly Frustrated		Frustrated	
	Community Satisfaction		Community Satisfaction		Community Satisfaction		Community Satisfaction		Community Satisfaction		Community Satisfaction	
Intentions to Migrate	−5	5+	−5	5+	−5	5+	−5	5+	−5	5+	−5	5+
	%	%	%	%	%	%	%	%	%	%	%	%
Definite intention to stay	31.4	48.9	26	52.6	6.7	20	0	11.1	5.9	10	3.2	20
Indefinite whether will stay or leave	49	34.4	37	15.7	71.1	55	36.4	50	35.3	10	12.9	13.3
Definite intention to leave	19.6	16.7	37	31.6	22.2	25	63.6	38.9	58.8	80	83.9	66.7
TOTAL %	100	100	100	99.9	100	100	100	100	100	100	100	100
N	51	90	27	19	45	10	33	18	17	10	62	15
Gamma =	− .250		− .303		− .144		− .504		+ .373		− .464	

TABLE LXX: The Relationship between Occupational (and Income) Frustration and Plans to Migrate by Levels of Community Satisfaction

	Community Satisfaction								
	Low Levels 0 to 3			Medium Levels 4 to 6			High Levels 7 to 9		
	Occupational Frustration			Occupational Frustration			Occupational Frustration		
Plans to Migrate	Not Frustrated	Partly Frustrated	Frustrated	Not Frustrated	Partly Frustrated	Frustrated	Not Frustrated	Partly Frustrated	Frustrated
Definite plans to stay	% 17.8	% 2.1	% 2.3	% 39.1	% 8.5	% 8.7	% 54.4	% 22.5	% 10
Indefinite whether will stay or leave	64.4	58.3	9.1	43.7	57.6	21.7	27.2	47.5	15
Definite plans to leave	17.8	39.6	88.6	17.2	33.9	69.7	18.4	30.0	75
Total % N	100 45	100 48	100 44	100 87	100 59	100.1 46	100 103	100 40	100 20
	Gamma = 0.775			Gamma = 0.616			Gamma = 0.585		

TABLE LXX (cont.)

	Community Satisfaction								
	Low Levels 0 to 3			Medium Levels 4 to 6			High Levels 7 to 9		
	Income Frustration			Income Frustration			Income Frustration		
Plans to Migrate	Not Frustrated	Partly Frustrated	Frustrated	Not Frustrated	Partly Frustrated	Frustrated	Not Frustrated	Partly Frustrated	Frustrated
Definite plans to stay	31.8	5.0	3.8	47.3	11.9	13.6	57.8	21.7	30.0
Indefinite whether will stay or leave	50.0	75.0	23.8	29.1	61.0	38.3	27.7	43.5	25.0
Definite plans to leave	18.2	20.0	72.5	23.6	27.1	48.1	14.5	34.8	45.0
TOTAL %	100	100	100	100	100	100	100	100	100
N	22	40	80	55	59	81	83	46	40

Gamma = .729   Gamma = .415   Gamma = .446

TABLE LXXI: THE RELATIONSHIP BETWEEN FAMILY OBLIGATIONS AND PLANS TO MIGRATE

Migration Plans		Levels of Family Obligation				Total
		None	Very Slight	Medium	High	
Definite plan to stay		% 11.7	% 26.5	% 34.4	% 51.6	128
Indefinite whether will stay or leave		43.3	38.8	40.6	25.8	213
Definite plan to leave		45.0	34.6	25.0	22.6	194
TOTAL	% N	100 180	99.9 260	100 64	100 31	535

Gamma = −.305

TABLE LXXII: THE RELATIONSHIP BETWEEN OCCUPATIONAL (AND INCOME) FRUSTRATION AND PLANS TO MIGRATE, BY LEVELS OF FAMILY OBLIGATION

	Level of Respondent's Family Obligations								
Plans to Migrate	None			Very Slight			Medium-High		
	Occupational Frustration			Occupational Frustration			Occupational Frustration		
	Not Frustrated	Partly Frustrated	Frustrated	Not Frustrated	Partly Frustrated	Frustrated	Not Frustrated	Partly Frustrated	Frustrated
Definite plans to stay	% 19.0	% 8.2	% 4.4	% 43.4	% 7.2	% 9.8	% 60.4	% 23.5	% 0.0
Indefinite whether will stay or leave	55.2	54.8	13.3	37.2	59.5	15.7	31.3	53.0	21.4
Definite plans to leave	25.9	37.0	82.2	19.4	33.3	74.5	8.3	23.5	78.6
TOTAL % N	100.1 58	100 73	99.9 45	100 129	100 69	100 51	100 48	100 17	100 14
	Gamma = .502			Gamma = .661			Gamma = .781		

Plans to Migrate	Income Frustration			Income Frustration			Income Frustration		
	Not Frustrated	Partly Frustrated	Frustrated	Not Frustrated	Partly Frustrated	Frustrated	Not Frustrated	Partly Frustrated	Frustrated
Definite plans to stay	34.5	6.3	6.9	51.8	12.9	17.2	70.3	26.1	16.7
Indefinite whether will stay or leave	34.5	67.2	24.7	29.4	58.1	25.8	21.6	52.2	33.3
Definite plans to leave	31.0	26.6	68.5	18.8	29.0	57.0	8.1	21.7	50.0
TOTAL %	100	100.1	100.1	100	100	100	100	100	100
TOTAL N	29	64	73	85	62	93	37	23	30
	Gamma = .535			Gamma = .513			Gamma = .662		

R.E.—I.

TABLE LXXIII: THE RELATIONSHIP BETWEEN ATTITUDES TOWARD THE COMMUNITY'S SOCIAL PROVISIONS AND MIGRATION INTENTIONS

| Migration Intentions | Attitude towards the community's social provisions | | | | | | TOTAL |
| | Positive | | | | Negative | | |
	0 and 1	2 and 3	4 and 5	6 and 7	8 and 9		
Definite intention to stay	% 32.1	% 27.3	% 20.2	% 28.2	% 20.9		127
Indefinite whether will stay or leave	46.4	45.5	50.0	34.4	36.7		208
Definite intention to leave	21.4	27.3	29.8	37.4	42.3		190
TOTAL % N	100 28	100 44	100 94	100 163	100 196		525

Gamma = 0.137

Appendix IV:
Tables for Chapters 5 and 6

TABLE LXXIV: THE RELATIONSHIP BETWEEN THE LEVEL OF OCCUPATIONAL ASPIRATION AND THE LEVEL OF FRUSTRATION OF OCCUPATIONAL AND INCOME ASPIRATIONS

	Level of Occupational Aspiration			
	Higher and lower Professional	Intermediate Non-manual	Skilled and Service	Unskilled and Semiskilled
Occupational Frustration	%	%	%	%
Not frustrated	25.9	31.3	42.3	44.2
Frustrated	33.3	25.0	19.0	41.9
*TOTAL %	100	100	100	100
N	54	176	142	43

Gamma = −.123

	Higher and lower Professional	Intermediate Non-manual	Skilled and Service	Unskilled and Semiskilled
Income Frustration	%	%	%	%
Not frustrated	18.2	20.8	27.6	33.3
Frustrated	40.0	44.6	42.5	53.3
*TOTAL %	100	100	100	100
N	55	168	134	45

Gamma = −.027

* The proportions "partly frustrated" are excluded from the table, but can easily be calculated by subtraction from 100%.

TABLE LXXV: The Relationship between the level of Income Aspiration and the level of Frustration of these Aspirations

Income Frustration	Level of Income Aspiration (Pounds per week)							
	Up to 6	7–8	9–10	11–12	13–14	15–20	20 plus
Not frustrated	% 52.3	% 40.3	% 30.7	% 29.4	% 32.6	% 21.7	% 22.9
Partly frustrated	23.1	23.9	24.2	33.8	30.2	27.0	31.3
Frustrated	24.6	35.8	45.1	36.8	37.2	51.3	45.8
Total % N	100 65	100 67	100 91	100 68	100 43	100 115	100 48

Gamma = .202

Table LXXVI: The Relationship between Occupational Aspiration and
Plans to Migrate

Plans to Migrate	Lowest level of Occupational Aspiration				
	Higher and lower professional	Intermed. non-manual	Skilled	Service	Semiskilled and unskilled
Definite plans to stay	% 8.8	% 10.7	% 24.1	% 7.1	% 15.2
Indefinite whether will stay or leave	47.4	44.9	41.4	46.4	30.4
Definite plans to leave	43.9	44.4	34.5	46.4	54.3
Total % N	100 57	100 178	100 58	99.9 84	99.9 46

$X^2 = 14.8$ (full table); $P > .90 < .95$. But $X^2 = 5.3$ (with service and skilled categories aggregated); $P = .50$.   Gamma $= .010$

Table LXXVII: The Relationship between Income Aspirations and Plans
To Migrate

Plans to Migrate	Level of Income Aspiration (Pounds per week)		
	15 and over	9–14	Up to 8
Definite plans to stay	% 17.7	% 23.7	% 32.8
Indefinite whether will stay or leave	42.1	34.3	41.8
Definite plans to leave	40.2	42.0	25.4
Total % N	100 164	100 207	100 134

Gamma $= -.189$

TABLE LXXVIII: The Relationship between the levels of Occupational Aspiration or current Occupational Achievement and (1) Occupational Frustration, (2) Migration Plans

Level of Occupational Achievement or beliefs about achievement	Level of Occupational Aspiration or Achievement					
	Professional and Semi-Professional	Farmers	Intermed. Non-Manual	Skilled manual	Service	Semiskilled and Unskilled
	%	%	%	%	%	%
Aspirations not frustrated; plus aspirations already achieved	25.9	95.6	32.0	56.8	53.5	56.4
Aspirations partly frustrated	40.7	2.2	43.3	29.6	30.7	10.9
Aspirations frustrated	33.3	2.2	24.7	13.6	15.8	32.7
Total % / N	99.9 / 54	100 / 45	100 / 178	100 / 81	100 / 101	100 / 55

(Excluding Farmers) Gamma = .239

Plans to migrate						
Definite plans to stay	8.8	88.9	10.2	37.0	17.0	28.1
Indefinite whether will stay or leave	47.4	6.7	44.6	38.3	44.0	29.8
Definite plans to leave	43.9	4.4	45.2	24.7	39.0	42.1
Total % / N	100.1 / 57	99.9 / 45	100 / 177	100 / 81	100 / 100	100 / 57

(Excluding Farmers) Gamma = — .140

TABLE LXXIX: THE RELATIONSHIP BETWEEN THE LEVEL OF EDUCATION ACHIEV-
ED AND THE LEVEL OF OCCUPATIONAL ASPIRATIONS OR OCCUPATIONAL ACHIEVEMENT

Level of Occupational Aspiration or Achievement	Level of education achieved		
	Primary only	Vocational	Secondary
	%	%	%
Professional, lower professional workers and proprietors	3.2	2.8	26.2
Farmers	20.5	3.3	5.9
Intermed. non-manual workers	4.5	27.1	61.5
Skilled manual workers	11.5	33.1	1.1
Service workers	26.9	28.7	4.8
Semiskilled and unskilled workers	33.3	5.0	0.5
TOTAL %	99.9	100	100
N	156	181	187

(Excluding Farmers)   Gamma = .808

TABLE LXXX: THE RELATIONSHIP BETWEEN THE LEVEL OF EDUCATION ACHIEVED
AND THE LEVEL OF INCOME ASPIRATIONS OF RESPONDENTS

Level of Income Aspiration	Level of education achieved		
	Primary only	Vocational	Secondary
	%	%	%
Less than £6 per week	23.6	15.2	1.8
£7 to £10	32.4	35.9	27.3
£11 to £14	21.6	21.7	24.8
Over £15	22.3	27.2	46.1
TOTAL %	99.9	100	100
N	148	184	165

Gamma = .339

TABLE LXXXI: THE RELATIONSHIP BETWEEN THE LEVEL OF EDUCATION AND MIGRATION INTENTIONS, CONTROLLING FOR THE LEVEL OF OCCUPATIONAL FRUSTRATION

Levels of Occupational Frustration

Intentions to Migrate	Not Frustrated			Partly Frustrated			Frustrated		
	Education received			*Education received*			*Education received*		
	Primary	Vocational	Secondary	Primary	Vocational	Secondary	Primary	Vocational	Secondary
	%	%	%	%	%	%	%	%	%
Definite intention to stay	56	40.9	20.3	7.1	10.1	9.8	6.3	9.4	4.1
Indefinite whether will stay or leave	29.8	37.6	57.8	57.1	60.9	51.2	15.6	15.6	20.4
Definite intention to migrate	14.3	21.5	21.9	35.7	29.0	39.0	78.1	75.0	75.5
TOTAL %	100.1	100	100	99.9	100	100	100	100	100
N	84	93	64	14	69	82	32	32	49

Gamma = .325　　　　　　Gamma = .106　　　　　　Gamma = .025

TABLE LXXXII: THE RELATIONSHIP BETWEEN THE LEVEL OF EDUCATION AND MIGRATION INTENTIONS, CONTROLLING FOR THE LEVEL OF INCOME FRUSTRATION

	Level of Income Frustration								
	Not Frustrated			Partly Frustrated			Frustrated		
Intentions to Migrate	Education received			Education received			Education received		
	Primary	Vocational	Secondary	Primary	Vocational	Secondary	Primary	Vocational	Secondary
	%	%	%	%	%	%	%	%	%
Definite intention to stay	52.8	52.6	35.3	44.4	12.7	3.8	17.5	14.7	6.6
Indefinite whether will stay or leave	29.2	28.1	50	5.6	63.6	73.1	40.4	33.3	18.4
Definite intention to migrate	18.1	19.3	14.7	50	23.6	23.1	42.1	52.0	75
TOTAL %	100	100	100	100	99.9	100	100	100	100
N	72	57	34	18	55	78	57	75	76

Gamma = .107   Gamma = .090   Gamma = .386

TABLE LXXXIII: THE RELATIONSHIP BETWEEN INCOME FRUSTRATION AND MIGRATION PLANS BY LEVEL OF EDUCATION AND OCCUPATIONAL FRUSTRATION

PERCENTAGES INDEFINITELY AND DEFINITELY PLANNING TO MIGRATE

Income Frustration	Level of education received								
	Primary and 1 year Vocational*			Vocational 2–3 years			Secondary 3–5 years		
	Occupational Frustration			Occupational Frustration			Occupational Frustration		
	Not frustrated	Partly frustrated	Frustrated	Not frustrated	Partly frustrated	Frustrated	Not frustrated	Partly frustrated	Frustrated
Not frustrated	% 38.9 (72)	% 80 (5)	% 100 (4)	% 50 (28)	% 62.5 (8)	% 0.0 (1)	% 68.1 (22)	% 50 (8)	% 75 (4)
Partly frustrated	36.4 (11)	100 (4)	100 (4)	75 (16)	93.5 (31)	100 (3)	91.4 (24)	97.4 (39)	100 (13)
Frustrated	58.3 (24)	100 (7)	94.2 (34)	76.5 (17)	95.5 (22)	87.5 (16)	81.3 (16)	96.6 (29)	96.8 (31)
TOTAL N	107	16	42	61	61	20	62	76	48
Relationship between occupational and income frustration for each educational level	Gamma = .763			Gamma = .534			Gamma = .472		

* This is a slightly different categorisation to the previous ones, in that 46 respondents who had received only one year's vocational education are here included with the primary educated. Their inclusion, however, makes little difference to the results.

TABLE LXXXIV: THE RELATIONSHIP BETWEEN SEX, AND OCCUPATIONAL BACKGROUND AND LEVELS OF OCCUPATIONAL FRUSTRATION

Occupational Frustration	Non-manual occupations		Farmers		Skilled and service		Semiskilled and unskilled	
	Males	Females	Males	Females	Males	Females	Males	Females
	%	%	%	%	%	%	%	%
Not frustrated	32.6	35.5	57.9	43.6	58.3	42.9	53.1	33.3
Partly frustrated	32.6	43.5	29.3	38.2	19.4	22.9	18.4	37.8
Frustrated	34.9	21.0	12.9	18.2	22.2	34.3	28.6	28.9
TOTAL %	100.1	100	100.1	100	99.9	100.1	100.1	100
N	43	62	140	110	36	35	49	45
	$X^2 = 2.60$ (n.s.) P (.50 — .75)		$X^2 = 5.2$ P (.90 — .95)		$X^2 = 1.9$ P (.50 — .75)		$X^2 = 5.4$ P (.90 — .95)	

TABLE LXXXV: THE RELATIONSHIP BETWEEN SEX, AND OCCUPATIONAL BACKGROUND AND LEVELS OF INCOME FRUSTRATION

Income Frustration	Non-manual occupations		Farmers		Skilled and service		Semiskilled and unskilled	
	Males	Females	Males	Females	Males	Females	Males	Females
	%	%	%	%	%	%	%	%
Not frustrated	20.5	26.2	43.3	28.0	31.4	28.6	29.8	20.0
Partly frustrated	34.1	39.3	22.7	31.8	34.3	22.9	19.1	33.3
Frustrated	45.5	34.4	34.0	40.2	34.3	48.6	51.1	46.7
TOTAL %	100.1	99.9	100	100	100	100	100	100
N	44	61	150	107	35	35	47	45
	$X^2 = 0.30$		$P > .95$		$X^2 = 1.70$		$X^2 = 2.25$	
	$P (.10 — .25)$				$P (.50 — .75)$		$P (.50 — .75)$	

TABLE LXXXVI: THE RELATIONSHIP BETWEEN SEX, AND OCCUPATIONAL BACKGROUND AND LEVELS OF COMMUNITY SATISFACTION

Community Satisfaction	Occupation of Father							
	Non-manual		Farmers		Skilled and Service		Semiskilled and unskilled	
	Males	Females	Males	Females	Males	Females	Males	Females
	%	%	%	%	%	%	%	%
Alienated (0–3)	31.1	23.8	20.7	29.4	34.3	32.4	31.9	34.1
Moderate (4–6)	33.3	38.1	34.7	44.0	40.0	35.3	44.7	41.5
Positive (7–9)	35.6	38.1	44.7	26.6	25.7	32.4	23.4	24.4
TOTAL %	100	100	100.1	100	100	100.1	100	100
N	45	63	150	109	35	34	47	41
	X² = .75		X² = 8.95		X² = .38		X² = .21	
	P:25–50		P > .95		P:10–25		P < .10	

TABLE LXXXVII: THE RELATIONSHIP BETWEEN SEX, AND OCCUPATIONAL BACKGROUND AND LEVEL OF FAMILY OBLIGATIONS

Family Obligations	Occupation of Father							
	Non-manual		Farmers		Skilled and Service		Semiskilled and unskilled	
	Males	Females	Males	Females	Males	Females	Males	Females
	%	%	%	%	%	%	%	%
None	52.3	53.1	27.1	26.8	33.3	37.1	25.5	31.8
Very slight	34.1	42.2	45.2	58.0	50.0	48.6	59.6	50
Medium—Heavy	13.7	4.7	27.8	15.1	16.7	14.3	14.9	18.2
TOTAL %	100.1	100	100.1	99.9	100	100.1	100	100
N	44	64	155	112	36	35	47	44
	X² = 2.87		X² = 6.7		X² = .14		X² = .84	
	P : .75 – .80		P > .95		P : .05 – 21		P : 25–50	

TABLE LXXXVIII: THE RELATIONSHIP BETWEEN SEX, AND OCCUPATIONAL BACKGROUND AND ATTITUDES TOWARD THE COMMUNITY'S SOCIAL PROVISIONS

	Occupation of Father							
Attitude toward social provisions	Non-manual		Farmers		Skilled and Service occupations		Semiskilled and unskilled occupations	
	Males	Females	Males	Females	Males	Females	Males	Females
Negative (7–9)	% 54.5	% 66.7	% 53.9	% 51.9	% 70.3	% 38.2	% 65.2	% 48.9
Moderate (4–6)	31.8	22.2	30.9	35.8	27.0	35.3	28.3	28.9
Positive (0–3)	13.6	11.1	15.1	12.3	2.7	26.5	6.5	22.2
TOTAL %	99.9	100	99.9	100	100	100	100	100
N	44	63	152	106	37	34	46	45
	$X^2 = 1.667$		$X^2 = .88$		$X^2 = 10.8$		$X^2 = 5.04$	
	$P > .50 < .75$		$P > 25 < 50$		$P > .95$		$P > .90 < .95$	

TABLE LXXXXIX: The Relationship between sex, and occupational background and Plans to Migrate

Occupation of Father

Intending to Migrate	Non-manual occupations		Farmers		Skilled and service occupations		Semiskilled and unskilled occupations	
	Males	Females	Males	Females	Males	Females	Males	Females
	%	%	%	%	%	%	%	%
Definite intention to stay	13.3	10.9	39.7	19.8	24.3	11.4	24.0	17.0
Indefinite	35.6	51.6	36.5	44.0	37.8	37.1	26.0	49.0
Definite intention to go	51.1	37.5	23.7	36.2	37.8	51.4	50.0	34.0
TOTAL %	100	100	99.9	100	99.9	99.9	100	100
N	45	64	156	116	37	35	50	47
	$X^2 = 2.75$ P (.50 − .75)		P > .95		$X^2 = 4.66$ P > .90		$X^2 = 5.47$ P (.90 − .95)	

TABLE XC: THE RELATIONSHIP BETWEEN SEX, THE LEVEL OF EDUCATION RECEIVED
AND THE LEVEL OF OCCUPATIONAL ASPIRATION

	Education of Respondent					
	Primary		Vocational		Secondary	
Level of Occupational Aspiration	*Sex*		*Sex*		*Sex*	
	Male %	Female %	Male %	Female %	Male %	Female %
All non-manual	1.9	26.7	5.4	52.6	86.8	97.2
Farmers	—	—	4.1	—	7.4	—
Skilled manual	13.2	3.3	64.9	2.1	2.9	—
Service	26.4	50.0	18.9	42.3	1.5	2.8
Semiskilled manual	50.9	20.0	6.8	3.1	1.5	—
Unskilled manual	7.5	—	—	—	—	—
TOTAL %	99.9	100	100.1	100.1	100.1	100
N	53	30	74	97	68	106

TABLE XCI: THE RELATIONSHIPS BETWEEN SEX, LEVEL OF OCCUPATIONAL ASPIRATION AND INTENTIONS TO MIGRATE

	Level of Occupational Aspiration							
	Professional		Non-manual		Skilled and service		Semiskilled and unskilled	
Intention to Migrate	Males	Females	Males	Females	Males	Females	Males	Females
	%	%	%	%	%	%	%	%
Definite intention to remain	3.7	13.3	10.4	10.8	16.5	11.7	16.7	10.0
Indefinite whether will stay or leave	51.9	43.3	39.6	46.9	41.2	51.7	27.8	40.0
Definite intention to migrate	44.4	43.3	50.0	42.3	42.4	36.7	55.6	50.0
TOTAL %	100	99.9	100	100	100.1	100.1	100.1	100
N	27	30	48	130	85	60	36	10

TABLE XCII: THE RELATIONSHIP BETWEEN SEX, LEVEL OF EDUCATION, AND LEVEL OF INCOME ASPIRATION

Level of Income Aspiration	Level of Education					
	Primary		Vocational		Secondary	
	Male	Female	Male	Female	Male	Female
	%	%	%	%	%	%
Up to £10 per week	41.7	88.9	18.9	81.9	8.4	44.7
More than £10 per week	58.2	11.1	81.1	18.1	91.6	55.3
TOTAL %	99.9	100	100	100	100	100
N	103	45	90	94	71	94

TABLE XCIII: THE RELATIONSHIP BETWEEN THE NUMBER AND PROPORTION OF UNCLES WHO ARE WORKING ABROAD AND THE LEVEL OF INCOME ASPIRATION OF THOSE WHO COME FROM A FARM AND WORKING CLASS BACKGROUND, AND HAVE RECEIVED ONLY A PRIMARY OR VOCATIONAL SCHOOL EDUCATION

A. LEVEL OF INCOME ASPIRATION OF RESPONDENTS	Number and location of uncles and aunts						
	1–6 uncles and aunts alive				Over 6 alive		
	All at home	1 away	2–3 away	4+ away	Less than 2 away	3–4 away	4+ away
	%	%	%	%	%	%	%
(1) *Farmers with primary or vocational education*							
Information not available							
Up to £10 per week	55.5	55.5	60.6	66.7	53.9	47.4	54.4
Over £10 per week	44.4	44.4	39.4	33.3	46.2	52.6	45.6
TOTAL %	99.9	99.9	100	100	100.1	100	100
N	9	27	33	9	26	19	46
(2) *Working class respondents with primary or vocational education*	%	%	%	%	%	%	%
Information not available							
Up to £10 per week	42.9	56.6	50.0	50.0	53.3	54.6	55.9
Over £10 per week	57.2	43.4	50.0	50.0	46.7	45.5	44.2
TOTAL %	100.1	99.9	100	100	100	100.1	100.1
N	7	23	26	10	15	11	43

TABLE XCIV: THE RELATIONSHIP BETWEEN THE NUMBER AND PROPORTION OF UNCLES WHO ARE WORKING ABROAD AND THE LEVEL OF OCCUPATIONAL AND INCOME FRUSTRATION OF THOSE WHO COME FROM A FARM AND WORKING CLASS BACKGROUND, AND HAVE RECEIVED ONLY A PRIMARY OR VOCATIONAL SCHOOL EDUCATION

| | Number and location of uncles and aunts | | | | | | |
| | 1-6 uncles and aunts alive | | | | Over 6 alive | | |
	All at home	1 away	2-3 away	4+ away	Less than 2 away	3-4 away	4+ away
B. OCCUPATIONAL FRUSTRATION							
(1) Respondents from farm backgrounds	%	%	%	%	%	%	%
Not frustrated	44.4	59.3	71	75	66.7	55.6	57.8
Partly frustrated	33.3	22.2	22.6	25	33.3	27.8	24.4
Frustrated	22.2	18.5	6.5	—	—	16.7	17.8
TOTAL %	99.9	100	100.1	100	100	100	100
N	9	27	31	8	24	18	45
		X² = 4.04				X² = 2.44	
		P > .75 < .90				P > .25 < .50	
(2) Respondents from working class backgrounds	%	%	%	%	%	%	%
Not frustrated	28.6	36.4	61.5	40	60	45.5	47.7
Partly frustrated	28.6	22.7	19.2	10	33.3	18.2	25
Frustrated	42.8	40.9	19.2	50	6.7	36.4	27.3
TOTAL %	100	100	99.9	100	100	100.1	100
N	7	22	26	10	15	11	43
		X² = 2.90				X² = .578	
		P > .75 < .90				P = .25	

TABLE XCIV (cont.)

| | Number and location of uncles and aunts | | | | | | |
| | 1–6 uncles and aunts alive | | | | Over 6 alive | | |
	All at home	1 away	2–3 away	4+ away	Less than 2 away	3–4 away	4+ away
C. INCOME FRUSTRATION							
(1) Respondents from farm backgrounds	%	%	%	%	%	%	%
Not frustrated	22.2	35.7	54.3	62.5	51.9	40	40
Partly frustrated	33.3	28.6	22.9	12.5	18.5	35	17.8
Frustrated	44.4	35.7	22.9	25.0	29.6	25	42.2
TOTAL %	99.9	100	100.1	100	100	100	100
N	9	28	35	8	27	20	45
		X² = 4.355				X² = 2.284	
		P > .75 < .90				P > .50 < .75	
(2) Working class respondents	%	%	%	%	%	%	%
Not frustrated	28.6	31.8	40	30	33.3	18.2	27.9
Partly frustrated	14.3	13.6	24	—	40.0	18.2	25.6
Frustrated	57.1	54.5	36	70	26.7	63.6	46.5
TOTAL %	100	99.9	100	100	100	100	100
N	7	22	25	10	15	11	43
		X² = .567				X² = .231	
		P > .10 < .25				P > .10 < .25	

TABLE XCV: THE RELATIONSHIP BETWEEN THE NUMBER AND PROPORTION OF SIBS WHO ARE WORKING OUTSIDE THE COMMUNITY AND THE LEVEL OF INCOME ASPIRATION OF RESPONDENTS WHO COME FROM FARM AND WORKING CLASS BACKGROUNDS, AND WHO HAVE RECEIVED ONLY A PRIMARY OR VOCATIONAL EDUCATION

Level of Income Aspiration of Respondents	None working as yet	1–3 working			4 and over working		
		All working at home	1 working outside the community	2–3 working outside	All at home or just 1 away	2–3 working outside the community	4 or more working away
(1) Farmer respondents with primary or vocational education	%	%	%	%	%	%	%
Up to £10 per week	54.8	51.9	61.5	66.7	50	56.5	53.3
Over £10 per week	45.2	48.1	38.5	33.3	50	43.5	46.7
TOTAL %	100	100	100	100	100	100	100
N	31	54	26	12	10	23	15
		X² = 1.248 P > .25 < .50			X² = .127 P > .05 < .10		
(2) Working class respondents							
Up to £10 per week	64.3	60.7	58.3	62.5	44.4	45	35
Over £10 per week	35.7	39.3	41.7	37.5	55.6	55	65
TOTAL %	100	100	100	100	100	100	100
N	14	28	24	16	9	20	20
		X² = 0.072 P < .05			X² = .475 P > .10 < .25		

(Column group heading: No. and location of working sibs)

TABLE XCV (cont.)

(B) Income Frustration	None working as yet	1–3 working			4 and over working		
		All working at home	1 working away from home	2–3 working away from home	All at home or just 1 away	2–3 working away	4 or more working away
(1) Farm respondents with primary or vocational education	%	%	%	%	%	%	%
Not frustrated	45.2	50.9	51.7	50	45.5	34.8	18.8
Partly frustrated	19.4	24.5	13.8	33.3	27.3	13.0	37.5
Frustrated	35.5	24.5	34.5	16.7	27.3	52.2	43.8
TOTAL %	100	100	100	100	100.1	100	100.1
N	31	53	29	12	11	23	16
		$X^2 = 2.928$ df = 2 P > .25 < .50			$X^2 = 2.228$ df = 2 P > .25 < .50		
(2) Working class respondents with a primary or vocational education							
Not frustrated	28.6	51.7	37.5	33.3	33.3	10.0	15.0
Partly frustrated	28.6	17.3	20.8	26.7	22.2	20.0	20.0
Frustrated	42.7	31.0	41.7	40.0	44.4	70.0	65.0
TOTAL %	100.1	100	100	100	99.9	100	100
N	14	29	24	15	9	20	20
		$X^2 = 1.904$ df = 2 P > .25 < .50					

Number and location of working sibs

TABLE XCVI: The Relationship between the number and proportion of sibs who are working outside the community and the level of Occupational and Income Frustration of Respondents who come from farm working class backgrounds and have received only a vocational or primary school education

Occupational Frustration	Number and location of working sibs						
	None working as yet	*1–3 working*			*4 and more working*		
		All working at home	1 working outside the community	2–3 working outside	All at home or just 1 working away	2–3 working away	4 or more working away
(1) Farm respondents with primary or vocational education	%	%	%	%	%	%	%
Not frustrated	76.7	73.1	52	61.5	54.5	55.6	26.7
Partly frustrated	16.7	19.2	28	30.8	36.4	38.8	26.7
Frustrated	6.7	7.7	20	7.7	9.1	5.6	46.7
TOTAL %	100.1	100	100	100	100	100	100.1
N	30	52	25	13	11	18	15

*X² = 3.43   df = 2   P > .75 < .90

*X² = 3.247   df = 2   P > .75 < .90

TABLE XCVI (cont.)

Occupational Frustration	None working as yet	1-3 working			4 and more working		
		All working at home	1 working outside the community	2-3 working outside	All at home or just 1 working away	2-3 working away	4 or more working away
(2) Respondents from working class backgrounds	%	%	%	%	%	%	%
Not frustrated	11.1	65.5	50	52.9	44.4	38.1	31.6
Partly frustrated	44.4	17.2	20.8	23.5	22.2	23.8	26.3
Frustrated	44.4	17.2	29.2	23.5	33.3	38.1	42.1
TOTAL %	99.9	99.9	100	99.9	99.9	100	100
N	9	29	24	17	9	21	19

1-3 working: *X² = 1.449 df = 2 P > .50 < .75

4 and more working: *X² = .463 df = 2 P > .10 < .25

* The partly frustrated and the frustrated categories are aggregated for the purpose of computing the statistic.

TABLE XCVII: THE RELATIONSHIP BETWEEN THE NUMBER AND PROPORTION OF RESPONDENTS' SIBS WHO ARE WORKING OUTSIDE THE COMMUNITY AND RESPONDENTS' INTENTIONS TO MIGRATE

INTENTIONS TO MIGRATE	None working as yet	1–3 working			4 and more working		
		All working at home	1 working outside the community	2–3 working outside	All at home or just 1 away	2–3 working away from home	4 or more working away
	%	%	%	%	%	%	%
(1) Farm respondents with primary or vocational education							
Definite intention to remain at home	48.6	41.8	27.6	35.7	45.5	29.2	18.8
Indefinite whether will remain or migrate	31.4	41.8	34.5	35.7	45.5	50.0	37.5
Definite intention to migrate	20.0	16.4	37.9	28.6	9.1	20.8	43.8
TOTAL %	100	100	100	100	100.1	100	100.1
N	35	55	29	14	11	24	16
		X² = 1.661 df = 2 P > .50 < .75			X² = 2.236 df = 2 P > .50 < .75		
(2) Working class respondents with primary or vocational education							
Definite intention to remain at home	20.0	44.8	12.0	23.5	33.3	9.5	20.0
Indefinite whether will remain or migrate	53.3	27.6	44.0	23.5	33.3	38.1	20.0
Definite intention to migrate	26.7	27.6	44.0	52.9	33.3	52.4	60.0
TOTAL %	100	100	100	99.9	99.9	100	100
N	15	29	25	17	9	21	20
		X² = 7.383 df = 2 P > .95			X² = 1.80 df = 2 P > .50 < .75		

TABLE XCVIII: The Relationship between the number and proportion of sibs who are working outside the Community and the Migration Intentions of Respondents

Respondents' intentions to migrate	Number and location of working sibs						
		1–3 working			4 and more working		
	None working as yet	All working at home	1 working away	2–3 working away	All at home or just 1 away	2–3 working away	4 and more working away
	%	%	%	%	%	%	%
Definite intention to stay	19.7	35.5	19.1	21.8	33.3	20.3	17.5
Indefinite whether will stay or leave	46.2	36.3	41.6	32.7	41.7	39.0	38.6
Definite intention to migrate	34.1	28.2	39.3	45.5	25.0	40.7	43.9
TOTAL %	100	100	100	100	100	100	100
N	132	124	89	55	24	59	57

X² = 10.368
P > .95
Gamma = .243

X² = 3.655
P > .50 < .75
Gamma = .150

TABLE XCIX: The Relationship between the number and proportion of uncles and aunts who are working outside the Community and the Migration Intentions of Respondents

Respondents' intentions to migrate	Number and location of Respondents' uncles and aunts								
	1–3 uncles and aunts			4–6 uncles and aunts			Over 6 uncles and aunts		
	All in the home community	1 living away	2–3 living away	All at home or just 1 away	2–3 away	4–6 away	Up to 2 away	3–4 away	5 and more away
	%	%	%	%	%	%	%	%	%
Definite intention to stay	14.3	40	28.6	22.2	30.7	20	33.3	18.6	18.8
Indefinite whether will stay or migrate	28.6	6.7	33.3	46.3	34.7	45	41.3	44.1	42.9
Definite intention to migrate	57.1	53.3	38.1	31.5	34.7	35	25.4	37.3	38.2
TOTAL %	100	100	100	100	100.1	100	100	100	99.9
N	21	15	21	54	75	40	63	59	191

$X^2 = 2.875$
$P > .25 < .50$

$X^2 = 7.213$
$P > .95$

Index